Russia's Oil and Natural Gas

Advance Reviews

'A "grab bag" full of choice prizes offered by a stellar collection of European and American scholars. All are present, timely and durable analyses and will reward careful attention. The volume also contains a number of valuable economic time series. I recommend the collection to all serious students of the Russian economy.'

James R. Millar
Director of the Institute for European, Russian and Eurasian Studies, The George Washington University

'This volume examines the implications of the Russian oil boom for the country's development by drawing together contributions from a number of leading specialists on the Russian economy... should be the recommended first read for anyone wishing to obtain knowledge and insights on the implications of the oil boom for Russia.'

John Litwack
Chief Economist for Russia, The World Bank

'A very timely and provocative research conducted by a group of highly qualified experts, the monograph highlights on one of the most critical challenges of national and global development. This is a comprehensive study into the core of the "mineral trap" and an excellent guidance and reference book for global and national policy makers, economic and political experts and all those who seek the key to understanding of modern economic growth and global development.'

Leonid Todorov
Institute for the Economy in Transition

Russia's Oil and Natural Gas

Bonanza or Curse?

Edited by

MICHAEL ELLMAN

School of Economics
Universiteit van Amsterdam

Anthem Press

Anthem Press
An imprint of Wimbledon Publishing Company
www.anthempress.com

This edition first published in UK and USA 2006
by ANTHEM PRESS
75-76 Blackfriars Road, London SE1 8HA, UK
or PO Box 9779, London SW19 7ZG, UK
and
244 Madison Ave. #116, New York, NY 10016, USA

British Library Cataloguing in Publication Data
A catalogue record for this book is available from the British Library.

Library of Congress Cataloging in Publication Data
A catalog record for this book has been requested.

1 3 5 7 9 10 8 6 4 2

ISBN 1 84331 226 3 (Pbk)
ISBN-13 978 1 84331 226 0 (Pbk)

Cover photograph: © Sergey Burasovsky,
The Moscow House of Photography.

Printed in India

CONTENTS

LIST OF TABLES AND FIGURES

PREFACE

Earlier versions of most of the chapters in this book were presented at the VIIth World Congress of ICCEES (International Council for Central and East European Studies) in Berlin in July 2005. They have been revised and updated for this publication. It was decided to produce a book on this issue in view of its importance and topicality, the variety of opinions expressed by the authors, and the quality of their contribution to the debate. There are some minor discrepancies between the data cited by various contributors, e.g., for the value of oil and gas exports in particular years. This results from such factors as revision of official statistics as more data becomes available, differences between customs and balance of payments statistics, and the inclusion or otherwise of Belarus as an export destination. The official Russian statistical organization was known as *Gosudarstvennii komitet po statistike* (State Committee for Statistics – usually abbreviated to Goskomstat) until April 2004, when it was transformed into the *Federal'naya sluzhba gosudarstvennoi statistike* (Federal State Statistics Services – usually abbreviated to Rosstat). In this book it is generally referred to as Rosstat.

Amsterdam
1 November 2005

A. OVERVIEW

1

THE ISSUES

Michael Ellman

Russia is the world's second largest producer and exporter of oil. It is also the largest producer and exporter of natural gas. At times of low world market prices for oil and natural gas, such as 1986–88 (for natural gas 1987–89) and 1998, it experiences economic crises. The balance of payments crisis caused by the low energy prices during the first of these periods contributed to the failure of Gorbachev's perestroika and the collapse of the USSR. The second period of low energy prices was an element in the macroeconomic crisis of 1998 when the exchange rate fell sharply, the government defaulted on its internal debt and was forced to reschedule its external debt, many Russian entities defaulted on their external commitments, and real wages and living standards fell sharply. When prices are high, as in 2004–05, it enjoys a bonanza. The budget is in surplus, public sector salaries are increased and paid on time, there is an enormous surplus on the current account of the balance of payments, foreign exchange reserves shoot up, and living standards rise as the population consumes imported consumer goods and foreign holidays.

Any visitor to Moscow or St. Petersburg in 2005 might have taken it for granted that for Russia high world market prices for energy are an unmixed blessing. Such a visitor would have seen the luxury flats already constructed and under construction, the abundance of new cars on the streets and new TVs and DVD players in people's flats, the shiny new supermarkets with a wide variety of produce, and the large number of people recently returned from, or busy planning, holidays in Europe or on the Red Sea coast of Egypt.

However, things are not so simple. Although some countries with abundant energy resources (USA, Canada, Norway, UK) have indeed benefited substantially from this, it is well known that they can also have negative effects. This phenomenon (with respect to silver and gold) seems to have been first observed in sixteenth-century Spain. That country received a substantial influx of silver and gold, looted or mined in Mexico and Peru.

These resources of bullion were the envy of the other European countries. However, they did not benefit the Spanish economy. They triggered an inflation which undermined Spanish exports and encouraged Spanish imports. At the same time, talent was distracted from economic entrepreneurship in a market economy into fighting, the organization of dependent labour and colonial administration. Spain went into a deep economic decline despite the inflow of treasure.

In the Netherlands, which in the 1960s began the exploitation of the large Groningen natural gas field, the initial experience of these riches was wholly favourable. It removed the balance of payments constraint on growth, the income constraint on public expenditure, and provided abundant cheap energy. However, experience soon showed that there were also negative effects. The budgetary revenue permitted the expansion of a variety of social welfare programmes. However, when oil prices fell, the budget came under great strain and these programmes became difficult to finance. Furthermore, people adjusted their behaviour to take advantage of these programmes. For example, the benefits provided for invalids produced a remarkable increase in the number of officially registered 'invalids'. The export earnings from the natural gas exports generated substantial imports, which partially displaced domestic production. Since natural gas production employs very few people, this had the effect of reducing employment and increasing unemployment. The export earnings also exerted upward pressure on the exchange rate, which tended to reduce exports and increase imports. The structure of the economy changed, to natural gas and away from non-gas exports and non-gas production. This had the effect of increasing the proportion of the population depending on income transfers from the state and on state employment, reducing employment in the market sector and increasing unemployment. This unexpected phenomenon, in which an abundance of riches undermines the market sector and makes much of the population worse off, came to be known as 'the Dutch disease'.

Furthermore, experience throughout the world in recent decades has shown that countries without natural resources are the fast-growing ones, and that countries with substantial energy exports tend to be the slow-growing ones. It is resource-poor countries such as China and South Korea (and previously Japan) that have grown rapidly in recent decades. Resource-rich countries such as Nigeria, Venezuela, Mexico and Saudi Arabia have experienced substantial economic fluctuations, in line with world energy prices, but relatively modest long-run average growth rates. It is this contrast which has generated the term 'the resource curse' and the growing literature analysing it.

The negative experience of certain other countries raises the question of what will be the long-run effect of Russia's enormous energy riches on the structure of the economy and the welfare of the population. Will they undermine manufacturing and agriculture and swell the ranks of civil servants, the military and the unemployed? Or will they be used to develop an internationally competitive tradeables sector that generates well-paid market-sector employment for the population? This is the central question dealt with in this book. It contains data about the Russian energy sector and its role in the Russian economy, about actual and possible economic policies, and also about the relationship between energy riches and the political system. In this respect it is similar to previous writing on this subject,[1] but is more up to date, includes more economic analysis and devotes more attention to financial flows.

Chapter 2 by Oppenheimer and Maslichenko provides an overview of the Russian oil (and gas) industry and its economic significance. It contains a mass of factual material which will be invaluable for anyone seeking information on these matters. This chapter, inter alia, draws attention to the superior record of private companies in the Russian natural gas sector compared with Gazprom (the state-controlled and overwhelmingly-dominant player). It also points out the success of the private sector in restructuring the coal industry. This chapter (and Chapter 6) also draws attention to the accumulation of debt by quasi-sovereign borrowers such as Gazprom, whose appetite for borrowings is large but whose commercial orientation is at best partial.

Section B is about financial flows. In Chapter 3, Tabata provides detailed information on the beneficiaries of price 'subsidies', about the balance of trade and fiscal impacts of the energy sector, and about the Stabilization Fund. For example, in 2004 the gain to domestic users of natural gas from not having to pay world market prices but only the much lower domestic prices was equal to the remarkable sum of 6.5 per cent of GDP. Another example is that, according to preliminary data, in 2004, oil, oil products and natural gas accounted for 55 per cent of Russian exports of goods. Tabata provides detailed information about the taxes paid by oil and gas companies, noting that, 'The tax regime for oil and natural gas companies can be thought of as the outcome of a repeated game in which the state tries to maximize its revenues and the companies strive to minimize their taxes.' He also estimates the sensitivity of tax revenues to fluctuations in world market prices for oil. It should be noted that Tabata's conclusion that 'the current tax burden on the oil and gas sector should not be regarded as high' refers to the situation in the early years of the twentyfirst century. In the mid-90s, before the 1998 currency

---

[1] Lane, D, ed., 1999, *The Political Economy of Russian Oil*, Lanham, MD; Kim, Y, 2003, *The Resource Curse in a Post-Communist Regime*, London; Dienes, L, 2004, Observations on the problematic potential of Russian oil and the complexities of Siberia, *Eurasian Geography and Economics*, No. 5.

depreciation and at the then prevailing level of world oil prices, after allowing for depreciation and using inflation accounting, oil extraction and processing, and gas extraction, were very lossmaking.[1]

The purpose of a stabilization fund, such as was introduced in Russia at the beginning of 2004, and about which Tabata provides data, is to prevent the volatility of energy prices destabilizing a country's economy. A particularly important issue confronting energy exporters (and other commodity exporters) is how to deal with fluctuations in world market prices. There is a danger that such countries will expand their public expenditures when prices are high and contract them when they are low, thus accentuating the fluctuations caused directly by price fluctuations. To follow a stabilizing, counter-cyclical policy, requires accumulating assets in the upswing which can be spent in the downswing, thus smoothing out the impact of commodity prices. The Russian government is attempting this with its current budget surplus, build-up of a stabilization fund and repayment of foreign debts. This policy will be tested when energy prices fall. The current high prices are likely to encourage alternatives (tar sands, nuclear, shale oil, tidal, biomass), exploration for new fields and energy conservation, leading to a decline in prices from their 2005 highs. This will benefit consumers but destabilize the energy exporters such as Russia if prices fall too low for too long. If this happens, the Stabilization Fund will be available to finance government expenditure in the lean years. This should assist in preventing a decline in energy prices generating an economic crisis in Russia.

In Chapter 4 Bernstam and Rabushka argue that the key factor enabling the Russian economy to recover from the depression of the 1990s was the decision of the Central Bank of Russia of 16 October 1998 requiring exporters to remit 50 per cent of their earnings to Russia. It was this that, according to them, led to an influx of money in Russia which remonetized the economy and permitted its subsequent economic growth. This is a matter of great importance. What is important as far as the Russian economy is concerned, is not the value of exports as shown in balance of payments statistics, but the flow of funds to Russia.

Bernstam and Rabushka focus on a distinctive feature of the Russian economy in the Yeltsin era, unpaid bills. During the Yeltsin era, companies frequently did not pay their bills for a long time, frequently delayed wage payments and frequently delayed tax payments. Where payments were made, they were often made in kind rather than in money. Consequently, a large share of transactions took the form of barter rather than of monetary

---

[1] Ivanenko, V, 2005, The statutory tax burden in Russia and its avoidance in transitional Russia, *Europe-Asia Studies* no. 7 table 6 p. 1035.

exchange. This was a strange and quite unexpected development in an economy supposedly making the transition to a market economy. It led to a situation in which many enterprises, even potentially healthy ones, were in permanent financial difficulties, many employees were in great financial difficulties, and the state experienced a large and chronic budget deficit. The financial difficulties of firms, households and the state were a major cause of the great Russian depression of the 1990s. The inability of the state to collect adequate taxes was the main cause of the macroeconomic crisis of August 1998. Since then, these unusual features of the Russian economy have largely disappeared. Bills, wages and taxes are now generally paid more or less on time. Barter no longer plays an important role. At the same time economic growth has resumed, as households, enterprises and the state spend their increased incomes.

The 'non-payments crisis' has frequently been commented on. The best-known explanation of it up till now was the Gaddy–Ickes 'virtual economy' thesis.[1] This argued that mutual non-payment was a way of propping up negative value-added enterprises. Events since the 1998 crisis have shown that this explanation was wrong.[2] Under conditions of macroeconomic growth and (initially) a depreciated currency, many Russian enterprises have been able to flourish. Large swathes of the economy, far from being negative value-added sectors, are able to pay wages and taxes and generate profits for their owners.

Bernstam and Rabushka, on the other hand, see the 'non-payments crisis' as a result of a number of coincident factors. These were, an inheritance of state-owned enterprises for whom ability to make payments and the availability of money had never been an effective constraint; an environment in which the economy was dominated by state-owned and former state-owned enterprises; a state policy of liberalization and privatization of existing state-owned enterprises; capital flight which denied the economy much of its export earnings; and a combination of inflation and monetary policy which led to a sharp fall in the real money supply.

Another relevant factor was a combination of taxes, inflation, and demand, which made most of the economy unprofitable. Ivanenko has shown that in 1995, at statutory tax rates, allowing for depreciation and with inflation accounting, and given actual output levels, virtually all sectors of the economy were loss-making, most very substantially so.[3] The only ways most firms could

---

[1] Gaddy, C G, and Ickes, B W, 1998, Russia's virtual economy, *Foreign Affairs*, No. 5; Gaddy, C G, and Ickes, B W, 1999, An accounting model of the virtual economy in Russia, *Post-Soviet Geography and Economics*, No. 2.

[2] For an early criticism of the 'virtual economy' thesis see Woodruff, D, 1999, It's value that is virtual, *Post-Soviet Affairs*, No. 2 and Woodruff, D, 1999, Erratum, *Post-Soviet Affairs*, No. 3.

[3] Ivanenko, V, 2005, The statutory tax burden in Russia and its avoidance in transitional Russia, *Europe-Asia Studies* no. 7 table 6 p. 1035.

survive were by capital consumption (i.e. disinvestment), or delaying or obtaining exemption from taxes, or delaying payment of bills and wages, or operating in the informal sector (which enabled taxes to be evaded), or by some combination of these strategies. Hence the 'non-payments crisis' can be seen as an ingenious and successful survival mechanism for an economy which, due to a combination of adverse circumstances, was not viable under conditions of normal payments discipline. Had payments discipline been insisted on, as many external advisors suggested, most of the economy would have had to close down.

Bernstam and Rabushka also argue that the transition of the Russian economy from depression to recovery was not caused by wise IMF advice, nor by sound government policy, but was the byproduct of a decision of the Central Bank of Russia taken with a different end in mind.

Furthermore, Bernstam and Rabushka point out that under certain circumstances liberalization can have unfavourable consequences and restricting economic freedom positive consequences. This goes against the currently popular neo-liberal orthodoxy, which suggests that liberalization is always and everywhere a good thing. However, it is undoubtedly true and has been previously pointed out by others. For example, Kornai has stated that the managers of state enterprises, if given more autonomy in all areas, are likely to use it not only to raise efficiency but also in socially harmful ways and that therefore they have to be closely supervised.[1] Similarly, McKinnon has argued that liberalization should follow a careful order, and that if that order is violated it may have very negative economic consequences.[2]

Whether it really was just one regulation of the Central Bank of Russia which turned the Russian depression into sustained growth, is unclear. Russia is not well known as a country in which business firms faithfully and rapidly implement changes in official regulations. Perhaps the gradual return of business confidence in 1999–2000 was more important. However, it is certainly the case that the influx of export remittances has played a crucial role in Russia's recent growth, as Chapter 6 confirms. Probably it was the combination of new central bank regulations, increased attempts to enforce them, increased business confidence, and rising export prices, that did the trick.

Section C is about economic policy. In Chapter 5, Ahrend argues that Russia's current energy dependence is inevitable and that further increases in energy exports (particularly natural gas) would be sensible. To overcome possible negative macroeconomic consequences, he recommends a cautious fiscal

---

[1] 'The state sector must not be "liberalized" unconditionally; instead we must watch it carefully'. Kornai, J, 1990, *The Road to a Free Economy*, New York, p. 60.
[2] McKinnon, R, 1993, *The Order of Economic Liberalization* 2nd edn, Baltimore.

policy, a large Stabilization Fund, repayment of external debt, sterilization of excessive export earnings, policies aimed at keeping inflation on a downward path and taxation of the natural resource rent combined with low general taxation. In this way it should be possible to avoid the Dutch disease and use the energy riches to benefit the population in the long run.

For continued economic growth and avoidance of the resource curse, Ahrend recommends structural reforms, such as the breakup of Gazprom; reform of the banking sector; administrative reform; strengthening civil society, the rule of law, property rights and press freedom; government accountability; and reduced corruption. He considers economic diversification justified for both economic and political reasons. In addition to creating an enterprise-friendly economic environment, as specific instruments to achieve it he suggests taxation policy, the development of a venture capital sector, and possibly 'new style' industrial policy (e.g., support for science parks, academic spin-offs, etc.). He warns against any government attempt at large scale state investment in pet industrial projects ('picking winners') on the ground that international experience shows that this does not work.

Ahrend's arguments are conventional in the international financial institutions and among mainstream economists. They tend to be recommended to all energy-rich countries. However, it is possible that specific aspects of the Russian economy, resulting from such fundamental factors as the path dependent nature of economic processes and/or Russia's geographical situation, may make Russia special and require country-specific policies. Hedlund has argued strongly for the importance of path dependence in the Russian case.[1] Kontorovich found that when investigating regional variations in small business density, the regulatory climate appeared to be of little importance and the main explanatory factors were geographical ones, such as the share of urban population in the region, its population density, and the presence/absence of a seaport.[2]

The chapters by Gavrilenkov and Khanin offer two very different perspectives on the future. Gavrilenkov (Chapter 6) considers that market forces, particularly the capital market, will allocate a considerable part of the income derived from energy exports to other sectors of the economy, thus bringing about a spontaneous diversification of the economy. Domestic and foreign banks, and the capital markets, together with retained earnings, will provide the funds for substantial investments in the non-energy sectors. No special

[1] Hedlund, S, 2005, *Russian Path Dependence. A People with a Troubled History*, London.

[2] Kontorovich, V, 2005, Small business and Putin's federal reform, in Reddaway, P, and Orttung, R, eds, *The Dynamics of Russian Politics*, Vol. 2 *Putin's Reform of Federal-regional Relations*, Lanham, MD.

government measures are necessary. The state only has to confine itself to ensuring macroeconomic stability, keeping tax rates low (and if possible reducing them), protecting private property, continuing the programme of liberal economic reforms as recommended by the IMF and other Western advisers, and market forces will ensure economic growth and economic diversification. If the state attempts to substitute itself for market forces the result will be much less efficient than spontaneous diversification. The reason for this is that the Russian state is very corrupt and its investment projects are not profit-oriented. According to Gavrilenkov, the main results so far of government rhetoric about strengthening the role of the state in the economy are to worsen the investment climate and reduce the rate of growth of the economy.

A positive feature of Gavrilenkov's argument is that he is both a good economist and currently working in the heart of the Russian capital market. Hence he is very well informed about his topic and has inside knowledge about the contribution of the capital market to diversification. However, his position is controversial in Russian policy debates, where Soviet-period attitudes remain widespread. Gavrilenkov's very title ('The road to spontaneous diversification') expresses his liberal and anti-Communist orientation (for Lenin 'spontaneous' processes were inherently inefficient and had to be replaced by conscious direction and planning). The Soviet-era economist Nikolai Shmelev, academician and currently director of the Europe Institute of the Academy of Sciences, has argued that under Russian conditions the state must play a major role in the investment process. He gave three reasons for this. First, privatization under Russian conditions means giving away state enterprises for very low prices to dubious people who are only interested in investment in a small number of highly profitable activities (energy, trade, vodka, gambling, building, crime). Second, there is no alternative, since the private sector is not interested in investment in manufacturing. Third, it is necessary to repopulate and develop eastern Siberia and the Far East, and only the state can do this.[1]

Khanin (Chapter 7) offers a quite different perspective to that of Gavrilenkov. He begins by stressing the unreliability of Russian economic statistics. In Soviet times, he was the foremost critic of Soviet economic statistics, and in recent years he has become a trenchant critic of Russian economic statistics. According to Khanin, although the official statistics understate the *level* of the national income (because of the importance of the shadow economy or informal sector) they exaggerate the *growth* of the national income (as well as distorting the value of many other important economic variables). In his chapter, Khanin briefly summarizes his recalculations, which have been set out at length in a number of Russian publications.

---

[1] Shmelev, N, 2005, Kliuchevye voprosy Rossii, *Svobodnaya mysl'-XXI*, No. 9.

On the basis of his calculations, and of his interpretation of the economic history of Russia over the last three centuries, Khanin sketches his policy proposals. Essentially he argues for a new leap forward, as in the times of Peter the Great and Stalin. It should primarily consist of a massive investment programme, to be financed by a massive reduction in the consumption of the highest incomes and utilization of the foreign trade surplus. He points out that the state would probably play the central role, and that it would probably have to be an authoritarian state since this kind of programme is unlikely to win an election. However, in his view it is essential to overcome Russian economic backwardness.

It is worth noting that, according to some liberal economists, Russian economic policy has already begun moving in the direction proposed by Khanin. In September 2005, Andrei Illarionov (then economic advisor to President Putin) gave an interview in which he warned against what he regarded as the dangerous move towards greater state involvement in the economy apparent in the second Putin term.[1] He even referred to 2004 as 'the year of the great break', a deliberate comparison with 1929, described by Stalin as 'the year of the great break'. In the year1929 Stalin broke decisively with the (partial) market economy of the NEP period and launched the Stalinist leap forward based on massive investment, coercion and mass terror. A milder version of Illarionov's interpretation is also to be found in Gavrilenkov's Chapter 6.

The two crucial issues raised by Khanin's policy proposals are their political feasibility and economic attractiveness. The proposed redistribution of income from the higher income groups will strike many people as fair. However, it does not seem politically feasible. The well-off are hardly likely to give up easily their current life style and aspirations for the future. In particular, the huge redistribution of income away from Moscow (and to a lesser extent St. Petersburg) and in favour of the provinces, is hardly politically realistic. Furthermore, if a variant of this programme ever came to be attempted, it would be essential from the standpoint of economic efficiency to ensure that the investments implemented would be in projects that in due course benefited the population. High-cost manufacturing plants (as resulted from Latin American import-substitution) or high-tech rearmament (as under Stalin and Reagan) or an enlarged space programme (on the lines of Bush's manned Mars proposal) could soak up a huge volume of resources without improving welfare. On the other hand, high investment rates were and are characteristic of the successful East Asian economies. In addition, the investment programme Khanin advocates is not just a matter of traditional industrial physical capital (buildings and machinery) but also includes the urban infrastructure (e.g., housing, sewers,

[1] *Rossiiskaya gazeta*, 23 September 2005.

heating) and the allocation of substantial resources to education and health. These are programmes which directly improve human development.

The two chapters by Gavrilenkov (who is the chief economist and managing director of a Moscow brokerage house) and Khanin (who is a professor at a Novosibirsk university) span the range of Russian opinion about economic policy and the future of Russia. The former looks to the market and the Western world and hopes that Russia will make progress without leaps and will gradually become just another country, albeit a very large and energy-rich one with a rather special history. The latter considers that the market has failed, looks with approval at the specifically Russian phenomenon of the state-led economic development leap, and has favourable words for Stalin and his economic successes.

It is obvious that an assessment of the relative merits of the Gavrilenkov and Khanin scenarios depends very much on one's judgement of the reliability of official statistics. If the official macroeconomic statistics are reliable, then economic growth in recent years has been fast, and maybe spontaneous diversification is a successful and very sensible strategy. On the other hand, if Khanin is right that the official growth statistics are substantially exaggerated, then spontaneous diversification would seem much less attractive and the case for the mobilization model would be strengthened.

Much discussion of possible economic policies implicitly assumes that economic outcomes are exclusively determined by economic policy. However, economic outcomes are actually determined by a variety of factors, of which domestic economic policy is just one. A major factor determining economic outcomes is the geographical situation of the country concerned. That is why this book includes Kontorovich's Chapter 8, which draws attention to one of the geographical factors determining the future of the Russian economy, its low population density. The purpose of including this chapter is to stress that Russia's energy riches are just one of the factors determining its economic future.

Russia is very large. Indeed it is the largest country in the world. Russians tend to be proud of this. It is endlessly repeated in speeches and publications. However, it has a downside. Due to its size, its population density is low. In most of the country this is a disincentive to business formation. If the total Russian population were concentrated in a much smaller area, it is likely that the rate of new business formation would be much higher, with corresponding benefits for economic growth. Furthermore, the large area brings high transport costs with it. The abundance of energy is just one specifically Russian economic feature. The huge size of the country is another, which also has important economic consequences. Another geographical factor, which recently has been much discussed, and which also has important economic consequences (short growing season, additional heating and building costs) is the cold weather which prevails over much of the country for a large part of each year.[1]

In Section D, Tompson (Chapter 9) discusses the internal political aspects of the Russian oil and natural gas riches. He points out that in Russia the 'resource shock' did not arise from discoveries of natural resources (as in the Dutch, Norwegian and British cases) but from the adjustment of relative prices in the post-Soviet period resulting from opening up the economy to international trade. Adjusting relative prices from their Soviet levels to levels more in line with those of the world market, completely changed the relative profitability of the raw materials and manufacturing sectors. His main finding is that the argument that Russia today is experiencing Venezuelaization is an exaggeration. He argues that the energy riches themselves are not a problem, but what is a problem is the combination of those riches with an institutional environment that is not well equipped to cope with the problems generated by huge energy riches. This argument underlines the importance of political–institutional developments in co-determining Russia's future.

Tompson also draws attention to the role of energy in Russian foreign policy. The specific features of the USSR's foreign policy were initially the Communist International and subsequently its massive armed forces. Till almost its end the USSR remained the carrier of a specific ideology which found numerous adherents abroad, at first workers and intellectuals in the advanced countries and then revolutionary movements and dictators in the third world. As late as the 1980s, Marxism–Leninism was attractive in much of Africa and also in the Caribbean and provided the USSR with allies throughout the world. This ideology repelled some countries and political movements and attracted others, thus playing a major role in shaping the USSR's relations with the rest of the world. The military might of the USSR increasingly constituted the main source of its role as one of the two great powers in the world. Its nuclear weapons, intercontinental rockets and large armed forces were a major aspect of its international status.

The Russian Federation (unlike the USA) is not engaged in exporting a specific ideology and has downsized its armed forces. The specific feature of its foreign policy is its huge energy exports. This is a legacy from the USSR which the Putin administration is consciously exploiting. In view of the large and growing demand for energy throughout the world, these exports give it a

---

[1] Parshev, A P, 2001, *Pochemu Rossiya ne Amerika*, Moscow; Hill, F and Gaddy, C, 2003, *The Siberian Curse*, Washington DC. For a critique of the latter book see Shenfield, S, ed., 2005, *JRL Research and Analytical Supplement*, No. 31, October, Parts 4 and 5 (www.cdi.org/russia/johnson/jrl-ras.cfm). A recent book stressing Russia's 'illiberal geography' is Lynch, A, 2005, *How Russia is not Ruled*, Cambridge.

potent political instrument. For the EU, the large oil and natural gas imports from Russia are an important reason for maintaining good relations with Russia, even if Russia is scarcely a model democracy, human rights are violated in the war in Chechnya and elsewhere, and the new members of the EU are suspicious of Russia and some of them have poor relations with Russia. Similarly, for China, Japan and South Korea current and prospective imports of oil and natural gas from Russia are an important reason for keeping on good terms with Russia.

Although Russia today plays a much reduced role in the world compared with the USSR, its energy exports ensure that it is still a major player in international politics. Its decisions on pipeline routes, choice of foreign partners for energy projects, and choice of export markets, are closely followed in foreign capitals and give it considerable political influence. Similarly, the foreign investments of its oil and gas companies, both downstream (e.g., oil refineries and petrol stations) and upstream (exploration and development of oil and gas fields) are carefully assessed by anxious governments. In the twenty-first century, Russia's energy riches make it a major player on the world scene. In this way its role in the world is much more constructive than was that of the USSR. Instead of generating problems for the West all over the world, as the USSR did, Russia today helps solve the problem of domestic energy shortages which plague many countries. Hence today Russia, like Norway, Nigeria, or Venezuela, but on a bigger scale, is a major contributor to world stability and the welfare of the energy importers.

2

ENERGY AND THE ECONOMY: AN INTRODUCTION

Peter Oppenheimer and Sergiy Maslichenko

Post-crisis Economic Growth in Russia

In 2005 Russia experienced a seventh successive year of relatively strong GDP increase, reaching 6.4 per cent. Real incomes rose by an estimated 8.8 per cent and poverty rates declined further. The federal budget ran a record surplus in 2005 of 7.5 per cent of GDP (Table 2.1). The external surplus on trade in goods and services was USD 106 billion (14% of GDP), twenty per cent higher than in 2004. The foreign exchange reserves of the Central Bank of Russia increased by over 40 per cent to USD 182 billion as of 1 January 2006. Total employment was 68.2 million and estimated unemployment decreased to 5.7 million or 7.7 per cent of the workforce.

Table 2.1 Macroeconomic Indicators

	1999	2000	2001	2002	2003	2004	2005	1999–2005 (average)
GDP, % increases	6.4	10.0	5.1	4.7	7.3	7.1	6.4	6.7
Industrial production, % increases	11.0	11.9	4.9	3.7	7.0	6.1	4.0	6.9
Fixed capital investment, % increases	5.3	17.4	8.7	2.6	12.5	10.9	10.5	9.7
Inflation (CPI), %	36.5	20.2	18.6	15.1	12.0	11.7	10.9	–
Real disposable income, % increases	n.a.	12.0	8.7	11.3	13.7	7.8	8.8	10.4
Federal budget balance, % GDP	–1.1	2.3	3.0	2.3	1.7	4.2	7.5	–

Note: The data for 2005 are preliminary.
Source: Rosstat.

The upswing has been broadly based (Table 2.2). Production of goods in 2004 grew by 6.3 per cent (compared with 8.2 per cent in 2003) and of services by 7.9 per cent (6.9 per cent). Dividing industrial production growth into its natural resource (export oriented) and manufacturing (domestically oriented) components shows the two developing in roughly parallel fashion over the years (Table 2.3 & Figure 2.3). In 2004 the industrial growth leaders were engineering (11.7 per cent), chemicals (7.4 per cent), fuel and energy (7.1 per cent), construction materials (5.3 per cent) and ferrous metallurgy (5.0 per cent) (Figure 2.4).

Table 2.2 Growth in the Russian Economy, 2002–04, % p.a.

	2002	2003	2004	2002–04 (average)
GDP	4.7	7.3	7.1	6.4
Industry	4.0	7.5	6.1	5.9
Construction	2.8	14.3	10.2	9.0
Agriculture	2.9	5.7	2.9	3.8
Transport	3.4	5.6	5.0	4.7
Communication	16.6	20.7	24.7	20.6
Trade	8.2	10.9	10.1	9.7
Other services	2.2	4.0	2.3	2.8

Source: Rosstat.

Table 2.3 Annual Growth Rates in Resource and Manufacturing Industries (%)

	1999	2000	2001	2002	2003	2004
Non-ferrous metals	10.0	15.0	4.9	6.0	6.2	3.6
Ferrous metals	17.0	16.0	−0.2	3.0	8.9	5.0
Fuel and energy	2.4	5.0	6.1	7.0	9.3	7.1
Wood and wood processing	18.0	13.0	2.6	2.4	1.5	3.0
Weighted average	**9.3**	**10.4**	**4.2**	**5.5**	**7.8**	**5.7**
Electricity	−1.0	1.8	1.6	−0.7	1.0	0.3
Chemical	24.0	15.0	5.0	1.6	4.4	7.4
Engineering	17.0	20.0	7.2	2.0	9.6	11.7
Construction materials	10.0	13.0	5.5	3.0	6.4	5.3
Light industry	12.1	21.0	5.8	−3.4	−2.3	−7.5
Food	4.0	14.0	8.4	6.5	5.1	4.0
Weighted average	**10.6**	**14.3**	**6.3**	**2.5**	**5.6**	**6.1**

Source: World Bank; own estimates.

Size of the Oil and Gas Sector

Discussion of the role of oil and gas extraction in the country's economic performance requires a variety of statistical and conceptual clarifications.

Consider first the proportion of GDP constituted by the sector, and recall that output in the national accounts is defined as value-added. For the early 2000s Russian official national accounts data (illustrated in Figure 2.1) have shown the sector contributing a mere 8 or 9 per cent of GDP. This is inconsistent with a series of other statistics—notably the 50-per cent-plus share of oil and gas in Russia's exports (Table 2.4), when total exports have comfortably exceeded imports in value, most imports consist of consumer goods, and imported items account for 40 or 50 per cent of consumers' cash outlays. The inconsistency is resolved by the finding (reported by the World Bank in its Country Economic Memorandum—CEM—for Russia in 2004) that a large part of the upstream oil and gas sector's profits was being misattributed to commerce (wholesale trade), in order to escape taxation.[1] Some of this activity was doubtless illegal (evasion of tax through the use of phantom companies and the like), but a good deal was legal avoidance through the establishment

Figure 2.1 Structure of GDP: Official Shares (2003), %

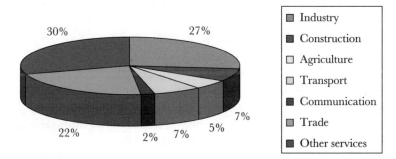

30%   27%

□ Industry
■ Construction
□ Agriculture
□ Transport
■ Communication
■ Trade
■ Other services

7%

22%   2%   7%   5%

Source: Rosstat.

Table 2.4 Hydrocarbon (Oil and Gas) Exports

	1998	1999	2000	2001	2002	2003
Oil and gas exports (USD billion)	27.9	31.0	52.8	52.1	56.3	74.0
Share of total exports, %	32.2	36.6	46.1	46.1	46.4	49.2
Ratio to GDP, %	10.4	15.8	20.3	17.0	16.3	17.1

Source: Gurvich (2004), p. 9.

[1] The point had been previously uncovered by Tabata (2002). See also Kuboniwa *et al.* (2005). We are grateful to Michael Ellman for pointing this out.

Figure 2.2 Structure of GDP: Official and Adjusted Weights (2003), %

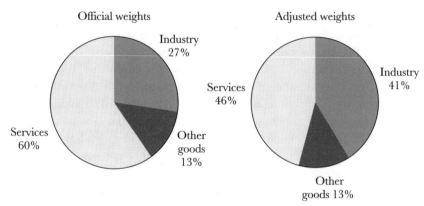

Source: Rosstat, World Bank and OECD.

of trading subsidiaries in regions offering special local tax reliefs (so-called 'internal offshores'). The latter was effectively abrogated in 2004, essentially by bringing a larger part of the tax system under federal control.

Adjusting for the anomaly by applying oil-sector profit margins normal in western countries (Canada, Netherlands, Norway, the UK) brings the oil and gas sector's share of Russia's GDP to the 20–25 per cent range. By the same token, industry's aggregate share rises from 28 to well over 40 per cent, and that of trade drops from 27 per cent to 15 or less. Figure 2.2 illustrates this adjustment.

While these are now plausible orders of magnitude, the foregoing by no means exhausts the list of problem issues affecting Russia's national accounts. For the time being internal market prices of fuel, particularly natural gas and the electricity derived from it, remain not merely below world market prices (which are not a critical benchmark) but below their cost of production properly calculated, i.e., including capital cost (which is a critical benchmark). Correction of this would raise the oil and gas sector's share of GDP still further. On the other hand, other adjustments would have an opposite effect. Russian national accounts data almost certainly understate real income accruing from housing and probably also from subsistence horticulture. For the time being it suffices to note that a GDP share for oil and gas of 20–25 per cent is more than three times as large as the share of British GDP contributed by the North Sea at its short-lived production peak in the 1980s.

Russia's Oil Sector and Living Standards in the 1990s

Before further considering economic expansion after 1998, a comment is in order on the change in GDP and living standards during the preceding

Figure 2.3 Growth Rates in Manufacturing and Resource-based Industries

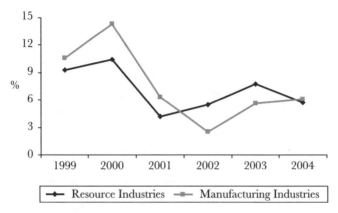

Source: World Bank; own estimates.

Figure 2.4 Leaders of Industrial Growth, 2004

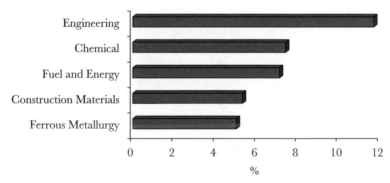

Source: Rosstat.

decade. The disintegration of the Soviet Union was accompanied by a major fall in production. Between 1989 and the mid-1990s Russia's GDP fell by more than 40 per cent. In most ordinary circumstances, movements of GDP can be taken as a good indicator of changes in living standards. However, in Russia of the 1990s there was little connection between the two. To a first approximation, average living standards hardly changed despite the drop in output. To be sure, the word 'average' conceals a multitude of sins. Dispersions around the average became a lot wider—over time (with sharp fluctuations in the real purchasing power of people's money income, as inflation alternately raced ahead of and lagged behind earnings), in space (with some regions, notably Moscow and oil-producing areas, more prosperous than others) and across the population (with income distribution becoming considerably more uneven than before).[1]

Food consumption indices showed per capita declines in meat, fish, eggs and dairy products, arguably reflecting hardship among lower income groups, a larger percentage of whose budget goes on food; yet the legitimacy of this interpretation is unclear, since the trend began not in 1991 but at least a decade earlier. Moreover, on the other side of the ledger, ownership of private cars rose from 59 vehicles per 1000 of the population in 1990 (itself double the 1980 figure) to over 100 from 1997 onwards. Also, ownership of household durables, already at a high level for most items in the 1980s, continued on an upward trend. Furthermore, the index numbers do not show the big improvement in quality brought by increased import penetration (of which more in a moment).

Admittedly the greater variability in living standards is also not captured by conventional indices. Economic life became more uncertain, more insecure, less predictable, all the more so in view of widespread arrears in wage payments and recourse to barter. This presumably had some direct and also—through increased liquor consumption—indirect responsibility for the accelerated decline in the life expectancy of Russians, especially males, in the 1990s. In 2001 Russian life expectancy was 58.6 years for males and 72.1 for females. (World Bank, CEM., p. 18)

Be that as it may, the maintenance of material living standards in the face of a massive fall in output was the result, in a positive sense, of the large-scale opening of Russia's economy to foreign trade. A big upsurge of consumer imports was more than paid for by expanded hard-currency export earnings, of which oil and gas generated the largest slice. In a negative sense, the maintenance of living standards was assisted by the fact that a good part of the fall in output was in military and quasi-military items which had never contributed much to living standards anyhow. This evidently includes, be it noted, much of the drop that occurred in oil output itself. Russia's annual production of crude in the second half of the 1990s was about 6.2 million barrels a day, compared with over 11 million at its peak in the late 1980s.

The opening of the economy is by far Russia's most important form of post-Communist adjustment to date. It was easily undertaken because it was achievable without significant physical restructuring of the country's domestic capital stock. Indeed, the 1990s, and to some extent the years after 2000 as well, were conspicuous for the absence of large-scale industrial fixed investment. This, of course, has to change sooner or later. It should be emphasized that

---

[1] Russia's reported Gini coefficent—the standard index of inequality, with outer limits of 0 and 1—increased from 0.27 in 1990 to 0.48 in 1996. (EBRD, *Transition Report*, 1999, p. 260) For additional data on Russian income inequality see pp. 165–166.

the low investment level has been due to market uncertainties and institutional conditions in Russia (the dysfunctional credit system, lack of trust, poor corporate governance, etc.), and not to balance-of-payments limitations. Russia's export receipts, even in the 1990s, would have been sufficient to finance substantial imports of investment goods on top of the consumer import boom which actually occurred. As it happens, instead of domestic investment, the additional export receipts financed multi-billion dollar outflows of capital into western markets.

The 1998 Threshold

The turning point of August 1998 to some extent marks the arrival of accustomed relations among macroeconomic variables. The full story, however, is more complicated.

The 1998 upheaval itself stemmed basically not from external factors but, in Latin American fashion, from domestic fiscal ones. True, Russia's balance of payments on current account went briefly into deficit as oil prices experienced a low (USD13 a barrel for Brent), following the East Asian financial crisis of 1997. That crisis also led to global portfolio shifts away from other emerging markets including Russia. However, these international factors would not have caused major turmoil for Russia if the government's budget and the Russian banking system had been in a sustainable condition.

The key point behind the August 1998 defaults and devaluation was the Federal authorities' failure to match government spending commitments with tax revenues. The gap had been filled for a few years with short-term borrowing—chiefly via ruble Treasury bills, the so-called GKOs—at exorbitant interest rates reflecting (in part) the properly restrictive monetary policy of the Central Bank. Russian commercial banks financed large-scale purchases of such government paper by borrowing abroad in foreign currency, thus exposing themselves to major foreign-exchange risk as well as to the possibility (likelihood?) of government default. When default appeared imminent, banks and others rushed to cover their foreign-exchange obligations, thereby of course precipitating the very collapse that they feared.

The majority of Russia's larger participating commercial banks were swept away (Alpha Bank being the main exception). A considerable part of the Russian government's ruble debt was eliminated. At the same time, the ruble fell sharply and in a few months lost about two-thirds of its value against western currencies.

A Different Adjustment Process

A sequel to the events of August 1998 was a textbook Keynesian (as developed for the open economy by Meade, Swan and others) macroeconomic adjustment process. Expenditure reduction was accompanied by expenditure switching. Reduction was achieved by a combination of restrictive monetary and fiscal policies. The Central Bank strongly resisted the temptation to revert to permissive monetary management in the face of the inflationary impetus imparted by ruble depreciation. And the federal government followed suit by refusing full indexation of its expenditure commitments while striving for maximum increases in revenue. The oil sector was of critical importance in the enhancement of revenue (Table 2.5). This occurred initially through the effect of devaluation in raising the ruble value of oil exports—which indeed had constituted the major prior case for ruble devaluation irrespective of the August financial crisis. Subsequently the high level of international oil prices had an equal effect (continuing, of course, to 2005 at least).

Expenditure switching was achieved likewise through the rise in the ruble price of traded goods—in this case particularly imported consumer articles—and the associated fall in the real wage, which initially was in the order of 30 per cent. This stimulated domestic production (and restrained imports) of a range of manufactures, from processed foods to building materials to pharmaceuticals. Much of it also involved, or led to, fixed investments in the relevant industries though not necessarily large-scale or on a continuing basis.

Initially a switching effect was probably significant on the export side as well. At the world oil prices and ruble exchange rate of the first half of 1998 Russian oil exports were not strongly profitable. The high oil prices prevailing from 2000 onwards were unforeseeable; in their absence the lower ruble exchange rate would have been decisive in underpinning production.

The overall result was to kick-start a period of economic expansion and financial soundness whose main features were summarized in the opening section of this chapter. No doubt output and incomes could have grown still faster. The one specific blemish, however, has been that consumer-price inflation has remained in double figures. Over the whole seven-year period that has hitherto elapsed since 1998 oil and gas production has maintained its 20–25 per cent share of GDP. After somewhat losing share in the earlier part

Table 2.5 Budget Revenues from Oil and Gas Sector (% of GDP)

	1999	2000	2001	2002	2003
Oil sector	3.2	5.8	5.6	5.6	5.9
Gas sector	1.9	2.0	2.5	2.1	1.9
Pipeline transport	0.5	1.0	1.1	0.4	0.4
Total oil & gas sector	5.6	8.7	9.2	8.1	8.2
Other revenues	28.6	28.6	27.9	28.9	28.2

Source: Gurvich (2004), p. 14.

Table 2.6 Oil and Gas Sector: % of GDP Growth

	2000	2001	2002	2003	2000–2003
Oil sector	9.7	13.2	47.9	34.9	24.8
Gas sector	−3.6	−9.0	1.7	5.9	−0.8
Oil & gas sector	6.1	4.2	49.6	40.8	24.0

Source: Gurvich (2004), p. 28; own estimates.

of the period, the sector accelerated and fully regained its earlier position (Table 2.6 and Chapter 5).

Sustaining the Process

There was, and is, nothing inevitable about expansion continuing at this pace, whether for seven years or longer. What factors explain it?

One, at least permissively, has been the economy's margin of spare capacity. The term 'economic growth' has not so far been strictly applicable to post-Communist Russia. This is because the term normally refers to (the medium- and long-term trend of) an economy's maximum potential, 'full-employment' or 'ceiling' output. Its determinants are—at their simplest and most aggregative—the rates of growth of the working population and of labour productivity (output per worker) respectively. These concepts have had little or no relevance to Russia over the past 15 years. During that time the country has undergone not a period of growth but an oversized fluctuation, albeit one in which structural change has been sufficient to leave most of the population better off than it was at the outset. Real wages are reckoned to have increased during 1999–2003 by over 80 per cent, leaving them 28 per cent higher than on the eve of the 1998 crisis. (Ahrend 2004 and Chapter 5)

Aggregate output, however, having fallen by 40–50 per cent in the near-decade to 1998, has still to regain its previous peak. In Yegor Gaidar's (2003) terminology, we are talking about 'recovery growth'. This statement applies also to the individual sector of upstream oil (though not, as it happens, to natural gas, production of which has fluctuated around a more or less stationary level). Russia's oil production in 2004 at a little under 9.3 m.b.d. was still 15 per cent below the 1989 total.

What is unclear is where the country's current productive potential lies in relation to these previous peaks. For one thing, population has declined in the interim, albeit only slightly. Between 1989 and 2002 a natural fall of 5 per cent (7.4 million) reflecting a lower birth rate and shorter life spans appears to have been three-quarters offset by net inward migration. Arrivals from the FSU (many of them doubtless ethnic Russians) substantially outnumbered emigrants to Germany, Israel and the United States. The quality of the labour force was probably unaffected by these movements (World Bank, 2004).

For another, much more important thing, business fixed investment was at a low ebb through the 1990s. Ageing capital stock was not replaced when in demand. And previously non-existent or underdeveloped sectors were held back by capacity shortages and a business climate unfavourable to risk-taking and finance for new enterprises: The situation improved somewhat from 1999 onwards. Expansion was supported by fixed investment outlays increasing at nearly 10 per cent per annum over five years. The expansion itself signified improved utilization of labour across the economy. Increases in open unemployment during the 1990s had been slight, largely because employees with nowhere else to go had an incentive to remain on the books of an enterprise even when unpaid. By the same token, higher GDP after 1998 showed up preponderantly as productivity gains. Existing enterprises were once again able to make use of their workers; or else the workers themselves were able to move to new employers, both in import-substitute industries and in the non-traded services sector.

All this represented a measure of progress in the development of market mechanisms and institutions as well as of macroeconomic polices. However, the improvement must not be exaggerated. The conspicuous output and investment performance of the oil industry after 1998, for example (Table 2.7, Figure 2.5 and Chapter 5), was a consequence mainly of the termination of primitive battles for corporate control, which previously monopolized the attention of enterprise executives. It illustrates the power of the profit motive. But it does not signify a breakthrough in establishing law-abidingness or security of shareholder and other property rights in a business context. Still less does it signify the emergence of well-functioning credit and capital markets in Russia, capable of intermediating between savers and investors and thereby financing the wholesale transformation—beginning with a good deal of demolition—of the mainly military 'rust belt' industries which still physically

Table 2.7 Annual Changes in Fixed Capital Investment (%)

	2000	2001	2002	2003	2000–03 (cum.)
Oil production	51.1	23.6	−15.1	19.2	89.0
Oil processing	140.0	15.6	−9.5	−1.9	146.3
Gas production	44.4	5.0	−1.0	24.8	87.3
Pipeline transport	69.6	22.8	−18.2	−11.7	50.4
Oil & gas Sector	**58.9**	**19.5**	**−13.4**	**10.2**	**81.2**
Total in economy	*17.4*	*10.0*	*−1.7*	*11.1*	*41.0*

Source: Gurvich (2004), p. 27.

Figure 2.5 GDP Components Growth (%)

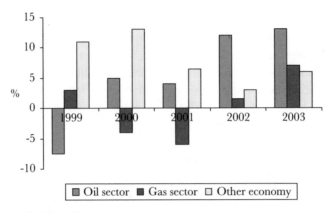

Source: Gurvich (2004), p. 27.

dominate many Russian towns. Business costs continue to be hugely inflated by bribery and corruption (Myers 2005); and where channels of corruption are not well developed, business dealings are limited by lack of trust.

Progress in these matters is being hampered by political factors, but not by them alone. Moreover, where politics are an obstacle, it is not invariably the authorities who are at fault. Mikhail Khodorkovsky and Yukos are unfortunate victims of on-going deficiencies in Russia's economic, political and judicial mechanisms. Unfortunate indeed, but not innocent. And their fate is not a sign of sweeping rejection of capitalist economics and market principles by President Putin and his colleagues (Browder 2005).[1]

The Terms of Trade

As already noted, Russia's economic upswing coincided with major strengthening of international oil (and gas) prices. Russia's terms of trade as an exporter have benefitted accordingly. The initial form of the benefit was a further increase

[1] Prior to its dismemberment, Yukos was one of the tiny number of Russian companies with shares quoted on western stock markets, a small proportion of the company's capital having been publicly floated for this purpose by Khodorkovsky and associates. The main motive for this fractional flotation was to boost the company's overall net worth—and hence the wealth of Khodorkovsky and associates—by plugging into western market valuation of upstream oil reserves. Further share sales by the controlling Russian shareholders could well have followed in due course, and indeed a major sell-out to western partners was rumoured to be impending or under negotiation at the time of Khodorkovsky's arrest in autumn 2003. This prospect may well have affected the timing of the Russian regime's move against Khodorkovsky.

in the oil industry's rental income, bringing the government still greater tax revenue from that source (Table 2.5). More generally, the enlarged international purchasing power of the country's GDP meant that real disposable incomes were able to increase much faster than real GDP itself (Table 2.1) without upsetting the external accounts. Indeed, the Central Bank added more than USD100 billion to its currency reserves, while the government prepaid a substantial share of Russia's external borrowings. On top of that the government established a Stabilization Fund to sterilize part of its oil-based receipts, with an immediate view to dampening inflation and limiting the real-terms appreciation of the ruble.

The foregoing paragraph takes the rate of increase of real GDP as given. The question, however, which has exercised various analysts is whether the growth of GDP itself was, or will be, significantly affected by higher oil prices. Among the bodies that have sought quantitative answers to the question are the OECD (Ahrend 2004 – see Table 2.8), the Economic Expert Group in Russia (Gurvich 2004, 2005) and the World Bank (2004). Most of the econometric results reported are spurious, because based on inadequate qualitative formulation of the complex and contradictory economic forces involved. The most egregious error is that of Christof Rühl and colleagues at the World Bank, who wrote (World Bank 2004, para 35):

> No matter how it is estimated, the share of oil and gas in GDP only measures the direct contribution to growth of changes in the international price for these commodities. The indirect effect is larger and harder to estimate.

Alas, the alleged 'direct contribution' is merely a conceptual blunder. It does not actually exist. The movement of real GDP over time measures physical changes in output. Accordingly it is—has to be—calculated at constant prices and is directly no more altered by changes in the terms of trade than it is by inflation.[1] The confusion presumably arises from the habitual identification

Table 2.8 Actual and Simulated GDP Growth Rates

	Actual	Simulated*
2000	10.0	6.3
2001	5.1	6.1
2002	4.7	4.5
2003	7.3	6.2
Average	*6.8*	*5.8*

* Assuming constant oil prices at long-term average levels (USD19 Urals) in 2000–2003.
Source: Ahrend (2004).

of changes in real disposable national income with changes in real GDP (or rather, real GNP). This equivalence holds, however, only when the terms of trade remain constant. If the terms of trade move, there is an instantaneous rise or fall in real disposable national income, but no change in real GDP.

To avoid a different kind of misunderstanding, let it be said that Russia's export and import prices, and therefore terms of trade, are determined by world market conditions, upon which Russia itself has no perceptible influence (the 'small country' case). More complex analysis is needed if a country partially determines its own term of trade—for instance because of the weight of its exports or imports of commodity X in the world total. This would be the 'large country' case. But it still would not signify any 'direct contribution' of terms-of-trade changes to economic growth.

The indirect effects are another matter. However, here there is a conflict between 'export-led growth effects' and 'Dutch disease' effects. The former give a boost to growth through the added consumption and investment activity stimulated by the expenditures of the leading sector. The latter act as a drag on growth by inducing real appreciation of the currency and thus handicapping the advance of traded-goods industries other than the leading sector. Both apply, by the way, with second-order variations, not merely to price (terms-of-trade) changes, but also to output (GDP) growth of the leading sector. And in both cases a key element of the economic mechanism is the set of incentives perceived by entrepreneurs in the various parts of the economy to expand or contract productive capacity under their management.

To disentangle and assess the working of these factors in the Russian context would be a highly complex exercise, and its value for policy purposes questionable. However, there is certainly no presumption—contrary to what the abovementioned authors are inclined to suppose—that an improvement in the terms of trade has a positive rather than a negative effect on GDP growth.

Energy-sector Policy and Prospects

The central and critical role of the energy sector in Russia's current economic performance is a focus of dilemmas for the government. In a word, the authorities do not trust unfettered market freedom and private enterprise to serve the national interest. Or alternatively, they do not believe that taxation

[1] It appears necessary to state that this point is not dependent on any restrictive assumptions, and in particular is unaffected by the precise method used for computing a change in real GDP. Any method involves evaluating two non-identical bundles of output—namely, output produced in period 2 and in period 1, respectively—at one and the same set of prices, be they prices of period 1, those of period 2, those of a third period or something in-between. Whatever the choice, the computation abstracts from any movement of prices occurring either between periods 1 and 2 or at any other time.

plus arms-length regulation of enterprise behaviour can be sufficient to secure an acceptable outcome from the national point of view.

This is despite—or perhaps because of—the clear achievements of private firms in expanding output in all parts of the energy sector. The major rebound of oil production has been brought about overwhelmingly by private business (see Chapter 5). In coal and gas, the achievements are on a smaller scale but equally striking. In the restructured and privatized coal industry, state budget subsidies have been all but eliminated—from almost USD3 billion in 1993 to USD200 million in 2003. At the same time the decline in production was halted and reversed (Figure 2.7). The gas industry remains obviously dominated by Gazprom. Yet independent gas producers (mostly private companies) managed, despite poor initial conditions (green-field, no export outlets), to double their gas production in 1999–2004. Gazprom's much larger output stagnated (Figure 2.8), in spite of the company receiving windfall income from high European gas prices since late 1999. Gazprom output would, moreover, have been less than reported without the enforced takeover of the independent gas company Purgaz (Gubkinskoye gas field). This had been acquired as a green-field project in 1999 by the somewhat mysterious independent company Itera, which proceeded to invest over USD200 million in its development. (Milov 2005).

Gazprom's export commitments—volumes to Western Europe in 2004 up 13.4 per cent from 1999; those to CIS countries up 1 per cent—left its

Figure 2.6 Russian Oil and Condensate Production (1913–2004)

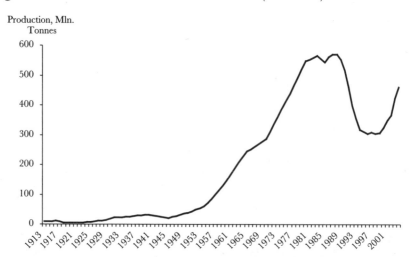

Source: Robert Campbell, Thane Gustafson, Interfax, *Neft' i Kapital*, BP Statistical Review of World Energy, 2004.

Figure 2.7 Coal Sector: Subsidies and Production, 1993–2003

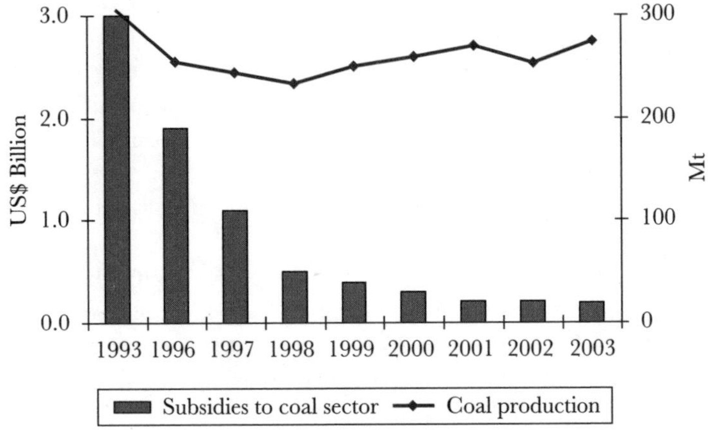

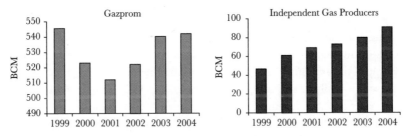

Source: Ministry of Industry and Energy statistics, own estimates.

Figure 2.8 Russian Gas Production, 1999–2004: Gazprom versus Independent Gas Producers

Note: Gas production of Gazprom includes independent gas producers taken over in the 1999–2004 period.
Source: Rosstat, TsDU TEK.

supplies to the domestic market in 2004 some 70 bcm short of demand, a gap expected to reach 100 bcm in 2005 or 2006. It is precisely the private independent gas producers which have so far filled this gap (Figure 2.8).

Kremlin suspicion of large-scale private ownership in the energy sector is reinforced by the presence of foreign companies, notably the 50 per cent partnership of TNK with BP in Western Siberia. The years 2003–05 have seen a series of moves to reassert or widen state control (Milov 2005). This includes:

1. Dismemberment and renationalization of Yukos, partly no doubt because it was serving as the vehicle for Mr Khodorkovsky's political designs, but not only for that reason.

2. Acquisition of Yuganskneftegaz, formerly the major production unit of Yukos, by the state company Rosneft through a questionable auction procedure.
3. Increased Kremlin interference in the approval of major foreign investment deals by Russian energy companies (the Kremlin is believed to have directly approved stake acquisitions in 2004 by ConocoPhillips in Lukoil and by Total in the gas producer Novatek, while refusing acquisitions by ExxonMobil in Yukos and by Total in Sibneft).
4. Announced restrictions on foreign participation in oil and gas upstream and pipelines.
5. Large-scale intrusion by Gazprom in the power sector, believed to be directly inspired by the Kremlin. Gazprom currently holds a 10.3 per cent stake in RAO UES and over 25 per cent in Mosenergo: this represents ownership of 30–40 GW of installed generation capacity, nearly 20 per cent of total generation capacity in Russia.
6. Kremlin-inspired but economically controversial acquisitions of energy assets in FSU countries by Russian state enterprises (RAO UES in power, Gazprom in gas).
7. In late September 2005, Gazprom announced its impending acquisition of just over 75 per cent of the share capital of Sibneft, a company accounting for roughly 10 per cent of Russia's oil production. Three per cent was being purchased for USD500 million from Gazprom's own subsidiary Gazprombank; the other 72 per cent for USD13 billion from Millhouse Capital, the holding company of Roman Abramovich. Most of the purchase is initially to be funded by credits of USD12 billion from a syndicate of western banks; about 40 per cent of this (USD5 billion) is to be repaid within months out of the USD5.7 billion proceeds of a Russian Government purchase of Gazprom treasury shares.

There is little synergy between Gazprom and Sibneft; the former produces little oil, the latter virtually no gas, and both have been criticized for poor management of their resources. This was basically a further case of the Russian Government asserting itself, and incidentally making a mockery, at least for the present, of suggestions that Gazprom should be broken up in the interests of competitive market structures and improved efficiency. Instead, Russian government spokesmen emphasized that Gazprom would now be 'the world's largest energy company'. As a sop— or potential bribe—to international markets, it was simultaneously suggested that wider foreign shareholdings in Russian state companies including Gazprom and Rosneft would soon be facilitated. However, Gazprom is burdened with substantial debts (quite apart from those incurred to finance the purchase of Sibneft), and faces huge capital outlays on the development of new gas fields to replace declining output from

Figure 2.9 Average Daily Oil Output, Russia, 2004–05

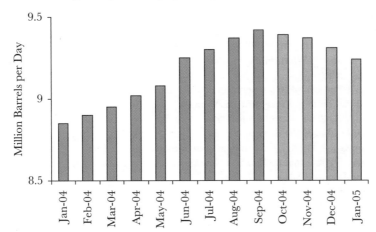

Source: Neft' i Kapital.

existing 'super giants'. Furthermore, a shareholding in a Russian state-controlled company, with its multiple objectives and use as a Kremlin political instrument, is less attractive than one in a profit-maximizing one.

As regards the terms of the Sibneft deal, it did not escape attention that the Russian state, having a decade previously allowed its major oil assets to pass to oligarch purchasers for a song (that indeed was the origin of the term 'oligarch' in the Russian context), is now paying serious money to buy some of them back, even while effectively expropriating others (Yukos).

The net result of all these energy-sector developments has been some immediate deterioration in the Russian business climate. Crude oil output showed an unforeseen setback (Figure 2.9; Blas and Gorst 2005). Fixed investment decisions were discouraged. This applies to state companies almost as much as to private ones, where their future organizational basis is uncertain (for instance Rosneft, for a time expecting to be merged with Gazprom and still preoccupied with the task of establishing operational control of Yuganskneftegaz following its acquisition).

It is mildly ironical that a sense of insecurity about shareholder rights and corporate governance procedures should have been rekindled by state action. This makes President Putin's complaints about the country's flagging or inadequate growth rates sound all the more hollow. Russia still has a long way to go in establishing the basic institutions and framework conditions for the market economy. Progress to date has been significant and visible, but also somewhat fragmentary and inconsistent.

Bibliography

Ahrend, R, 2004, Accounting for Russia's post-crisis growth, *OECD Economics Department Working Paper No. 404*, September.

Ahrend, R, and Tompson, W, 2005, Fifteen years of economic reform in Russia: what has been achieved? What remains to be done?, *OECD Economics Department Working Paper No. 430*, May.

American Chamber of Commerce in Russia, Expert Institute, 2005, *The Economy and Investment Climate in Russia*, Ernst & Young.

Belousov, A R, 2004, Razvitie rossiiskoi ekonomiki v srednesrochnoi perspektive: analiz ugroz, *Problemy prognozirovaniya*, No. 1.

Blas, J and Gorst, I, 2005, Oil production in Russia stagnates, *Financial Times*, 2 June.

Browder, W F, 2005, *How the West has Gotten Russia Wrong* (presented at the Russia Economic Forum, London, April).

Cordonnier, C, 2005, Russia: natural resource rent and competitiveness, *RECEP Working Paper*.

European Bank for Reconstruction and Development, 2003, Transition Report, London.

Gaddy, C G and Ickes, B W, 2002, *Russia's Virtual Economy*, Washington DC, Brookings Institution Press.

Gaidar, E, 2003, Recovery growth and some peculiarities of the contemporary economic situation in Russia, *Post-Communist Economies*, 15, No. 3, pp. 299–311.

Georgieva, K, 2004, Russia's economic developments in facts and figures, *World Bank presentation*, IX Berlin Finance Conference, June.

Granville, B E and Oppenheimer, P M (Eds), 2001 *Russia's Post-Communist Economy*, Oxford University Press.

Gurvich, E T, 2004, Makroekonomicheskaya otsenka roli rossiiskogo neftegazovogo sektora, *Voprosy Ekonomiki*, No. 10.

Gurvich, E T, 2005, Udvoenie VVP: Pravitel'stvo bessil'no, *Vedomosti* No.11, 25 January.

Institute for the Economy in Transition, 2005, Rossiiskaya ekonomika v 2004 godu: Tendentsii i perspektivy, Moscow.

Kuboniwa, M, Tabata, S and Ustinova, N, 2005, How large is the oil and gas sector of Russia? A research report, *Eurasian Geography and Economics*, 46, No. 1, pp. 68–76.

Mandil, C, 2005, Securing the Russian–European energy partnership, *International Energy Agency*.

Milov, V, 2005, Russian energy sector and its international implications, *Institute of Energy Policy*, Discussion Paper, March.

Myers, Steven Lee, 2005, In Russia bribery is the cost of business, *International Herald Tribune*, August 10.

Salnikov, V A and Galimov, D I, 2005, Itogi razvitiya promyshlennosti v 2004 g., *Centre for Macroeconomic Analysis and Short-term Forecasting*, Working Paper, March.

Tabata, S, 2002, Russian revenues from oil and gas exports: flows and taxation, *Eurasian Geography and Economics*, 43, No. 8, pp. 610–27.

World Bank, 2003–2005, *Russian Economic Report*, various issues (Nos. 6–10).

World Bank, 2004, *From Transition to Development: A Country Economic Memorandum for the Russian Federation*.

Yasin, E G, 2003, Nerynochnyi sector: strukturnye reformy i ekonomicheskii rost, *Higher School of Economics*, June.

B. FINANCIAL FLOWS

3

PRICE DIFFERENCES, TAXES AND THE STABILIZATION FUND[1]

Shinichiro Tabata

The Hypothesis of 'Subsidies' Caused by Price Differences

This chapter analyses some financial aspects of the Russian oil and gas industries under circumstances of a rapid increase in oil and gas export revenues (Table 3.1). It begins by considering the following hypothesis: domestic users of oil are receiving 'subsidies', because domestic oil prices have not risen sharply in comparison with world prices. Hence domestic non-energy producers are receiving assistance from the oil and gas industries which helps their international competitiveness and restricts the spread of the Dutch disease in contrast to the depression of the 1990s (Tabata, 2000).

The difference between world market prices and domestic purchasers' prices of crude oil increased from USD 5.2 per barrel in 1998 to USD17.2 per barrel in 2004 (Figure 3.1). We can therefore deduce that domestic users of crude oil received huge subsidies. Since domestic users of crude oil are limited to consumers in the oil-refining industry,[2] prices of petroleum products are examined in the next section.

The Case of Petroleum Products

Curiously, we can see in Figures 3.2 and 3.3 that domestic purchasers' prices are higher than export prices in the case of gasoline and diesel fuel, while in

[1] Partial funding for this research was provided by the Japanese Ministry of Education and Science in 2005 in the form of a grant for research on Russian capitalism and the flow of financial resources.
[2] According to the input–output table for 2002 (*Sistema* 2005, pp. 84–87), the oil refinery industry used 38.4 per cent of oil output; 57.8 per cent of oil output was exported; and other uses were only 3.8 per cent, including chemical industry (1.9 per cent) and the oil extraction sector itself (1.2 per cent).

Table 3.1 Production and Export of Oil and Gas in Russia

	Units	1995	1996	1997	1998	1999	2000	2001	2002	2003	2004[c]
Oil, including gas condensate											
Production	million tons	306.8	301.2	305.6	303.3	305.2	323.5	348.1	379.6	421.3	459.1
Export[a]	million tons	127.4	126.0	127.3	137.2	134.5	144.4	162.1	188.4	223.4	257.4
Ratio of export to production	per cent	41.5	41.8	41.6	45.2	44.1	44.6	46.6	49.6	53.0	56.1
Export[a]	billion dollars	13.3	15.9	14.8	10.3	14.1	25.3	24.6	28.9	38.8	59.3
Share in total export	per cent	16.1	17.7	17.0	13.8	18.7	24.1	24.1	26.9	28.6	32.4
Natural gas											
Production	billion cubic meters	570	575	544	564	564	555	551	563	581	591
Export[a]	billion cubic meters	194.3	198.5	200.9	203.4	205.4	193.9	180.9	185.6	189.4	200.4
Ratio of export to production	per cent	34.1	34.5	36.9	36.1	36.4	34.9	32.8	33.0	32.6	33.9
Export[a,b]	billion dollars	12.1	14.7	16.4	13.5	11.3	16.6	17.8	15.9	20.0	21.9
Share in total export	per cent	14.7	16.4	18.9	18.1	14.9	15.8	17.5	14.8	14.7	12.0
Petroleum products											
Production	million tons	182	176	177	164	169	173	179	185	190	195
Export[a]	million tons	47.1	57.0	61.3	53.9	50.8	62.6	63.5	75.4	77.7	82.1
Ratio of export to production	per cent	25.9	32.4	34.6	32.9	30.1	36.2	35.5	40.8	40.9	42.1
Export[a]	billion dollars	5.0	7.5	7.3	4.3	4.7	10.9	9.4	11.2	14.0	19.3
Share in total export	per cent	6.0	8.4	8.3	5.7	6.2	10.4	9.2	10.4	10.3	10.5
Oil, natural gas and petroleum products											
Export	billion dollars	30.4	38.1	38.5	28.1	30.1	52.8	51.8	56.0	72.8	100.5
Share in total export	per cent	36.9	42.5	44.3	37.7	39.8	50.3	50.8	52.2	53.6	54.9
Total foreign trade of Russia											
Exports of goods	billion dollars	82.4	89.7	86.9	74.4	75.6	105.0	101.9	107.3	135.9	183.2
Imports of goods	billion dollars	62.6	68.1	72.0	58.0	39.5	44.9	53.8	61.0	76.1	97.4
Balance of trade in goods	billion dollars	19.8	21.6	14.9	16.4	36.0	60.2	48.1	46.3	59.9	85.8

[a] Since the data on 2002–2003 from *Tamozhennaia* does not include trade with Belarus, they are derived from *Belarus' i Rossiia*, 2003, pp. 113–14; 2004, pp. 117–18 and added to the *Tamozhennaia* data.

[b] For the same reason as noted in footnote a, data on trade with Belarus in 1998–2000 are derived from *Belarus' i Rossiia*, 2001, p. 107.

[c] Preliminary data obtained from *SEP*, 2004, No. 12, pp. 21–2; 2005, No. 1, p. 126; website of the Central Bank of Russia.

Source: Compiled by the author from *RSE*, 2004, pp. 377–9; *Tamozhennaia*, various years. Total foreign trade data of Russia are from the website of the Central Bank of Russia.

Figure 3.1 Prices of Crude Oil

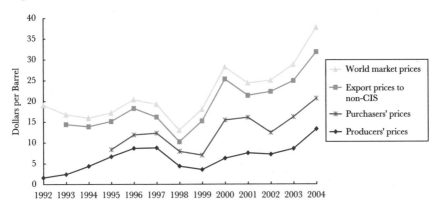

Note: Annual average; data in tons are converted into those in barrels by 1 ton = 7.3 barrels.
Source: World market prices: *IFS*; Export prices: *Rossiia* 2005, pp. 410–11; *RSE* 2000, p. 593;
2001, p. 621; 2002, p. 630; 2004, p. 669; *Tseny* 1995, p. 198; Purchaser's prices: Data at
the end of year (*Tseny* 1998, p. 144; 2000, p. 126; 2002, p. 120; 2004, p. 137; *SEP* 2004,
No. 12, p. 152) are converted into dollars by official rates (*IFS*), and their average was
calculated; Producers' prices for 1992–2003: Data of annual average (*Kratkosrochnye*) are converted
into dollars by official rates (*IFS*; World Bank 1995, p. 433); for 2004: Calculated from the data
at the end of year (*Kratkosrochnye*) through the same process by which Purchasers' prices are
calculated.

Figure 3.2 Prices of Gasoline

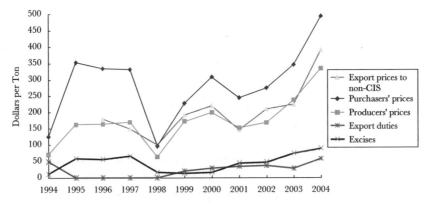

Note: At the end of year.
Source: Export prices: Average data in December. *SEP* 1997, No. 1, p. 79; 1998,
No. 1, pp. 103–4; 1999, No. 1, pp. 131–2; 2000, No. 1, p. 91; 2001, No. 1, p. 99; 2002, No. 1,
p. 104; 2003, No. 1, p. 111; 2004, No. 1, p. 109; 2005, No. 1, p. 132; Purchasers' prices: *Tseny*
1998, p. 144; 2000, p. 126; 2002, p. 120; 2004, p. 137; *SEP* 2004, No. 12, p. 152. Converted
into dollars by official rate (*IFS*); Producers' prices: *Kratkosrochnye*. Converted into dollars by official
rate (*IFS*); Excises and export duties: Federal Laws and Government Resolutions.

Figure 3.3 Prices of Diesel Fuel

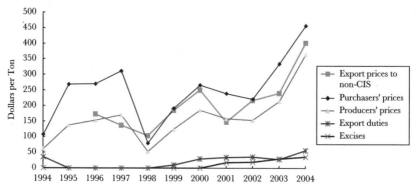

Note: At the end of year.
Source: The same sources as noted in Figure 3.2.

Figure 3.4 Prices of Heavy Fuel Oil

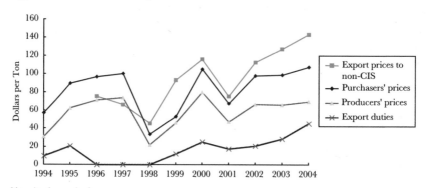

Note: At the end of year.
Source: The same sources as noted in Figure 3.2.

the case of heavy fuel oil, export prices have been higher than purchasers' prices since 1998 (Figure 3.4). This is due to the domestic taxation on petroleum products. Value-added taxes (VAT) and excises have been levied on domestic purchases of petroleum products,[1] while exports to non-CIS countries have been exempted from these taxes. The difference between gasoline and diesel fuel, on the one hand, and heavy fuel oil, on the other, is explained by the absence of excises on heavy fuel oil.[2] Although export prices to non-CIS countries include export duties, these data seem to suggest that domestic taxation

---

[1] The rate of VAT was 28 per cent in 1992, 20 per cent since 1993 and 18 per cent since 2004. VAT is levied on the price of the product, taking account of excises (Article 154 of Tax Code).
[2] Excises have been levied on gasoline since 1994 and on diesel fuel since 2001 (see Appendix).

on gasoline and diesel fuel by excises and VAT is heavier than taxation by export duties.[1]

Thus, in the case of gasoline and diesel fuel, the hypothesis of subsidies does not seem to be proved. In the case of heavy fuel oil, the difference between export prices and domestic purchasers' prices increased from USD8.0 per ton in 2001 to USD36.4 in 2004 (Figure 3.4). The hypothesis of subsidies proves to be true in this case.

In considering the prices of petroleum products, we should remember that we are dealing with transaction prices within vertically integrated oil companies. The structure of Russia's oil industry is characterized by vertically integrated companies (Shiobara 2004, pp. 23–47; Kuboniwa *et al.* 2005, pp. 69–70). In most cases a holding company owns oil-well drilling companies, oil-refining companies and trading companies; and the holding company supplies oil to its own oil refineries and receives petroleum products from them (Figure 3.5). In this situation transaction prices between the holding company and its subsidiaries are consciously set, usually at an extremely low level, in order to minimize tax payments. On the other hand, the holding company, as a major player in an oligopolistic industry, is in a position whereby it can choose the selling prices for the domestic market (P4).[2] Therefore, even though producers'

Figure 3.5 Structure of Oil Company and Prices of Petroleum Products

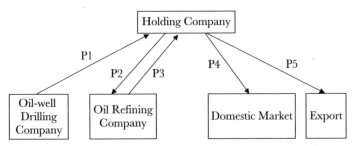

Note: P1=Purchasers' price of oil; P2=Transaction price of oil; P3=Transaction price of petroleum products in vertically integrated companies or producers' prices of petroleum products; P4=Purchasers' price of petroleum products; P5=Export price of petroleum products.

---

[1] These three taxes do not explain the price difference completely. For example, if we deduct from the purchasers' price of gasoline at the end of 2004 (492.9 USD per ton) excises (88.6 USD) and VAT (72.8 USD), and then we deduct from the export price to non-CIS countries in December 2004 (389.9 USD) export duties (57 USD), we obtain 315.6 USD and 332.9 USD, respectively (note that the amount of VAT is a rough estimate). Needless to say, there are other factors, including other taxes that contribute to the price difference.

[2] Gurvich (2004, pp. 10, 17) suggested a hypothesis of equal profitability of exports and domestic supply, meaning that the difference between export prices and domestic selling prices is explained by export duties.

prices or production costs of petroleum products seem to have increased rapidly in recent years (Figures 3.2–3.4), it does not necessarily mean a decrease in the profitability of oil companies.[1]

Thus, we might conclude that the advantage of low oil prices was mostly enjoyed by oil refineries, i.e., oil companies themselves, and that the hypothesis of subsidies is therefore only partially true.

The Case of Natural Gas

The hypothesis of subsidies is undoubtedly true in the case of natural gas. World market prices of natural gas increased by 2.1 times from 1999 to 2004 in tandem with prices of oil (Figure 3.6). The difference between world market prices and domestic purchasers' prices widened from USD 50.0 per 1,000 cubic meters in 1999 to USD 96.6 in 2004. Since gas is used by various industries, many producers are receiving these price subsidies. If we regard all of these price differences as subsidies, the total subsidies in 2004 can

Figure 3.6 Prices of Natural Gas

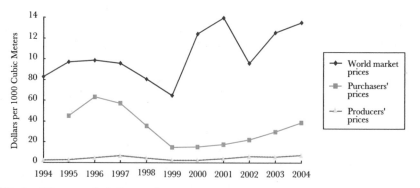

Note: Annual average; includes petroleum gas.
Source: World market prices: Prices of Russian natural gas reported in *IFS*; Purchaser's prices: Data at the end of year (*Tseny* 1998, p. 144; 2000, p. 126; 2002, p. 120; 2004, p. 137; *SEP* 2004, No. 12, p. 152) are converted into dollars by official rates (*IFS*), and their average was calculated; producers' prices for 1994–2003: Data of annual average (*Kratkosrochnye*) are converted into dollars by official rates (*IFS*); for 2004: Calculated from the data at the end of year (*Kratkosrochnye*) through the same process by which purchasers' prices are calculated.

[1] The producers' prices of petroleum products reported in Rosstat's statistics and used in the charts are prices of P3, when oil-refining companies are not owned by the holding company. If the refining companies are subsidiaries of the holding company, transaction prices are not reported at all. Usually, the producers' prices recorded in this way are considerably higher than transaction prices. I owe this footnote to Toshihiko Shiobara.

be calculated as USD 37.7 billion or 1.09 trillion rubles, or the equivalent of 6.5 per cent of GDP.[1]

Tax Revenues from Oil and Gas

Recent Increases in Tax Revenues

Since oil and gas companies try to avoid tax payments by changing their organizational structure and transferring a substantial amount of profits to their subsidiaries in the trade and transportation sectors, the tax system has been repeatedly revised by the Government. The tax regime for oil and natural gas companies can be thought of as the outcome of a repeated game in which the state tries to maximize its revenues and the companies strive to minimize their taxes. The present taxation system for oil and gas is summarized in the Appendix. Since 2004, the major taxes from oil and gas have been imposed as mineral extraction fees (severance taxes) and export duties (Table 3.2). Due to the absence of detailed tax revenue data, I made 'statutory estimates' in this table, using statutory tax rates and the production and export data in each year.

Revenues from customs duties have increased significantly in recent years, especially, in 2003 and 2004. Their share in total revenue increased from 7.1 per cent in 1999 to 15.8 per cent in 2004 (Table 3.2). This was due to the increase in export duties, mostly from oil. Since February 2002, rates of export duties on oil have been adjusted using a formula tied to international market prices, and the coefficient in this formula was raised in June 2004 (see Figure 3.7 and Appendix). As shown in Figure 3.8, actual rates increased sharply from the second half of 2004, due to rapid increases in oil prices and the increase in the coefficient mentioned above. Export duties on gas are ad valorem taxes. Their revenues increased considerably in 2004 (Table 3.2), because their tariff was raised from 5 to 30 per cent in the beginning of 2004. Simultaneously, excises on gas were abolished.

Severance taxes were introduced in 2002. Since then they have accounted for major parts of the payment for the use of natural resources, revenues of which have increased significantly in recent years. As shown in Table 3.2, most severance taxes have been obtained from oil.[2] Rates of severance taxes on oil have

---

[1] The price difference (96.6 USD per 1,000 cubic meters) is multiplied by domestic consumption (390.6 billion cubic meters), obtained from Table 3.1.

[2] According to FNS (2005, p. 4), total federal budget revenues of severance taxes reached 425.0 billion rubles in 2004; of which those from oil—355.1 billion rubles (83.6 per cent); from gas—58.9 billion rubles (13.9 per cent); and gas condensate—3.0 billion rubles (0.7 per cent). Note that a part of severance tax revenues from oil was included in the regional budgets (see Appendix).

Table 3.2 State Budget Revenues from Oil and Gas

	1999	2000	2001	2002	2003	2004
	(In billion rubles)					
Total state budget revenue	1,213.6	2,097.7	2,683.7	3,519.2	4,138.7	5,427.3
Excises	109.1	166.4	243.3	264.1	343.4	244.3
Oil and gas condensate	5.7	8.7	11.9	—	—	—
Natural gas	58.1	88.8	117.7	129.5	157.4	—
Petroleum Products[a]	7.1	12.2	36.7	55.9	97.9	100.5
Gasoline	7.1	12.2	25.2	40.8	72.8	...
Diesel fuel	0.0	0.0	11.5	15.1	25.1	...
Customs duties	86.2	229.2	331.3	323.4	452.8	859.7
Import duties	47.4	64.4	...	...	158.0	204.2
Export duties	38.8	164.8	...	...	294.8	655.6
From oil[b]	16.0	77.7	108.6	99.6	192.0	380.7
From gas[b]	—	21.6	31.7	23.0	28.2	139.6
Payment for the use of natural resources	45.3	77.6	135.7	330.8	395.8	579.5
Severance tax	—	—	—	275.2	331.6	...
From oil[c]	—	—	—	246.1	301.7	436.7
From gas[c]	—	—	—	16.3	15.7	58.9
	(in per cent of total revenue)					
Total state budget revenue	100.0	100.0	100.0	100.0	100.0	100.0
Excises	9.0	7.9	9.1	7.5	8.3	4.5
Oil and gas condensate	0.5	0.4	0.4	—	—	—
Natural gas	4.8	4.2	4.4	3.7	3.8	—
Petroleum Products[a]	0.6	0.6	1.4	1.6	2.4	1.9
Gasoline	0.6	0.6	0.9	1.2	1.8	...
Diesel fuel	0.0	0.0	0.4	0.4	0.6	...

(in per cent of total revenue)

Customs duties	7.1	10.9	12.3	9.2	10.9	15.8
Import duties	3.9	3.1	...	...	3.8	3.8
Export duties	3.2	7.9	...	...	7.1	12.1
From oil[b]	1.3	3.7	4.0	2.8	4.6	7.0
From gas[b]	—	1.0	1.2	0.7	0.7	2.6
Payment for the use of natural resources	3.7	3.7	5.1	9.4	9.6	10.7
Severance tax	—	—	—	7.8	8.0	...
From oil[c]	—	—	—	7.0	7.3	8.0
From gas[c]	—	—	—	0.5	0.4	1.1

a From 1999 to 2003, this figure represents the sum of gasoline and diesel fuel, excluding revenues from diesel and carburetor engine oil. For 2004, these figures are estimates based on these revenues of the federal budget (FNS, 2005) and on statutory rates of distribution between the federal and regional budgets.

b Calculated on the basis of statutory tax rates specified by Federal Laws and Government Resolutions, and production and export data obtained from *RSE* and *Tamozhennaia*. Hereafter we will call them statutory estimates.

c For 2004, these figures are obtained by the same process explained in footnote b. These estimated revenues are 82.8 per cent and 93.1 per cent of the statutory estimates (see footnote b) of oil (excluding gas condensate) and gas, respectively. As for 2003, statutory estimates of oil and gas are multiplied by 82.8 per cent and 93.1 per cent, respectively. As for 2002, sum of severance revenues from oil and gas is available from Kolesnik (2003, p. 84). Statutory estimates of oil and gas in 2002 are reduced proportionally in order to coincide with this sum.

Sources: Total, Excises, Payment, Severance tax and Customs duties for 1999–2003: *RSE* 2004, p. 564; for 2004: *Rossiia* 2005, p. 317. Items of excises for 1999–2003: *SEP* 2001, No. 1, p. 158; 2002, No. 1, pp. 165–6; 2003, No. 1, pp. 171–2; 2004, No. 1, p. 171. Import and export duties for 1999–2000: Laws on the federal budget execution (Federal Laws No. 80 of 19 June 2001 and No. 39 of 23 April 2002); for 2003–2004: FTS (2005).

been also linked to international market prices (Figure 3.7). In January 2005 these tariffs were raised by 12.9 per cent (see Appendix). As shown in Figure 3.8, these rates have been steadily increasing, due to the increase in oil prices and the increase in coefficients in the formula.

Figure 3.7 Tax Rates on Oil

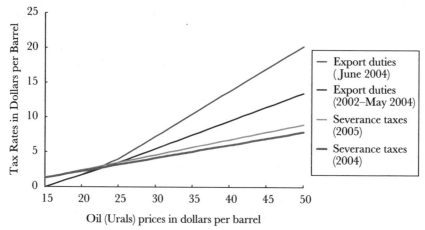

Source: Federal Laws: No. 126 of 8 August 2001; No. 190 of 29 December 2001; No. 33 of 7 May 2004; No. 102 of 18 August 2004.

Figure 3.8 Oil Prices and Tax Rates in Russia

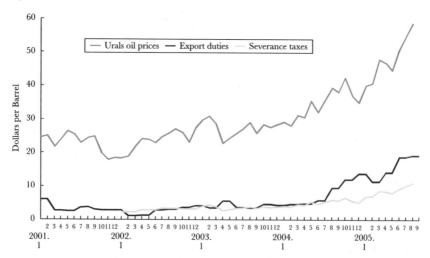

Source: Urals oil prices for January 2001–July 2002: *SEP*; for August 2002–present: *Rossiiskaia Gazeta.* Export duties: Government Resolutions. Severance taxes: Calculated on the basis of the formula stipulated by Federal Laws, using Urals oil prices.

Table 3.3 Stabilization Fund in 2004–05 (in Billion Rubles)

	Balance[a]	Receipts[b]	Expenditures	Notes
2004				
January	106.0	106.00		First deposit
February	122.1	16.08		
March	142.6	20.51		
April	171.0	28.38		
May	198.7	27.75		
June	229.2	30.44		
July	267.6	38.45		
August	305.9	38.33		
September	349.7	43.80		
October	404.4	54.69		
November	462.6	58.13		
December	522.3	59.71		
2005				
January 1	740.7	218.40		Remainder of the federal budget
January 31	647.2		93.5	Repayment of foreign debts
January	707.5	60.30		
February	768.4	60.95		
March	857.9	89.50		
April	954.4	96.50		
May	1,049.1	94.70		
June 7	1,047.8		1.3	Pay back to the federal budget[c]
June 30	622.0		425.8	Repayment of foreign debts (Paris Club)
June	725.2	103.20		
July	836.3	111.10		
August	964.9	128.60		
September	1,098.7	133.80		
October	1,236.4	137.70		
November	1,390.8	154.40		
22 December			30.0[d]	Payment to the Pension Fund of Russia
30 December			123.8	Write-off of the debts to Vneshekonombank
December	1,237.0			
2006				
1 January		222.1		Remainder of the federal budget
January	1,459.1			

Notes:

[a] As of the end of month, unless otherwise noted.

[b] Monthly receipts due to high oil prices, unless otherwise noted.

[c] Due to the final settlements of the federal budget for the previous year (See *Rossiiskaia gazeta*, August 16, 2005, p. 4).

[d] This amount was calculated as a residual.

Source: Minfin (2005).

Severance taxes on gas were changed from ad valorem taxes to specific taxes in January 2004. As a result, their revenues increased significantly in 2004 (Table 3.2). The corresponding tax rate was raised further in January 2005.

As excises on gas were abolished from the beginning of 2004, excises are now levied only on petroleum products from the oil and gas sector.

If we sum up severance taxes, export duties and excises from oil and gas (excluding export duties from petroleum products), they increased from 570.6 billion rubles in 2002 to 1,116.4 billion rubles in 2004, accounting for 16.2 per cent and 20.6 per cent of total state budget revenues, respectively.[1]

The Stabilization Fund

The Stabilization Fund was introduced in 2004.[2] A portion of revenues from export duties and severance taxes on oil were to be transferred into this fund, when world market prices on oil were above the base price (initially USD20 per barrel). The amount to be transferred would be determined by the difference between the revenues from export duties and severance taxes on oil assuming that world market prices are equal to the base price and actual revenues from them.

Resources from this fund were to be used, when they exceeded 500 billion rubles, for the financing of the deficit of the state budget when world market prices of oil fell under the base price. In 2005, it was prescribed by the federal budget law that they were to be earmarked for the financing of the deficit of the Pension Fund of Russia and the repayment of Russia's foreign debts.

As shown in Table 3.3, 'ordinary' monthly receipts of this fund have been increasing since the beginning of 2004. While the monthly average of 'ordinary' receipts in 2004 was 37.8 billion rubles, it tripled to 106.4 billion rubles in 2005. Financial resources from this fund were used in 2005 for the repayment of foreign debts and the payment to the Pension Fund of Russia.

Influence of the Increase in World Market Prices of Oil on Tax Revenues

As explained above, most tax revenues from oil have become dependent on world oil prices. Therefore, we can easily calculate the influence of the

---

[1] Berezinskaia (2005) estimated total tax payments (including profit taxes and VAT etc.) of the oil and gas sector in 2004 as 56.5 billion USD or 35.8 per cent of total revenue, or 9.6 per cent of GDP, while my estimates are equivalent to 38.7 billion USD and 6.7 per cent of GDP. The differences might be explained by the fact that my estimates include only the three taxes estimated in Table 3.2.

[2] Federal Law No. 184 of December 23 2003 inserted Chapter 13-1 'Stabilization Fund of the Russian Federation' in the Budget Code.

Table 3.4 Influence of an Increase in the World Market Price of Oil on the Tax Revenues of the State Budget from Oil

	Increase in tax revenues caused by an increase of one dollar per barrel in world market price of oil[a]		Increase in one year[b]	
	In dollars per barrel	In dollars per ton	In billion dollars	In billion rubles[c]
Export duties	0.65	4.745	1.12	32.4
Severance taxes	0.22	1.605	0.74	21.2
Sum	0.87	6.350	1.86	53.6

[a] Estimates based on the tax scheme in 2005 and assuming that world market price of oil is above 25 dollars per barrel.
[b] Estimated using the production and export data in 2004 obtained from *SEP*.
[c] Converted into rubles by official exchange rates (*IFS*).

increase in world market oil prices on tax revenues of the state budget. According to my estimates (Table 3.4), when world market prices of oil increase by one dollar per barrel, the Russian state budget receives an additional USD1.86 billion or 53.6 billion rubles in one year in the form of export duties and severance taxes.[1] These revenues are to be transferred to the Stabilization Fund, because at present world market oil prices are much higher than the base price. The base price was raised to USD 27 per barrel from the beginning of 2006 (Federal Law No. 127 of 12 October 2005).

Concluding Remarks

While we see some symptoms of the Dutch disease recently in the Russian economy, it has not advanced very much. 'Subsidies' for domestic energy users accruing from the differences between world market prices and domestic purchasers' prices are significant in the case of heavy fuel oil and natural gas. This might be regarded as one of the reasons why the Dutch disease has not progressed. However, in the case of gasoline and diesel fuel, oil companies themselves are the major beneficiaries of the extra revenues.

[1] This is 0.3 per cent of 2004 GDP. Gurvich (2004, p. 18) estimated the increase in tax revenues in 2003 from an increase of oil prices of one dollar per barrel as 1.57 billion USD or 0.36 per cent of GDP. His estimates included profit taxes and VAT, in addition to export duties and severance taxes. Valerii Mironov and Ol'ga Berezinskkaia of Tsentr razvitiia estimated that an oil price increase of one dollar per barrel brought about additional state budget revenues of 75 cents per barrel before July 2004. This increased to 91 cents after August 2004 and to 94 cents after January 2005. Their estimates included profit tax revenues, in addition to export duties and severance taxes (*Vedomosti*, November 22 2004 p. 4).

The recent changes in the tax system for oil and gas have contributed to its simplification and to significant increases in tax revenues from the oil and gas industry. However, as we (Tabata, 2002, pp. 622–23) and Gurvich (2004, pp. 15–16) pointed out, the current tax burden on the oil and gas industry should not be regarded as high, if we take into account the real size of the sector, i.e., including value added or profits transferred to the trade and transportation sectors.[1] Nevertheless, it is safe to say that recent changes in taxation on oil and gas significantly improve the situation, by levying taxes not on profits or other values expressed in domestic rubles, but on quantities and on export prices. The lion's share of energy windfall revenues now goes to the state.

The establishment of the Stabilization Fund in 2004 was an important initiative. The future perspectives for the Russian economy depend significantly on the use of the energy windfall revenues through the state budget and the Stabilization Fund.

Appendix on Taxation, 2003–2005[2]

Export Duties

Concerning export duties on oil, a new system for the determination of export tariffs that depends on world oil prices was introduced on 1 February 2002 (Federal Law No. 190 of 29 December 2001).

> When $P \leq 109.5$, $T = 0$.
> When $109.5 < P \leq 182.5$, $T = (P - 109.5) \times 0.35$.
> When $182.5 < P$, $T = 25.53 + (P - 182.5) \times 0.4$.

Where T is the export tariff, expressed in USD per ton and P is the oil price (Urals oil prices at the Mediterranean Sea and Rotterdam), expressed in USD per ton (see Figure 3.7).[3] Export tariffs have been set by Government Resolutions bimonthly (see Figure 3.8).

This scheme was revised in June 2004 (Federal Law No. 33 of 7 May 2004).[4] As a result, export tariffs on oil were raised, as shown in Figure 3.7.[5]

---

[1] See Vasil'eva and Gurvich (2005) for detailed discussion of tax burden on the oil and gas sector.

[2] See Tabata (2002, pp. 625–27) for taxation on oil and gas in 1995–2002.

[3] 109.5 USD and 182.5 USD per ton equal 15 USD and 25 USD per barrel, respectively.

[4] This law was put into effect one month after its official publication on 12 May 2004.

[5] 146 USD per ton equals 20 USD per barrel.

When $P \le 109.5$, $T = 0$.
When $109.5 < P \le 146$, $T = (P - 109.5) \times 0.35$.
When $146 < P \le 182.5$, $T = 12.78 + (P - 146) \times 0.45$.
When $182.5 < P$, $T = 29.2 + (P - 182.5) \times 0.65$.

Export tariffs on petroleum products were differentiated by product in the period 1999–2002.[1] From the beginning of 2003, it was specified that export tariffs on petroleum products would not exceed 90 per cent of those on crude oil (Article 8 of Federal Law No. 57 of 29 May 2002).[2] In addition, simultaneously, they were unified (Government Resolution No. 848 of 29 November 2002). This meant a reduction in export duties on gasoline and diesel fuel, and a rise in those on heavy fuel oil (see Figures 3.2–3.4). Since export tariffs on crude oil were revised bimonthly, as noted above, tariffs on petroleum products were also revised bimonthly and set precisely at 90 per cent of export tariffs on crude oil in the period from January 2003 through July 2004.

From January 2004, the provision of 90 per cent was deleted (Federal Law No. 159 of 8 December 2003).[3] Actually, export tariffs on petroleum products have been set at lower than 90 per cent, mostly 60–70 per cent, of those on crude oil since August 2004. In spite of the abolition of this 90 per cent regulation, average export tariffs on petroleum products increased from USD 27.4 per ton in 2003 to USD 39.2 in 2004. If tariffs on petroleum products had been set at 90 per cent of the tariff on crude oil in 2004, the average tariff would have been USD 50.2 per ton. Apparently, this was the reason for the abolition of the 90 per cent regulation. In addition, different tax rates have been applied to 'dark' and 'light' petroleum products since March 2005 (Government Resolution No. 79 of 16 February 2005).[4]

Export duties on natural gas have been ad valorem taxes since 1999. Their tariff was raised from 5 per cent (at least 2.5 euros per ton) to 30 per cent in the beginning of 2004 (Government Resolution No. 507 of

[1] In the period from August 1999 through February 2001, restrictions on exports of petroleum products, including gasoline, diesel fuel and heavy fuel oil, were imposed on oil-refining companies by specifying the percentage of domestic supply in the total production of these companies. Export duties on petroleum products were expected to play the same role as these restrictions.

[2] This law added one paragraph to Section 4, Article 3 of Federal Law on Customs Tariff, No. 5003 of 21 May 1993.

[3] This law was put into effect one month after its official publication on 15 December 2003.

[4] See Press Release of the Ministry of Industry and Energy on 11 August 2005 [http://www.mte.gov.ru/]. Actually, this differentiation seems to have occurred in November 2004, since Government Resolution No. 564 of 18 October 2004 which specified revised export duties on petroleum products did not include revised tariffs on heavy fuel oil.

19 August 2003). This was a compensation for the abolition of excises on gas at the same time.

Exports to the member-states of the Eurasian Economic Community (Belarus, Kazakhstan, Kyrgyzstan and Tajikistan) have been exempted from export duties since mid-1999. Export duties are exclusively federal budget revenues.

Mineral Extraction Fees (Severance Taxes)

In Chapter 26 of the Tax Code, severance tax rates on oil and gas were set at a uniform rate of 16.5 per cent of the value of realized products. However, with regard to oil, a special system that also depends on world prices was to be applied during 2002–2004 (Article 5 of Federal Law No. 126 of 8 August 2001).[1]

$$T = 340 \times (P - 8) \times R/252.$$

Where T is the severance tax rate, expressed in rubles per ton, P is the oil price (Urals oil prices at the Mediterranean Sea and Rotterdam), expressed in USD per ton and R is the official exchange rate of the ruble, expressed in rubles per dollar. $C = (P - 8) \times R/252$ is called a coefficient, reflecting the dynamics of world oil prices. This formula means that $C = 1$, when $P = 16$ and $R = 31.5$.[2]

The basic rate in this formula was raised by 2.1 per cent in January 2004 (Article 4 of Federal Law No. 117 of 7 July 2003).

$$T = 347 \times (P - 8) \times R/252.$$

In this law, the period of application of this system was prolonged until the end of 2006.

The basic rate and its coefficient, C, were revised in January 2005 (Article 4 of Federal Law No. 102 of 18 August 2004).[3]

[1] In the period from 2002 to 2003 this scheme was applied to gas condensate as well. Since 2004, a tax rate of 17.5 per cent has been applied to gas condensate (Federal Law No. 117 of 7 July 2003).

[2] It was written in Federal Law No. 126 of 2001 that this coefficient, C, is determined quarterly by taxpayers from the official values of P and R. However, C and T itself, along with P and R, were indicated in Letters of the Federal Tax Agency. In addition, since the beginning of 2003, C and T have been calculated and released monthly by the Federal Tax Agency.

[3] Article 2 of Federal Law No. 33 of 7 May 2004 specified that $T = 400 \times (P - 9) \times R/261$ would be applied from the beginning of 2005. However, this provision was nullified by Article 5 of Federal Law No. 102 of 18 August 2004. This meant an upward revision of the basic rate in January 2005.

$$T = 419 \times (P - 9) \times R/261.$$

Now, $C = (P - 9) \times R/261 = 1$, when $P = 18$ and $R = 29$.[1] As a result, the severance tax rate was raised by 12.9 per cent (Figure 3.7).[2] Severance tax tariffs on oil in the period 2002–05, expressed in USD, were shown in Figure 3.8.[3]

Severance taxes on gas became specific taxes in January 2004 (Federal Law No. 117 of 7 July 2003). Their tariff was set at 107 rubles per 1,000 cubic meters. This was not a temporary measure, as was the case of oil. This tariff was stipulated in Section 2, Article 342 of the Tax Code. This was also a compensation for the abolishment of excises on gas. However, it was raised to 135 rubles per 1,000 cubic meters in January 2005 (Article 1 of Federal Law No. 102 of 18 August 2004) and it is intended to raise it to 147 rubles in January 2006 (Federal Law No. 107 of 21 July 2005).

Ninety-five per cent of severance tax revenues from oil are included in the federal budget and 5 per cent—in the regional budgets (budgets of the subjects of the Russian Federation).[4] Severance tax revenues from gas are exclusively federal budget revenues.[5]

Excises

Excises on oil were abolished at the beginning of 2002, at a time when severance taxes were introduced. Rates of excises on gas were set at 15 per cent of the selling prices in the domestic market and 30 per cent for exports in the period 1999–2003.[6] Excises on gas were abolished at the beginning of 2004 simultaneously with considerable increases in tariffs of both export duties and severance taxes on gas.

---

[1] Concerning the change in 'standard ruble rates,' see 'Official information' of the Ministry of Finance on 11 January 2005 [http://www.minfin.ru/off_inf/1175.htm].

[2] This figure (12.9 per cent) was calculated on the basis of the tariff which might have been applied, if the previous formula had been used in January 2005.

[3] They were calculated by the author, while these tariffs, expressed in rubles, were available from Letters of the Federal Tax Agency issued every month.

[4] This was stipulated in Article 50 of the Budget Code amended by Federal Law No. 120 of 20 August 2004 and introduced on 1 January 2005. In 2004, 85.6 per cent of tax revenues were included in the federal budget and 14.4 per cent—in the regional budget. But, when it was extracted in an autonomous okrug, 81.6 per cent accrues to the federal budget, 13.4 per cent to the okrug budget, and 5.0 per cent to the krai or oblast in which the okrug is located (Article 8 of the federal budget law for 2004). In 2002 and 2003, larger portions went to the regional budget (see Tabata 2002, p. 627).

[5] This was stipulated by Article 8 of the federal budget law for 2004. In 2002 and 2003, the distribution of these tax revenues from gas was the same as those from oil.

[6] With respect to exports to Belarus, the domestic tax rate (15 per cent) was applied.

As for excises on petroleum products, they have been levied on gasoline since 1994, on diesel fuel, and diesel and carburetor engine oil since 2001, and they are to be levied on straight-run gasoline (*priamogonnyi benzin*) from January 2006.[1] They are specific taxes and their tax rates have been indexed almost every year by the revision of Article 193 of the Tax Code, as inflation continued.[2]

On 1 January 2003, excise tariffs on petroleum products were sharply raised, because these revenues were designated as one of the sources of regional road funds together with transport taxes introduced from the same day (Articles 1 and 9 of Federal Law No. 110 of 24 July 2002).[3] Another important revision made by the same federal law was that these excises would be levied not on producers, but on receivers of petroleum products, such as gas stations.[4] The aim of this revision was the intention that excise revenues would become revenues of consuming regions, not those of producing regions. In connection with this, while until 2002, 100 per cent of excise revenues from petroleum products were included in the federal budget, since 2003 only 40 per cent of these revenues have been included in the federal budget and 60 per cent in the regional budgets.[5]

Due to the lobbying of oil companies, the indexation of excise tariffs on petroleum products will not be carried out on 1 January 2006, while increases in excise tariffs on other commodities from January 2006 have been determined by Federal Law No. 107 of 21 July 2005.[6]

Exports of petroleum products are exempted from excises (Articles 183–4 of the Tax Code).

---

[1] According to Federal Law No. 107 of 2005, excise tariffs on straight-run gasoline were to be raised from 0 rubles to 2,657 rubles per ton in the beginning of 2006.

[2] Excises on gasoline were ad valorem taxes and their tariff was 10 per cent since March 1994, 20 per cent since March 1995 and 25 per cent since January 1997 (Government Resolutions No. 273 of 31 March 1994; No. 279 of 22 March 1995; No. 12 of 10 January 1997). They were changed into specific taxes and their tax rate was 290 rubles per ton since February 1998, 350 rubles since December 1998 and 455 rubles since January 2000 (Government Resolutions No. 29 of 14 February 1998; No. 192 of 29 December 1998; Federal Law No. 2 of 2 January 2000). Since 2001 their tax rates have been designated in the Tax Code.

[3] Article 5 of Federal Law No. 118 of 5 August 2000 decided that Federal Law No. 1759 'On Road Funds of the Russian Federation' dated on 18 October 1991 was to lose its validity on 1 January 2003. This Article, however, was deleted by Article 8 of Federal Law No. 110 of 24 July 2002. Finally, Federal Law No. 1759 of 1991 was nullified by Federal Law No. 122 of 22 August 2004.

[4] See Articles 182 and 183 of the Tax Code. Although Article 182 was revised again by Federal Law No. 191 of 31 December 2002, provisions concerning petroleum products remained intact.

[5] This was stipulated in Article 50 of the Budget Code amended by Federal Law No. 120 of 20 August 2004. Before this amendment their distribution was specified in the federal budget law of each year.

[6] See Press Release of the Ministry of Industry and Energy on 11 August 2005 [http://www.mte.gov.ru/].

Bibliography

Belarus' i Rossiia (Belarus and Russia), Moscow, Minstat Respubliki Belarus' and Rosstat, various years.

Berezinskaia, Ol'ga, Est' li u Rossii al'ternativa neftianomu kompleksu, ili stanet li gazovyi kompleks novym 'lokomotivom' promyshlennogo rosta? (Are there any alternatives to the oil complex or will the gas complex become the new 'locomotive' for industrial growth?) VEDI [http://vedi.ru/macro_r/macro1105_r.html].

FNS (Federal'naia nalogovaia sluzhba Rossii), 2005, *O postuplenii administriruemykh FNS Rossii dokhodov i vypolnenii zadaniia po ikh mobilizatsii v federal'nyi biudzhet za 2004 god (Revenues Administered by FNS of Russia and Fulfillment of Their Mobilization into the Federal Budget in 2004)* [http://www.nalog.ru/html/docs/budjet_2004.doc].

FTS (Federal'naia tamozhennaia sluzhba Rossii), 2005, *Otsenka platezhei v federal'nyi biudzhet (Evaluation of Payments in the Federal Budget)* [http://www.customs.ru/ru/docs/indexes/].

Gurvich, E T, 2004, Makroekonomicheskaia otsenka roli Rossiiskogo neftegazovogo sektora (Macroeconomic evaluation of the role of the Russian oil and gas sector), *Voprosy ekonomiki*, No. 10.

IFS, International Financial Statistics, International Monetary Fund, *annual and monthly.*

Kolesnik, M, 2003, Tekushchee sostoianie i perspektivy rentnogo nalogoblozheniia v Rossii (Current situations and perspectives of rent taxation in Russia), *Voprosy ekonomiki*, No. 6.

Kratkosrochnye ekonomicheskie pokazateli Rossiiskoi Federatsii (Short-term Economic Indicators of the Russian Federation), Moscow, Rosstat, monthly.

Kuboniwa, M, Tabata, S and Ustinova, N, 2005, How large is the oil and gas sector of Russia? A research report, *Eurasian Geography and Economics*, Vol. 46, No. 1.

Minfin, Ministerstvo finansov RF, *Predvaritel'naia otsenka ispolneniia federal'nogo biudzheta (Preliminary Evaluation of the Fulfillment of the Federal Budget),* monthly [http://www.minfin.ru/index.htm].

Rossiia v tsifrakh. 2005 (Russia in Figures. 2005), 2005, Moscow, Rosstat.

RSE, Rossiiskiy statisticheskiy ezhegodnik (Russian Statistical Yearbook), Moscow, Rosstat, various years.

SEP, Sotsial'no-ekonomicheskoe polozhenie Rossii (Socio-economic Situation of Russia), Moscow, Goskomstat Rossii, monthly.

Shiobara, T, 2005, *Economic Structure of Present Russia,* Tokyo, Keio UP (in Japanese).

Sistema tablits 'Zatraty-Vypusk' Rossii za 2002 god (System of Input–Output Tables for Russia in 2002), 2005, Moscow, Rosstat.

Tabata, S, 2000, The great Russian depressions of the 1990s: observations on causes and implications, *Post-Soviet Geography and Economics*, Vol. 41, No. 6.

Tabata, S, 2002, Russian revenues from oil and gas exports: flow and taxation, *Eurasian Geography and Economics*, Vol. 43, No. 8.

Tamozhennaia statistika vneshnei torgovli RF (Customs Statistics of Foreign Trade of the RF), Moscow, Federal'naia tamozhennaia sluzhba Rossii, various years.

Tseny v Rossii (Prices in Russia), Moscow, Rosstat, various years.

Vasil'eva, A A and Gurvich, E T, 2005, The industry structure of the Russian Fiscal System, *Studies on Russian Economic Development*, Vol. 16, No. 3.

World Bank, 1995, *Statistical Handbook 1995: States of the Former Soviet Union,* Washington, DC, World Bank.

4

RUSSIA'S ECONOMIC CONTRACTION AND RECOVERY 1992–2004: COMPULSORY REPATRIATION OF EXPORT REVENUES AND THE AMBIVALENCE OF LIBERALIZATION

Michael S. Bernstam and Alvin Rabushka

The conjunction of oil and Russia's economic recovery in 1999–2004 links many themes. On 16 September 1998, the Central Bank of Russia mandated repatriation of 50 per cent of foreign exchange revenues. On 31 December 1998, it raised the mandated repatriation rate to 75 per cent. This rule affected primarily fuels and metals exports. In the next several years, world oil prices started to climb. The Central Bank of Russia subsequently reduced the mandated repatriation rate from 50 to 30 to 25 per cent of foreign exchange revenues. Rising oil prices both incited this reduction and compensated for it. Russia's economy shifted from the great contraction in 1992–98 to a partial recovery in 1999–2004. Tables 4.1 and 4.2 provide the background data.

This chapter explains these developments.[1] It views Russia's economy as a new economic system that evolved from central planning after liberalization and privatization in 1992 and adapted to the policy shift in September–December 1998. We explore how, under this system, mandated repatriation of export revenues inadvertently became a quasi-fiscal policy, i.e., how it increased tax remittance and reduced subsidy extraction, which, in turn, shifted the economy from contraction to recovery. Oil and other tradeables, primarily natural resources, are important. Without their massive export, the issue of mandated repatriation of foreign exchange revenues would have been irrelevant. Oil on its own, however, was not the crucial factor.

[1] An extended version is available on-line at http://www.russiaeconomy.org/predation/pdf/pendulum.pdf.

Table 4.1 The Basic Data: The Money Stock, Receivables, and Output: Russia, 1990–2005

Year	Growth rate of real GDP	Index of real GDP (1991=100)	Monetary aggregate M2 (billion rubles)	Enterprise receivables (billion rubles)	The ratio of M2 to receivables, year-end (per cent)
1990	−3.0	105.3	n.a.	n.a.	762.5
1991	−5.0	100.0	0.456	0.060	656.2
1992	−14.5	85.5	0.958	0.146	149.0
1993	−8.7	78.1	6.4	4.3	92.2
1994	−12.5	68.3	33.2	36.0	79.5
1995	−4.1	65.5	97.8	123.0	76.3
1996	−3.6	63.1	220.8	289.3	52.1
1997	1.4	64.0	288.3	553.2	55.3
1998	−5.3	60.6	374.1	677.0	37.9
1999	6.4	64.5	453.7	1,198.2	48.9
2000	10.0	70.9	714.6	1,462.6	67.1
2001	5.1	74.5	1,154.4	1,721.4	78.9
2002	4.7	78.0	1,612.6	2,045.1	94.3
2003	7.3	83.7	2,134.5	2,262.7	126.5
2004	7.1	89.6	3,212.7	2,540.0	144.9
2005			4,363.3	3,010.5	

Note: All nominal values are denominated in billion 1998 rubles.
Sources: Money, Central Bank of Russia; Receivables and GDP, Rosstat, various releases.

Many observers, including the IMF, attribute Russia's recovery to rising world oil prices. Figure 4.1 documents the heterogeneous economic performance of the six major petroleum-exporting countries around the world in 1992–2004. In Russia and across countries, it is uncorrelated with oil price fluctuations. Figure 4.2 illustrates how economic recovery synchronized in Russia, Ukraine, Kazakhstan and other former Soviet states, both net oil exporters (Russia, Kazakhstan, Azerbaijan) and importers (Ukraine, Belarus, Moldova). The oil factor was neither necessary (viz., Ukraine) nor sufficient (viz., Venezuela) for economic recovery and growth in the early 2000s. The oil connection abstracted from the economic system and policy shifts is specious.

Russia's economic recovery raises a more fundamental, and incendiary, issue than oil. Figure 4.3 illustrates it. In Russia and similar post-centrally-planned economies, liberalization and privatization coincided with the great economic contraction in 1992–98. Partial de-liberalization and de-privatization in Russia, starting with mandated repatriation of export revenues, coincided with economic recovery in 1999–2004. The principal idea of this chapter is that the

Table 4.2 Receivables and their Financing as a Share of GDP: Russia, 1990–2005

Year	Enterprise receivables (billion rubles)	Receivables flow (billion rubles)	GDP (billion rubles)	Receivables flow as a percent of GDP (Claim on the tax subsidy)	Enterprise receivables including internal receivables within holding companies (billion rubles)
1990	n.a.	n.a.	0.644	n.a.	n.a.
1991	0.060	0.086	1.399	6.1	0.082
1992	0.146	4.15	19.0	21.8	0.204
1993	4.3	31.7	171.5	18.5	5.2
1994	36.0	87.0	610.7	14.2	43.8
1995	123.0	166.3	1,428.5	11.6	150.5
1996	289.3	263.9	2,007.8	13.1	362.0
1997	553.2	123.8	2,342.5	5.3	662.6
1998	677.0	521.2	2,629.6	19.8	846.1
1999	1,198.2	264.4	4,823.2	5.5	1542.0
2000	1,462.6	258.8	7,305.6	3.5	1999.7
2001	1,721.4	323.7	8,943.6	3.6	2450.8
2002	2,045.1	222.6	10,817.5	2.1	3211.0
2003	2,267.7	272.3	13,201.1	2.1	3663.3
2004	2,540.0	470.5	16,778.8	2.8	4138.7
2005	3,010.5				5174.4

Note: All nominal values are denominated in billion 1998 rubles.
Sources: Rosstat.

impact of economic freedom is ambivalent. It depends on the economic system. The freedom to create new wealth is eminently productive. However, the freedom for firms and some individuals to redistribute to themselves income from the government, other firms and other households, suppresses productive incentives and economic growth. Government restriction of such freedom, e.g., in China or in Russia after 1998, fosters economic performance.

Socialism from Below: Third-party Billing

To start with a quick frame of reference, one can view Russia's economy in the 1990s as third-party billing. X sells products to Y and charges Z. This operation is familiar on the sectoral scale in US health care services and higher education. Health care providers charge insurance companies or the

Figure 4.1 The Specious Oil Connection: Economic Performance of the Six Greatest Oil-exporting Countries vs. World Oil Prices, 1992–2004

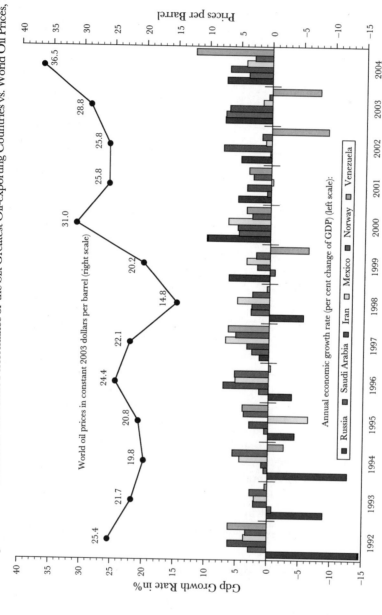

Note: The data for 2004 are provisional.

Sources: GDP growth rates: All countries except Russia: The IMF, *World Economic Outlook*, October 2000 (for 1992–1995) and October 2004 (for 1996–2004); Russia: Table 4.1. World oil prices in constant 2003 dollars: British Petroleum, at http://www.bp.com/sectiongenericarticle.do?categoryId=2012411&contentId=2018340.

Figure 4.2 The Specious Oil Connection: Economic Performance of Oil-exporting and Oil-importing Countries, Russia and Other States of the CIS, 1992–2004

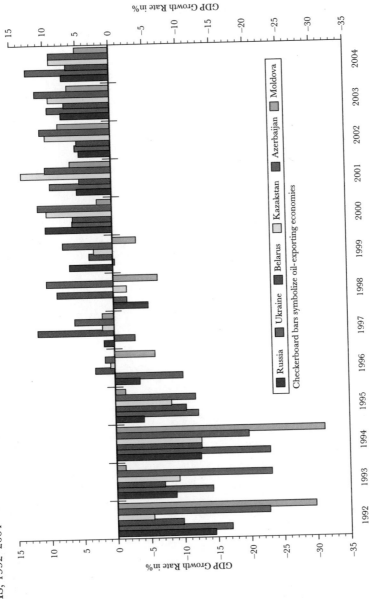

Note: The data for 2004 are provisional.
Sources: GDP growth rates: All countries except Russia: The IMF, *World Economic Outlook*, October 2000 (for 1992–1995) and October 2004 (for 1996–2004); Russia: Table 4.1.

Figure 4.3 Index of Real GDP (1991 = 100): Russia, 1990–2004

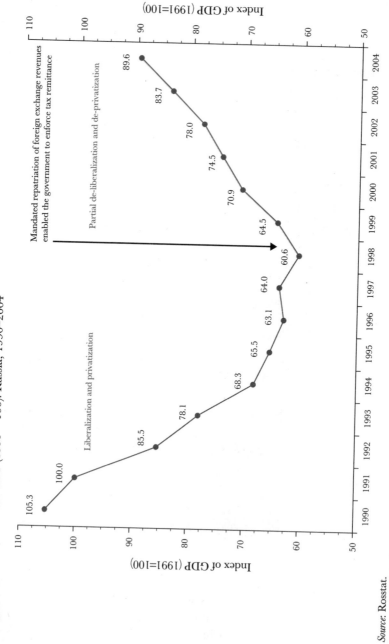

Source. Rosstat.

The data are reproduced in Table 4.1.

government. State colleges charge student tuition to the state government. Buyers receive products for free and do not economize on quantity and prices. Sellers can overcharge for their products when the third-party pays. This incentive structure is responsible for rapidly rising health care costs and tuition. After the abolition of central planning, a novel system of third-party billing evolved in Russia. It was national in scope and **runs from below**. Enterprises bill the government and the public.

Aggregate Third-party Billing

Figure 4.4 and Box 1 join forces on the next pages to explore step-by-step how this novel system had adapted and how it operates. In essence, enterprise X sells goods and services to enterprises Y and Z, receives some payments, and implicitly charges the unpaid balances to the government. Enterprise Y sells goods and services to enterprises Z and X, receives some payments, and implicitly charges the unpaid balances to the government. Enterprise Z sells goods and services to X and Y and to retailers, receives some payments, and implicitly charges the unpaid balances to the government. Circularly, all enterprises except retailers, various services, and outliers charge the government. In practice, enterprises X, Y and Z issue invoices to buyers and receive payments over time. As in the universal practice of trade credit, sales and their invoices precede payments. In accounting terms, the balances of the amounts invoiced net of payments constitute the outstanding balances of accounts receivables, or simply receivables. In most economies, the outstanding balances of receivables are paid by buyers. In Russia and similar countries, enterprises charge these balances to the government and the public at large, take the subsidy, and then pay each other. Enterprises Z, Y and X take the subsidy and pay X, Y and Z with public funds. This unique subsidy is taken, not given, charged, not solicited.

The monthly data in Figure 4.4 cover the period 1992–97 and truncate in 1998, for both presentation and substantive reasons. This was the period of the unfettered operation of aggregate third-party billing, before enterprise freedom to charge the government was restricted. Herewith a brief preview. When invoices outgrow payments, enterprises amass the balances of receivables. Enterprise income winds up to a great extent in receivables instead of cash. For many enterprises, receivables exceed net income. Enterprises increase payables, i.e., do not pay bills, lest their net cash flow turn negative. Tax arrears supplement payment arrears, especially for industries where receivables excee payables. Enterprises appropriate taxes withheld from workers and collect from consumers, which they do not remit to the government. The governm cannot enforce full tax remittance when enterprise bank accounts are dr down. Tax non-remittance on a national scale rules out government crackdown, seizing assets, or bankruptcy for it will wipe out the tax base. The government is forced to monetize tax remittance and enterprise payments (even if the government monetizes its budget deficit, itself due to tax non-remittance, the money is fungible). The banks transmit monetization through credit for payments, roll over and expand this credit.

Figure 4.4 highlights a regular empirical match between receivables and the subsidy they enforce. It shows how over time the outstanding balances of enterprise receivables match the sum of (1) tax non-remittance and (2) monetization multiplied through the banking system (approximated as the domestic money balances M2). These are the two principal channels of the subsidy wrung from the government. They sum up into a self-enforceable subsidy. The simple point of Figure 4.4 is that the government and, ultimately, the public are forced to pay the enterprise bill.

The Difference of Aggregate Third-party Billing

The national scale, across industries and enterprises, shifts third-party billing towards the government and the public (households, consumers) as the ultimate payers. In the supply chain over the stages of processing, every enterprise is both buyer and seller of products, and most enterprises, except retailers, various services, etc., issue invoices. The national scale aggregates third-party billing and enables the entire enterprise network to charge the government and the public at large (households and consumers) for its outstanding receivables.[1]

This marks the basic difference between sectoral and aggregate third-party billing. The former is voluntary and contractual. The latter forges a symbiotic bond in which enterprises take the initiative and the government is forced to pay. This feature is unique and extreme. Aggregate third-party billing charges from enterprises to the government, that is from below to above (in economic terms, it is endogenous). The subsidy is taken by the enterprise network from below, not given by the government from above. Ironically, this

party billing on the national scale is unique and extreme. It aggregates (1) various s of third-party billing and (2) cross-sectoral subsidies between enterprises and ough the mechanism of trade credit. The latter between individual sectors ome from sellers to buyers without billing the government. See Robert A id K Whitcomb, 1978, Implicit transfers in the extension of trade credit, lding and Thomas F. Wilson, eds., *Redistribution Through the Financial mics of Money and Credit*, New York, Praeger Publishers, pp. 191–208. billing, wherein the government is the third-party, extends cross-industry cross-sectoral operations. This creates the national scale m the government to the enterprise network.

system represents a traditional socialist economy in reverse, as if central planning flipped topsy turvy. Box 2 depicts this evolution.[1]

Central planning integrated a national assembly line. Individual enterprises acted as the shop floors on the assembly line of forced production under government output quotas. This was a veritable nation-enterprise. This system necessitated aggregate third-party paying. Whenever enterprise Y underproduced output or overspent inputs, lost income, run into a negative net cash flow problem, and missed the due date to pay its bills to enterprise X, the government financed enterprise Y to enable it to make payments to X. The government then punished enterprise Y for failing central plan output and input quotas. This financing of payment arrears (dubbed in the literature as the soft budget constraint) represented an automatic credit line. It served the government to enforce an uninterrupted flow of output, forced exchange and forced delivery on the vertical assembly line from X to Y and to enforce performance of Y. Third-party paying was from above, from the government to enterprises (in economic terms, exogenous). It was the government means to enforce forced production/exchange/delivery under central planning. It was thus a unique forced subsidy from the government. Like in making *foie gras*, it was the force-feeding of immediate production units in order to increase output quotas.[2]

Abolition of central planning could come in various ways. The government could phase-out the inherited nation-enterprise by phasing-in the new-entrant market sector and thus shrinking the share of the old state sector in GDP. China chose this strategy, bypassing liberalization and privatization of the preexisting state sector. Russia opted for liberalization of transactions and privatization of preexisting enterprises. This strategy subsumed the abolition of central planning. Inadvertently, it enabled the inherited assembly line of enterprises to evolve into a subsidy-extracting network. Individual enterprises (more precisely, their owners and managers) were free to join the subsidy network or survive and possibly perish without.

---

[1] The next two paragraphs summarize our book in http://www.russianeconomy.org/predation/pdf/chapter2.pdf and http://www.russianeconomy.org/predation/pdf/ch4add.pdf

[2] This treatment of the soft budget constraint under central planning is opposite to the standard literature which views the government as the benevolent and weak-willed dictator unable to commit himself to not subsidizing enterprises. See Janos Kornai, Eric Maskin and Gerald Roland, 2003, Understanding the soft budget constraint, *Journal of Economic Literature*, 41, No. 4, December, 1095–1136. This view begs the question how the government could maintain forced production. The standard view fits individual and sectoral bailouts in Western and developing economies, a species systemically different from central planning. It is incompatible with economy-wide third-party paying to enforce production quotas.

The enterprise network adapted aggregate third-party paying into aggregate third-party billing. This amounted to socialist devolution of fiscal and monetary authority from the government to the enterprise network. Aggregate third-party billing empowers the network to enforce its own subsidy from the government and the public. In effect, the enterprise network collects a tax from the public. This subsidy and this tax is one and the same, to wit, the tax subsidy. It represents the parallel taxation of the public by the enterprise network. One can call this new economic system Enterprise Network Socialism.[1]

How a mechanism operates often tells why it exists and how it came into existence. The evolution from central planning to Enterprise Network Socialism resulted from the fact that the inherited national assembly line, not scattered sectors or enterprises, can enforce third-party billing from below. This enables us to analyse what evolved historically as an adaptive operation of learning by doing. The next pages follow Box 1 and Figure 4.4 in laying out this operation step-by-step.

Facts: Fiscal Expectations, Surcharged Prices and the Self-enforceable Subsidy

Step 1. Surcharge

Step 1 is the easiest for enterprises to undertake and the hardest for observers to see and to explicate. It reveals itself through a chain of empirical observations. They compare the operation of accounts receivable in the US and Russia. To eliminate the influence of inflation, several diagrams of Figure 4.5 deflate nominal receivables and plot real receivables in inflation-adjusted values.[2]

---

[1] A quick taxonomic distinction. Aggregate third-party billing (1) is collective, all-encompassing, not of sectoral special interests; (2) entails a subsidy taken from below, not given from above; endogenous, not exogenous; (3) works automatically, not through the political process; and (4) subsidy extraction is cost-free to enterprises, does not involve spending resources of time, effort, and money. On each of these four counts aggregate third-party billing is opposite to what the literature calls rent-seeking. Also, the above point (2) indicates that aggregate third-party billing charges from below, endogenously, and is thus opposite to what the literature calls the soft budget constraint, which is operationally third-party paying. The latter can be total under central planning or sectoral in many other economies (e.g., bailouts), but it streams from above, and is exogenous in all cases. These are the taxonomic systemic differences between aggregate third-party billing under Enterprise Network Socialism and various other species of socialism (income redistribution). Ignoring these systemic differences leads to wrong diagnoses which beget wrong policies.

[2] The Consumer Price Index (CPI) is used as the deflator due to lack of other reliable indices for Russia.

Box 1 The Operation of the Total Third Party Billing under Enterprise Network Socialism.

One can follow the arrows in the flow chart in Figure 4.4 and proceed step-by-step thus:

Step 1. Trade credit is separated from sales and production. Invoices outgrow payments when enterprises add a third party surcharge to the price and bill the government. See Figures 4.5 and 4.6.

Arrow 1 in the flow chart leads to step 2.

Step 2. The flow of receivables for many enterprises exceeds net income. They increase payables lest their net cash flow turn negative. Aged receivables increase payment arrears and vice versa. This chain reaction circulates the payment jam across the economy. Enterprises whose flow of receivables exceeds that of trade payables must increase tax payables.

Arrow 2 in the flow chart leads to step 3.

Step 3. Enterprises do not remit taxes withheld from workers and collected from consumers. The government cannot enforce full tax remittance, as in the game of chicken. See Table 4.3, Figure 4.7 panel 1.

Arrow 3 in the flow chart leads to step 4.

Step 4. The government is forced to issue debt, i.e., securitize tax non-remittance. See Figure 4.10.

Arrows 4 and 5 in the flow chart lead to step 5.

Step 5. To delay the default, the government is forced to monetize the budget deficit, to wit, monetize enterprise tax remittance, as in the game of chicken. See Figures 4.4 and 4.7 panel 2.

Arrow 6 in the flow chart leads to step 6.

Step 6. Banks transmit, extend, roll over credit, which reduces aged receivables, but see step 8.

Step 7. Variable trade-offs between tax non-remittance and monetization of tax remittance, followed by credit rollover and extension, wind up in the self-enforceable subsidy. It sums up to the outstanding balances of receivables. See Figures 4.4, 4.8, and 4.9.

Corollary: A complementary array of cross-industry price subsidies accompanies this subsidy.

Arrows 7 and 8 in the flow chart lead to step 8.

Step 8. Which is identical to step 1. Stimulated by all these components, enterprises surcharge invoices with a network tax to extract the self-enforceable subsidy. See Figures 4.7 panels 1 and 3.

Corollary: This system becomes circular and self-reinforcing.

Figure 4.4 The Government and the Public are Forced to Pay the Enterprise Bill: Russia, 1992–1997

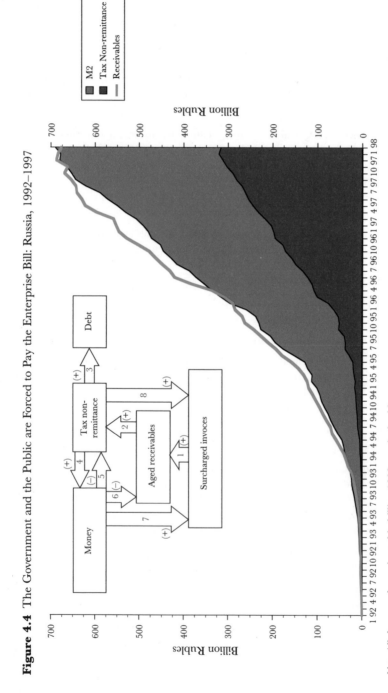

Note: All data are denominated in billion 1998 nominal rubles.

Sources: Receivables and tax non-remittance: Rosstat.

Money: Central Bank of Russia.

Box 2 The Evolution from Central Planning to Enterprise Network Socialism

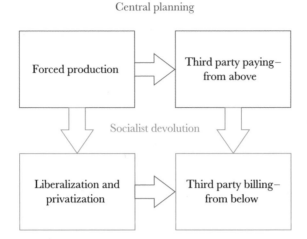

Central planning

Socialist devolution

Enterprise network socialism

• Observation 1. Separation

The first observation may seem to be blase and trivial. Figure 4.5 contrasts two patterns of trade credit in the US and Russia. To define these patterns, Figure 4.5 juxtaposes the annual indices of nominal or real receivables in 1991–2004 and the annual indices of real GDP.[1] Figure 4.5a and b compares the indices of nominal receivables in current rubles or dollars in the US and Russia against GDP growth. Figure 4.5c and d offers a sharper picture with real receivables in inflation-adjusted dollars or rubles on the same backdrop of GDP growth.[2]

Receivables in the US exhibit a cyclical pattern with short lags. Both nominal (Figure 4.5a) and real (Figure 4.5c) receivables increase during the years of economic growth and decline during recessions and their aftermath.

In Russia in 1991–2004, receivables display an idiosyncratic pattern. Both nominal and real receivables in Russia in Figures 4.5b and 4.5d show the

---

[1] The data are available on the web site of Rosstat at http://www.gks.ru/bgd/free/ b01_19/Main.htmhttp://www.gks.ru/bgd/free/B01_19/IswPrx.dll/Stg/d000/ i000330r.htm and http://www.statrus.info/catalog/edition .jsp?id=1821&uid=22, and on the web site of the Central Bank of Russia at http://www.cbr.ru/statistics/ credit_statistics/. Tables 4.1 and 4.2 offer annual summaries.

[2] Only Figure 4.5 and the discussion around it alternate nominal and real receivables. The rest of the figures, tables and discussion employ nominal receivables in current rubles or dollars. The qualifier 'nominal' is dropped for brevity except in Figure 4.5 and the surrounding discussion.

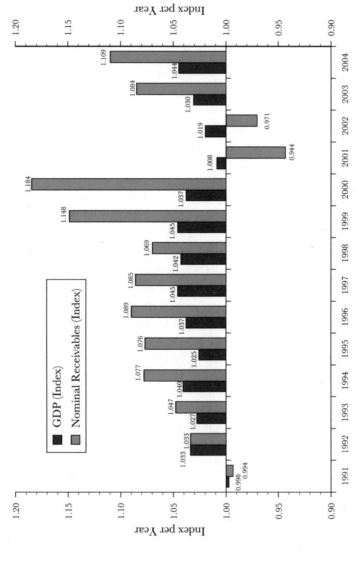

Figure 4.5a Indices of GDP and Nominal Receivables: U.S., 1991–2004

Sources: GDP: U.S. Department of Commerce, Bureau of Economic Analysis, at http://www.bea.gov/bea/dn/home/gdp.htm. Receivables: Board of Governors of the Federal Reserve System, The Flow of Funds Accounts of the United States, Table L.101, at http://www.federal-reserve.gov/releases/z1/Current/data.htm.

Figure 4.5b Indices of GDP and Nominal Receivables: Russia, 1991–2004

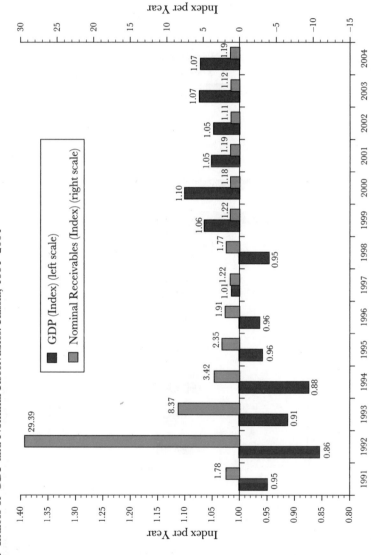

Figure 4.5c Indices of GDP and Real Receivables (Deflated by the CPI): U.S., 1991–2004

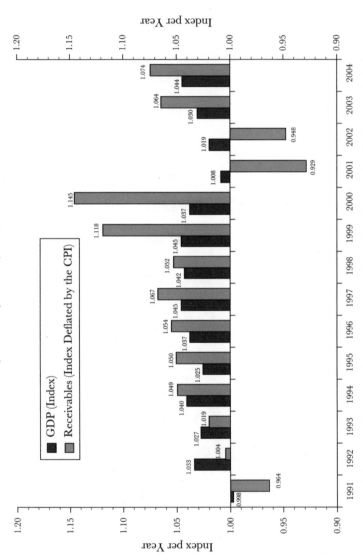

Sources: GDP: U.S. Department of Commerce, Bureau of Economic Analysis, at http://www.bea.gov/bea/dn/home/ gdp.htm. Receivables: Board of Governors of the Federal Reserve System, The Flow of Funds Accounts of the United States, Table L.101, at http:// www.federalreserve.gov/releases/z1/Current/data.htm. Consumer Price Index (CPI): U.S. Department of Labor, Bureau of Labor Statistics, at ftp://ftp.bls.gov/pub/special.requests/cpi/cpiai.txt.

Figure 4.5d Indices of GDP and Real Receivables (Deflated by the CPI): Russia, 1991–2004

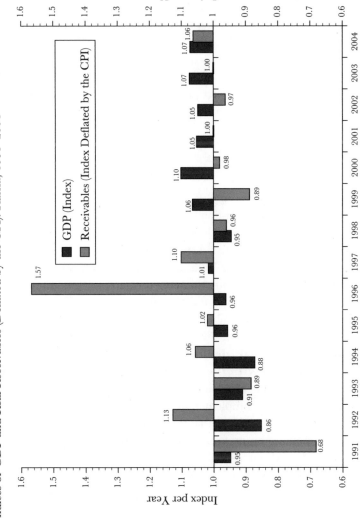

absence of any regular relationship with real output, with productive economic activity. Nominal receivables increased massively during the great contraction of 1992–98 and continued to increase moderately in 1999–2004. These increases correspond closely to increases in the annual price indices in Figure 4.6. This leaves real receivables vis-à-vis real economic activity in Figure 4.5d. **The indices of real receivables lack any relationship with the indices of real GDP.** Real receivables saw increases during the years of the great contraction of 1992–98 except 1993 and 1998 and declined or held unchanged during the years of the recovery of 1999–2004 except 2004. The pattern that arises here is detachment of real receivables from economic activity. Output declines and recovers but real receivables exhibit no participation in or reaction to production and sales. Trade credit and productive activity walk their own separate paths as if they operate on different planes of existence, detached from each other. Russia exhibits a unique pattern of separation of trade credit from production and sales.

• **Observation 2. Alignments**

The path of real receivables in Russia in Figure 4.5d is not only detached from output but, with the exception of the years 1991 and 1996, nearly stagnant. The year 1991 was before liberalization and the year 1996 is an evidential outlier, possibly a statistical error due to major changes in measuring the CPI in 1996.[1] Clipping the 1996 data from the path of real receivables charts a trend through 1992–2004 spanning the gap of 1996. All fluctuations in 1992–95 and 1997–2004 are minor, random and cancel each other over time. The index of real receivables actually hovered around unity and was stable within a narrow range. **The indices of real receivables are nearly invariant to GDP decline or growth. Real receivables in Russia seem to align with the index equal to unity, which implies zero growth of real receivables over time.**

Figure 4.6 displays the complementary part of this relationship during the same period 1992–2004. It shows that the separation pattern in Russia closely relates, indeed matches on an annual basis, the path of nominal receivables with the price index. Minor annual fluctuations which deviate from this match move randomly. A closer match of the two indices smoothes over time and forms a continuous relationship. This continuous relationship is consistent

[1] See Moscow Institute of Electronics and Mathematics, Laboratory of Econometric Studies, Zhikharev V et. al., How to measure living standards, at http://www.rau.su/observer/N05_99/5_15.htmhttp://www.rau.su/observer/N05_99/5_15.HTM). If their estimate is correct, the price index in 1996 was understated by 1.5 times and the index of real receivables is overstated in Figure 5.4 by the same 1.5 times. Then the spike of 1996 in Figure 4.5d is an error.

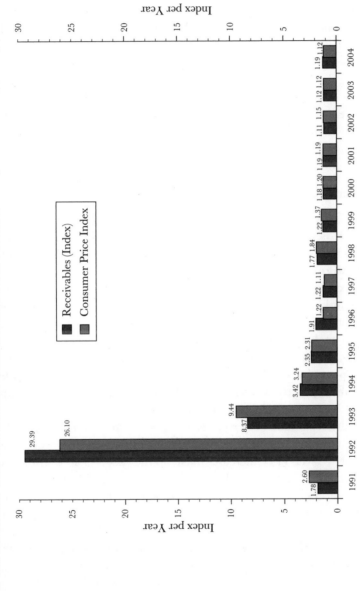

Figure 4.6 Receivables Grow with the Price Index: Receivables and Consumer Prices, Annual Indices, Russia, 1991–2004

Note: The index fraction of the price index over unity is the inflation rate.
Source: Rosstat.

with the indices of real receivables hovering around unity and converging towards it. **Tautologically, if the index of real receivables hovers around unity, the index of nominal receivables must align with the price index.**

In the US, the index of real receivables aligns with that of real GDP (e.g., both increased by 2.9 per cent per annum in 1990–2004 and about 3.2 per cent per annum during 1955–2004). The index of nominal receivables aligns with that of nominal GDP. There is no regular relationship between nominal receivables and the price indices.

Box 3 in the top matrix summarizes the contrasting alignments over time. Under the cyclical pattern of trade credit in the US, growth of real receivables aligns with growth of real output. Tautologically, growth of nominal receivables aligns with growth of nominal output. Under the separation pattern in Russia, real receivables stagnate within a stable narrow range and growth of nominal receivables aligns with price increases.

• **Observation 3. Invoicing**

The next observation is mechanical. Receivables are balances of invoices net of payments. **It is price increases in invoices in excess of payments that make up these balances in Russia and make nominal receivables grow in alignment with the price index**.

Box 3 explores this mechanical connection. It is depicted in the lower half of Box 3 and its side bars. It shifts focus from receivables to invoices as the source of empirical alignments. It is what is **in** invoices when they exceed payments and make up an increase in the outstanding balances of nominal receivables. **It can be output growth in current prices under the cyclical pattern in the US or it can be price increases *per se* under the separation pattern in Russia.** This decomposition makes both patterns mechanically consistent in the same mold.

Under the separation pattern in Russia, the mechanics transpire in nominal terms. New invoices raise prices and exceed past invoices valued at the previous price level. Price increases make up the excess of new invoices over payments on past invoices. When spending grows (the government never failed to print money) and payments increase, enterprises raise prices higher so that new invoices exceed payments on past invoices almost continuously. **Over time, in the overlapping flows of invoices and payments, invoices not only exceed but continuously outgrow payments by price increases.** This is the underlying mechanical meaning of the empirical observation in Figure 4.6 that the outstanding balances of nominal receivables grow at the rate of price increases. In short, all price excesses are in invoices.

Box 3 Facts and Mechanics of Two Patterns of Trade Credit

	U.S.: Cyclical pattern	Russia: Separation pattern
Real receivables	Align with growth of real output Figure 4.5c	Invariant, stable within a narrow range Figure 4.5d
Nominal receivables	Align with growth of nominal output Figure 4.5a	Align with price increases Figure 4.6

Mechanics

	New invoices exceed payments in real terms when output expands; payments exceed new invoices in real terms when output contracts	New invoices exceed payments in nominal terms by price increases. Invoices continuously outgrow payments by price increases
	Firms index invoices to payments and through them to spending. Output and prices increase (decrease) in one or another combination	Enterprises index invoices not to payments, not to spending but to fiscal expectations. They add a surcharge to prior prices

How can growth of real receivables align with growth of real output? Firms optimize cash flow. The ratio of nominal receivables to GDP is cyclical within a narrow stable range

How can real receivables stay invariant, stable? Enterprises maximize nominal receivables by price increases, subject to expected subsidy, which renders real receivables stable. The ratio of nominal receivables to GDP fluctuates

• Observation 4. Collection

What strategies of US firms and Russian enterprises stand behind their invoicing mechanics? One strategy makes possible the growth alignment of real receivables with real output in the US. The other strategy, in Russia, makes possible the alignment of the indices of nominal receivables with the price index (which holds real receivables nearly stable). These strategies are summarized in the left and right side bars in Box 3. They compare how and when (and hence why) invoices exceed payments by output growth in the US and by price increases in Russia.

Firms in the market economy strive to optimize their cash flow. This operation includes managing accounts receivable, that is, collecting payments and gearing invoices to payments collection. The average collection period is one of the major signs of the viability of the firm and a key indicator of its market valuation and credit worthiness. In the US, the average collection period decreased from 29 days in 1990 to 27 days in 1992–94, rising steadily with GDP growth to 37 days in 2000, and then gradually shortening to 31 days in 2003 and going up to 32 days in 2004. This is consistent with the pattern which the *Encyclopedia Britannica* cites to typify trade credit in market economies.[1] This is indeed the strategy of cash flow optimization: short collection periods, stability of payments collection, a narrow range and a cyclical pattern.

It literally pays to optimize the average collection period. Simpler yet, the firm cannot survive on income on the accrual basis alone. It is not sustainable. In brief, if its buyers do not pay their bills for a lengthy period (payments are in arrears), while the firm duly pays its bills within the due period, its net cash flow may run negative. When net cash flow is persistently negative, firms may face bankruptcy and no one would lend to them, or no one would lend them and firms may face bankruptcy, whichever sequence unravels. Most firms issue invoices in a cyclical pattern in order to receive payments within the due period and thus hold a manageable balance of receivables from the cash flow standpoint. Sellers make invoices exceed payments and increase the balance of receivables in alignment with output growth. They do not raise prices to make invoices exceed payments and expand the balances of receivables.

In Russia, the average collection period more than doubled from 24 days in 1991 to 51 days in 1992, shortened to 45–46 days in 1994–95 only to lengthen to 63 days in 1996, 66 days in 1997, and to a whopping 104 days in 1998.

---

[1] *Encyclopedia Britannica* in the article 'Business Finance,' section 'Accounts Receivable,' summarizes that the ratio of receivables to sales in US manufacturing ranges between 8 and 12 per cent, yielding the average collection period of approximately one month (around 36.5 days, to be exact).

Then a reversal, down to 69 days in 1999 and 54 days in 2000 and gradually to 44 days in 2003 and 40 days in 2004.

If the average collection period is lengthy and fluctuates separately from output, enterprises maximize nominal receivables subject to how much subsidy they expect to enforce in lieu of payments. They make invoices exceed payments to that end by price increases which amass the balance of receivables. It is this practice that undergirds the alignment of receivables and price indices in Figure 4.6. It also indicates that the causation in Figure 4.6 goes from growth of receivables (indeed from invoices) to price indices, not vice versa.

The mechanism of this subsidy extraction was introduced on pages 61–64 and in Figure 4.4. Figure 4.4 demonstrates how during the period from 1992 to 1998 the outstanding balances of receivables matched over time the sum of various subsidy channels, such as tax non-remittance and monetization multiplied through the banking system. This mechanism became more complicated in 1999–2004, but the pattern remained within, of which later. The next steps through Box 1 and its accompanying figures explore and document the mechanism of this subsidy extraction in detail.

- **Observation 5. Indexation**

The final observation of step 1 is straightforward, if unconventional. Box 3 summarizes it at the bottom. Optimization of cash flow in the US implies that firms index invoices to payments and through them to spending in the economy (that is, to the combined changes in the money supply and the velocity of its circulation). In the process, output and prices increase or decrease in one or another combination between them in the cyclical pattern. This indexation to payments and ultimately to spending does not let invoices exceed payments by separate price increases. That would expand the balance of receivables and undermine cash flow optimization. This is not sustainable. Firms could not survive thus.

In Russia, enterprises maximize nominal receivables by making invoices outgrow payments via price increases. This implies that, as they increase prices to make up the balances of nominal receivables, enterprises index invoices not to payments and hence not to spending. They index invoices to fiscal targets—how much subsidy enterprises expect to enforce. They learn by doing, by trial and error, as described earlier (see pages 61–64 above), and learn continuously over time, what these fiscal targets are. Those who learn survive and socialize the experience on the national scale. This is the collective survival of the fittest.

Ultimately, enterprises index invoices to fiscal expectations. In this pattern, price increases are detached from spending. Excess of invoices over payments, which is made up of price increases, is detached from spending. Fiscal expectations bypass current spending (money times velocity and their combined changes) and generate inflationary expectations directly,[1] through price increases in invoices in outgrowth of payments. These are self-fulfilling inflationary expectations. They materialize in the outstanding balances of receivables.

The simplest way to describe this procedure is to view price increases in invoices as a price surcharge added to the prior price listed in past invoices. This is a third-party surcharge, to be billed to the government and the public at large (households, consumers) in pursuit of the subsidy. One more inference which may seem outlandish but, on reflection, fits. Since this subsidy is collected (see Figure 4.4 again), the price surcharge in invoices constitutes a special tax levied by enterprises on the government and, eventually, on consumers and households. It acts like a quasi-value-added tax on sales over the stages of processing. It is quasi and not genuine value-added tax in the national income accounting sense because this tax is additive on enterprise fiscal expectations, not multiplicative at a preset rate. Hence it applies equally to output with positive and negative value-added. Which makes this unique tax from below (the endogenous tax) especially distortionary for, on top of income redistribution, it finances and perpetuates value subtraction.

Step 2. The Payment Jam

Mechanically, there are four potential responses to the problem of negative net cash flow: reduce receivables, obtain outside financing, increase trade

---

[1] A burgeoning literature inaugurates a new wave, which its practitioners call 'the fiscal theory of the price level.' It is possible that the Russian experience may fit as a special case with its own systemic particulars (the subsidy from below) and mechanics (trade credit). Only specialists in this innovative, sophisticated and extremely technical (not to say inscrutable) field can adjudicate if their approach is what explains the Russian case. The present authors believe so, but a true test would require substantial modeling and econometric analysis, beyond the scope of this chapter. Of a large body of literature, one can list only a few references here. Thomas J. Sargent and Neil Wallace, 1981, Some unpleasant monetarist arithmetic, *Federal Reserve Bank of Minneapolis Quarterly Review* 5, No. 3 (Fall), 1–17; Kiminori Matsuyama, 1991, Endogenous price fluctuations in an optimizing model of a monetary economy, *Econometrica* 59, No. 6 (November), 1617–31; Eric M. Leeper, 1991, Equilibria under active and passive monetary and fiscal policies, *Journal of Monetary Economics* 27, No. 1 (February), 129–47; Michael Woodford, 1995, Price level determinacy without control of a monetary aggregate, *Carnegie-Rochester Conference Series on Public Policy* 43 (December), 1–46; Joydeep Bhattacharya and Joseph H. Haslag, 1999, Monetary policy arithmetic: some recent contributions, Federal Reserve Bank of Dallas, *Economic and Financial Review* (Third Quarter), 26–36; Charles T. Carlstrom and Timothy S. Fuerst, 2000, The fiscal theory of the price level, Federal Reserve Bank of Cleveland, *Economic Review* 36, No. 1 (Quarter I), 22–32; Lawrence J. Christiano and Terry J. Fitzgerald, 2000, Understanding the fiscal theory of the price level, Federal Reserve Bank of Cleveland, *Economic Review* 36, No. 2 (Quarter II): 3–38; John Cochrane, 2000, Money as stock: price level determination with no money demand, National Bureau of Economic Research, *NBER Working Paper* no. 7498 (January).

payables and increase tax payables. Reducing receivables by factoring them can help occasionally, not continuously. Obtaining outside financing, such as borrowing and/or issuing equity, is not forthcoming when cash earnings are persistently negative.

One can increase trade payables. Initially, negative net cash flow does not halt operations because the business can draw on the money balances in the bank and dispose of other assets. After cash balances and other assets are run down, bills cannot be paid in full within the due period. Payables fall into arrears. Thus this business does automatically increase trade payables when its net cash flow turns negative. This happens by default. Unpaid bills automatically increase the outstanding balance of payables. Payment arrears (increased trade payables) turn net cash flow non-negative. Increasing trade payables helps trade debtors in the short run. This practice can last as long as trade creditors can and will sustain ageing and accumulation of their own receivables. Their own flow of receivables may exceed net income and net cash flow may turn negative. If and when trade creditors call in the debts owed them, bankruptcy arrives.

Finally, one can increase taxes payable. The business can stop or delay paying corporate income or profit tax. For quick cash, it can stop or delay remitting payroll and income taxes withheld from workers and value-added or sales taxes collected from consumers. This is illegal. If the government can enforce tax remittance and tax payments, it will, and this business will be no more.

• The Chain Reaction

One man's receivables are another man's payables. Money is fungible. These two basic propositions explicate that maximization of receivables (subject to the expected subsidy) in Russia was the source of the amassment of trade payables and that tax arrears supplemented payment arrears. As noted earlier, the average collection period expanded from 24 days in 1991 to 51 days in 1992, shortened to 45–46 days in 1994–95 only to lengthen to 63 days in 1996, 66 days in 1997, and to 104 days in 1998. It reversed to 69 days in 1999 and 54 days in 2000 and gradually decreased to 44 days in 2003 and 40 days in 2004. Since 1992, accounts receivables became and remained past due, or aged. Their counterpart is payment arrears. Days payable outstanding measure the average payment period (or non-payment period, as it were) the same way as the average collection period measures the unpaid length of receivables. Days payables outstanding doubled from 17 days in 1991 to 36 days in 1992, increased gradually to 55 days in 1996 and 61 days in 1997, and leaped to 102 days in 1998. A downward reversal started slowly afterwards, 72 days in 1999 and 56 days in 2000 and gradually shortened to 45 days in 2003, and 40 days in 2004. Since 1992, payables were in arrears.

Receivables amassed due to surcharged invoices generate payables that fall into arrears. It follows from the above discussion that maximization of receivables increases payables on two intertwined counts.

1. First, when receivables amass among sellers, trade payables amass among buyers. Aged receivables generate payment arrears.
2. Second, sellers themselves delay payments and thus increase payables and turn them into arrears to compensate for cash shortfalls when receivables take up the bulk of their net income.

A critical mass of payment arrears and aged receivables creates a payment jam. This is a situation on the brink of cessation of operating activities.[1] A marginal increase in payment arrears improves the cash flow position of buyers but worsens the cash flow position of sellers to the point where their net cash flow runs down to zero.[2] They, in turn, have to increase their payment arrears to stay afloat. However, this worsens the net cash flow position of their respective sellers and runs it down to zero. One can extend this exercise in rounds through the flow of funds until operating activities of some clusters of enterprises cease. This is a chain reaction. There is a recourse. Enterprises can maximize tax arrears, tax non-remittance.

Step 3. Third-party Payables

One can think of trade payables as second party payables. Most enterprises except retailers, various services, etc., are both sellers of output and buyers of inputs. In the flow of funds over the stages of processing, sectoral increases in payment arrears unleash a chain reaction of cash flow shortfalls. Tax arrears, in contrast, can be viewed as third-party payables. They harm the cash flow position of the government, reduce revenues and increase the budget deficit, which, in turn, delays government procurement payments, ages receivables of government suppliers and hurts their cash flow position. However, the government can sell bonds and/or print money to finance its budget deficits. Tax non-remittance and expected monetization not only offer enterprises a supplemental strategy of improving their cash flow position. They also constitute a pure subsidy. This is why enterprises which maximize profit in cash terms must maximize tax non-remittance.

[1] A detailed discussion is in Michael S. Bernstam and Alvin Rabushka, *From Predation to Prosperity*, Chapter 1, 'The Other Government,' at http://www.russianeconomy.org/predation/pdf/chapter1.pdf.
[2] This situation especially affects net creditor industries such as fuel energy, electric power, engineering (machine building), construction and transportation, but export revenues mitigate it for the crude oil and natural gas industries.

Other third-party payables include payroll arrears. Enterprise owners and managers treat them similarly to tax arrears but accumulate them to a lesser extent, if they want to maintain their core labor force. By the end of 1998, payroll arrears constituted 3 per cent of GDP, a significant income transfer from workers to enterprise owners and managers.[1]

Tax non-remittance is separate from tax evasion. It adds to tax evasion. Tax non-remittance is explicit and recorded. Enterprises withhold payroll and income taxes from workers and collect value-added and sales taxes from consumers. After that, enterprises impound part of this tax collection. In addition, they impound and do not remit their corporate income or profit tax which is also collected from households—consumers, workers and shareholders. In short, tax non-remittance is explicit confiscation of the tax base.

Table 4.3 documents the outstanding balances of tax arrears in Russia that rose from 0.6 per cent of GDP in 1992 to 18 per cent of GDP in 1998 and then reversed and declined to 2.2 per cent of GDP in 2004. The outstanding balances of taxes payable in the US ranged between 1.0 and 1.5 per cent of GDP.

Figure 4.7, panel 1 plots the relationship between tax non-remittance (the balances of tax payables, tax arrears) and the outstanding balances of receivables. This relationship is direct, strongly correlated and consistently proportional. This panel does not prove that amassment of receivables causes tax non-remittance. Correlation is not a causality. However, no proof of a one-directional causality is necessary. On the contrary, the relationship between the balances of aged receivables and tax arrears form a feedback loop as depicted in arrow 2 and the sequence of arrows 8 and 1 in the flow chart in Figure 4.4. Enterprises maximize receivables subject to expected subsidy (fiscal expectations), while tax non-remittance is part of this expected subsidy in the data plotted in Figure 4.4. An increase in tax non-remittance raises subsidy expectations and stimulates surcharged invoices (arrow 8 in the flow chart in Figure 4.4) which build up aged receivables (arrow 1 there). In turn, amassment and ageing of receivables render net cash flow negative without an automatic increase in trade payables and supplemental maximization of

[1] We list managers on a par with owners because, in Russia, state-owned enterprises did not remit profits or dividends to the government and, in terms of accrual of net income, qualified as private property of managers. One can also add state managers such as ministers of nuclear energy, railroads, etc. State enterprises also partially qualified as private property of managers in terms of exclusive control of the disposal value of net assets (equity). The existence of assets stripping of state enterprises effectively disqualifies the government as the owner. From this perspective, privatization of productive assets in Russia in the 1990s was nearly universal.

Table 4.3 Enterprise Money Balances and the Stock of Tax Non-remittance: Russia, 1992–2005

Beginning of year	(1) Enterprise money balances	(2) Tax non-remittance	(3) The ratio of (1)to(2)	(4) The ratio of tax non-remittance to GDP (%)
1992	0.221	0.010	22.1	0.6
1993	0.980	0.122	8.0	1.7
1994	5.9	3.0	2.0	2.5
1995	15.7	15.1	1.04	5.3
1996	19.6	75.1	0.26	10.1
1997	39.3	203.4	0.19	13.5
1998	58.5	316.6	0.18	18.0
1999	93.5	474.5	0.20	11.3
2000	169.0	572.6	0.30	9.2
2001	231.3	668.5	0.35	7.0
2002	337.1	625.2	0.54	4.7
2003	549.9	510.8	1.08	3.4
2004	509.7	444.7	1.15	2.2
2005	679.4	363.2	1.87	

Note: All nominal values are denominated in billion 1998 rubles.
Source: Rosstat, various releases.

tax non-remittance (arrow 2 in the same flow chart). Figure 4.7, panel 1 offers evidence for these relationships in both directions and for the entire feedback loop.

Under the payment jam, on the margin, the government cannot enforce tax remittance in full. All fiscal instruments are blunted. (It took the Central Bank of Russia to invent a sharp one in late 1998 and reverse the situation, but of this in due course). Of the possible menu of enforcements, one can think of fines and penalties, sequestration of enterprise money balances in the bank, lien and seizure of assets, placing in receivership, forced bankruptcy, prosecution of owners and managers and any other legal or fiscal recourse. During 1992–98, especially in 1996–98 when tax non-remittance exacerbated, the government tried, or at least tried to apply, all of these measures. They temporarily improved tax remittance by individually targeted enterprises, for a few months, but had all failed over time. On the national scale, under the payment jam, when enterprise X had to remit more taxes, it had to simultaneously reduce payments to enterprise Y, which then reduced its own remittance, netting little, if anything, for the government enforcement effort.

Figure 4.7 Panels 1–3. Tax Non-remittance, Money Stock, and Receivables, in Billion Rubles, Monthly Data, Russia, 1992–Mid-1999

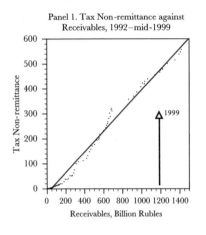

Panel 1. Tax Non-remittance against Receivables, 1992–mid-1999

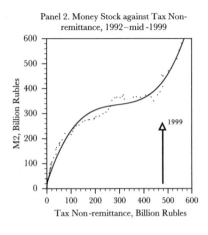

Panel 2. Money Stock against Tax Non-remittance, 1992–mid-1999

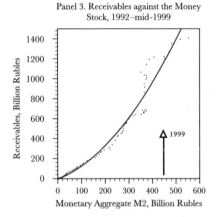

Panel 3. Receivables against the Money Stock, 1992–mid-1999

Sources: Receivables and tax non-remittance: Rosstat.
Money: Central Bank of Russia.

Not that the government did not try. Not that it was soft or weak-willed. Rather, it was impotent. Piling up fines and penalties could not induce payments when, as Table 4.3 shows, tax arrears in 1992–98 were growing unabated anyway. The data in Table 4.3 suggest why sequestration of enterprise money balances in the banks was not workable. Tax arrears were outgrowing enterprise money balances rapidly in 1992–98. Since 1996, the sequestration option evaporated altogether when tax arrears significantly exceeded enterprise money balances.

Lien and assets seizure, placement in receivership, forced bankruptcy, change of ownership, changing the form of ownership, prosecution of owners and managers, etc., are overlapping measures. In practice these measures meant renationalization. Apart from political constraints,[1] renationalization of enterprises and replacement of managers could not enforce tax remittance without changing incentives throughout the economic system. This implies no change without preventing surcharged invoices and accumulation of receivables. Both privately owned enterprises and those owned *de jure* by the government acted in the identical mode within the same network. Different ownership, different owners and different managers could not change the underlying systemic incentives. They indeed did not when the government made such changes from time to time in various industries.

Overall, under the payment jam, on the margin, any fiscal crackdown could improve tax remittance in specific sectors in the short run but jeopardize the flow of payments across the economy and the tax base in the long run. A major attempt to enforce tax remittance would have substituted additional payment arrears for tax arrears. A spillover effect through the flows of funds across industries would have brought down the net cash flow positions of net creditor enterprises and industries. This would have halted economic activity and wiped out the tax base.

The government options were between partial tax remittance by enterprises and the loss of the tax base. The options of the enterprise network were between partial tax remittance to the government (that is, maximization of receivables and the subsidy subject to fiscal constraints) and unpredictable consequences otherwise. Both the government and enterprises chose partial tax remittance. They were continuously engaged in the game of chicken over the **extent** of tax remittance, not over its completeness. As a rule, the government blinked.

This symbiotic arrangement worked for both until it engendered the great default of August 1998. The situation reversed in late 1998 after the Central Bank mandated repatriation and domestic sales of foreign exchange revenues. This reduction of capital outflow rapidly increased enterprise money balances (see Table 4.3). This, in turn, enabled the government to enforce more tax remittance in 1999–2000 in the flow sense, slow down the buildup of tax payables, and even reverse the trend and draw down the outstanding balances of tax arrears since 2001. This time, the enterprises blinked, first specific

[1] The government whose claim to existence was liberalization and privatization, could not renationalize enterprises and remain in power. Moreover, tax non-remittance was similar among enterprises which were *de jure* state-owned fully or partially (e.g., in oil, natural gas, electric power and other industries) and also among profit-making government agencies (nuclear energy, railroads, etc.). Renationalization of state-owned enterprises is absurd even under the Russian economic system. In sum, the government could not seize assets because it either already owned them, or had slated them for privatization, or just privatized them.

exporters, then the export sector at large, and, eventually, the entire enterprise network.

Step 4. Third-party Debt Transfer

A revenue shortfall due to tax non-remittance created an additional budget deficit which needed financing. All other sources of the budget deficit being equal and another source of financing, monetization, being also equal, the government had to issue bonds to finance this additional budget deficit. That is, the government had to securitize tax non-remittance. The monthly data demonstrate that the balances of tax non-remittance and government bonds issued from January 1995 to the default of August 1998 roughly converged.

Tax non-remittance is a pure subsidy. It is a transfer of income from workers and consumers to enterprise owners and managers. In the flows of funds, it is also a transfer of income from the government as the recipient of tax revenues, to the enterprise network. It is a subsidy because it would have been the same amount if all taxes were remitted and the equivalent outlay given to enterprises. The only difference with the latter case is that the subsidy via tax non-remittance is taken, not given. This subsidy is forced onto the government in the symbiotic arrangement discussed above. The government was then forced to securitize the tax non-remittance subsidy. Enterprise arrears were billed to the government via tax non-remittance and then charged to bond-holders when the government defaulted. This is a two-stage third-party debt transfer.

Step 5. Forced Monetization

A striking feature of panel 2 of Figure 4.7, which also shows in Figure 4.4, is that tax non-remittance and the money stock M2 were long-term complements and short-term substitutes in 1992–99. They grew in tandem at the same long-term rate and at different short-term rates. In 1992–95, money grew faster than tax non-remittance. In 1996–98, at a time of rapid bond financing of budget deficits, tax non-remittance grew faster than money. Since late 1998, money growth accelerated again relative to that of tax non-remittance. The semi-concave, semi-convex curve in panel 2 of Figure 4.7 fits the close correlation between the balances of tax arrears and money balances on identical scales. To wit, **they grew together ruble for ruble smoothed over time in the long run, substituting for each other ruble for ruble in the short run,** as if they were fungible in the fiscal pool.

Arrows 4 and 5 in the flow chart in Figure 4.4 capture their long-term and short-term feedback loop. It is not surprising that the government monetized budget deficits created, among other sources, by tax non-remittance—hence the plus sign from non-remittance to money. It is also not surprising that monetization dissipated the payment jam and reduced tax non-remittance in the short run—hence the minus sign from money to tax non-remittance. Also, bond receipts roughly matched tax non-remittance, which looked like they financed budget shortfalls from tax non-remittance. Why this double coincidence between money growth and tax non-remittance and between bonds and tax non-remittance?

There is no double indemnity. The government does not finance the fiscal cost of tax non-remittance twice, by issuing bonds and money. Recall the short-term trade-offs between money growth and that of tax non-remittance in panel 2 of Figure 4.7. When the money supply increased more, tax non-remittance increased less, and vice versa. One suggestion reconciles all the above observations. Under the payment jam, on the margin, **a ruble of bonds financed a ruble of tax non-remittance and a ruble of money growth financed a ruble of tax remittance**. The subsidy via tax non-remittance and the combined subsidy via tax non-remittance and financing additional tax remittance are the same. If one counts, as the practice of Western economies suggests, the entire money stock as implicit government debt, the debt created by both options is also the same.

To recapitulate, tax non-remittance forces bond financing of the resulting budget deficits. It forces government debt and leads to a default. The government is interested to delay this eventuality. It enforces tax remittance as much as it can under the payment jam. When this fails, the government monetizes tax remittance. **That is, the government pays enterprises to remit taxes they impounded**. In other words, the government subsidizes the amounts that would have become tax non-remittance but has thus become tax remittance. There is a ruble for ruble trade-off evidenced in the data in Figure 4.7, panel 2 and other figures. This secondary subsidy via monetization is forced onto the government by the first subsidy via tax non-remittance.

Step 6. Credit Transmission, Extension and Rollover

Banks transmit, extend and roll over credit to enterprises on the basis of the monetary base created by the Central Bank during monetization of tax remittance. Banks multiply monetization of tax remittance through re-intermediation between enterprises. Credit is issued for payments, not for investment. This proposition was covered and documented at length in the addendum to Chapter 4 of our book *From Predation to Prosperity*, 'Fixing China's Banks, not Russia's.'[1] When inflation is high and nominal interest rates are low, and hence

---

[1] http://www.russianeconomy.org/predation/pdf/ch4add.pdf.

real interest rates are highly negative, credit rollover and extension represent a pure subsidy.

Step 7. Aggregate Third-party Billing Pays

Various trade-offs between tax non-remittance and monetization of tax remittance, followed by credit rollover and extension, wind up in the self-enforceable subsidy. Tax non-remittance and monetization multiplied through the banking system sum up to the outstanding balance of receivables. Figure 4.4 demonstrated a close match in 1992–98 between enterprise subsidy claims through surcharged invoices, embodied in the balances of receivables, and the subsidy they force from the government through tax non-remittance and monetization.

Continuous short-term trade-offs between tax non-remittance and the money balances in the game of chicken between the government and enterprises (see again Figure 4.7, panel 2) make the subsidy self-enforceable. Fiscal expectations to which enterprises index invoices in pursuit of the subsidy become self-fulfilling. At the same time, long-term complementarity between tax non-remittance and the monetary aggregate as subsidy components makes the subsidy self-reinforcing over time until the policy reversal downgrades it.

This self-enforceable subsidy can be called the tax subsidy not only because it finances tax remittance and the fiscal costs of tax non-remittance. Also, when enterprises surcharge invoices they levy a tax over the stages of processing. The price surcharge in invoices which ends up in the balances of receivables is ultimately a tax on consumers and households. On top of that, it is the taxpayers who bear the cost of the subsidy through inflation and fiscal defaults. By forcing government subsidy, the enterprise network ultimately taxes the public at large.

Figures 4.8 and 4.9 break out of the 1992–98 time frame and extend the same relationship through the entire period of 1992–2004. Figure 4.8 uses the linear scale and Figure 4.9 the logarithmic scale. The linear scale enables us to show tax non-remittance and the monetary aggregate M2 as interacting components of the subsidy. However, due to high inflation in the early 1990s, the linear scale makes the data before 1994 invisible. The logarithmic scale demonstrates that the postulated relationship held since the beginning of 1992.

Tax non-remittance slowed down in 2000–01 and started to decline steadily in absolute terms since October 2001. The new policy initiated by the Central Bank which we mentioned earlier and will attend to shortly started to take effect. The subsidy has declined substantially in 2002–04. In the spirit of Figures 4.4, 4.8 and 4.9, one can estimate the claim on the subsidy as the ratio of the annual flows of receivables to GDP. This is not an actual subsidy which may be collected with a short lag but an annual claim on this subsidy. Table 4.2

Figure 4.8 The Self-enforceable Tax Subsidy: The Relationship between Enterprise Receivables, Tax Non-remittance, and Money, Russia, 1992–2005

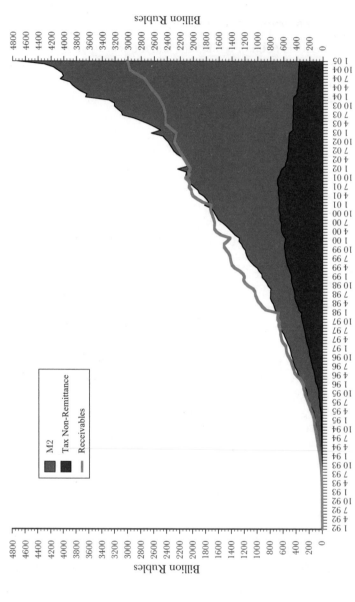

Notes:

1. All data are denominated in billion 1998 nominal rubles.

2. An increase in the deposit multiplier during 2000–2004, when tax non-remittance decreased and became negative and the subsidy to finance enterprise receivables decreased accordingly, makes the monetary aggregate M2 less suitable than M1 for approximating the quasi-fiscal component of the subsidy, which, together with tax non-remittance as a fiscal component, matches the outstanding balances of enterprise receivables. This change shows up in the excess of M2 over receivables in 2002–2004.

Source: Receivables and tax non-remittance: Rosstat; money: Central Bank of Russia.

Figure 4.9 The Self-enforceable Tax Subsidy: The Relationship between Enterprise Receivables, Tax Non-remittance, and Money (Logarithmic Scale), Russia, 1992–2005

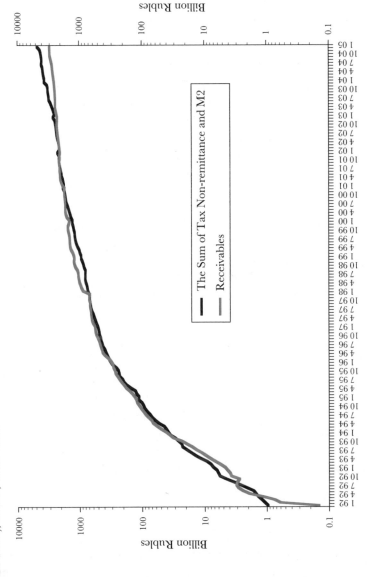

Note. All data are denominated in billion 1998 nominal rubles.
Sources: Receivables and tax non-remittance: Rosstat.
           Money: Central Bank of Russia.

estimates that the subsidy claim (and hence the subsequent subsidy) constituted 21.8 per cent of GDP in 1992, gradually declined to 13.1 per cent of GDP in 1996 and 5.3 per cent in 1997, and then increased to 19.8 per cent of GDP in 1998. Its gradual decline began from 5.5 per cent of GDP in 1999 to 2.1 per cent in 2002 and 2003. The claim increased to 2.8 per cent in 2004 but this upturn may represent a short-term fluctuation.

Step 8. The Circuit of Aggregate Third-party Billing

Step 8 is identical to step 1. Invoices outgrow payments and fall into the balances of aged receivables when enterprises surcharge invoices. They add a third-party surcharge to the price, subject to fiscal expectations and bill the government. Surcharged invoices carry a network tax on consumers and households. Now it is more evident why. The subsidy is self-enforceable under the payment jam created by aged receivables and payment arrears.

Fiscal expectations are self-fulfilling. The feedback from the subsidy to enterprise invoicing activity validates surcharged invoicing activity and stimulates more of it. It stimulates maximization of receivables subject to fiscal expectations. Arrows 7 and 8 in the flow chart in Figure 4.4 depict the feedbacks from the subsidy components, tax non-remittance and monetization, to surcharged invoices. Panels 1 and 3 of Figure 4.7 test empirical evidence for these feedbacks. Bivariate regressions can indicate causation running either and both ways. The flow of causation from receivables to tax non-remittance and monetization (multiplied by credit transmission) was discussed above. Now, this is a test of **fiscal expectations** stemming from the eventual subsidy to maximization of receivables.

A strong correlation between the balances of receivables and tax arrears in panel 1 was discussed earlier. Panel 3 regresses the monthly balances of receivables in 1992–mid-1999 against the monetary aggregate M2, the second major component of the subsidy. It shows a strong positive relationship between the balances of receivables and the money balances. This implies that a mechanical short-term effect, that monetization and credit would dissipate payment arrears and aged receivables, is totally overwhelmed by subsidy expectations. Panel 3 demonstrates a strong incentive for the subsidy-extracting strategy of the enterprise network. Panel 1 offers the same finding on the side of the tax non-remittance channel of the subsidy.

This discussion has come full circle. It is convenient to incorporate the fiscal circuit in the flow chart in Figure 4.4 into a general mechanism of Enterprise Network Socialism. This mechanism in Box 4 connects the fiscal circuit of aggregate third-party billing with its impact on real output (GDP) and with policy reversals in 1999–2004. The arrows numbered in blue, from 1 to 11,

Box 4 The Mechanism of Enterprise Network Socialism

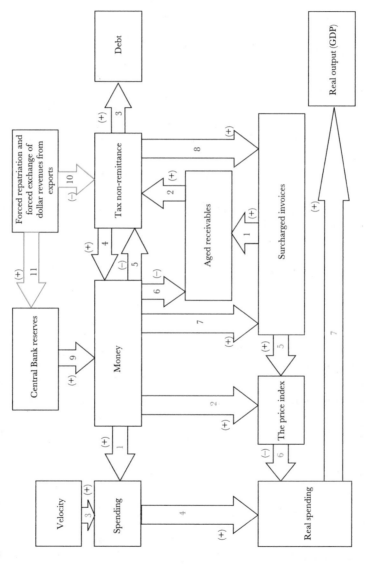

Note: The red arrows emphasize the relationship which became empirically dominant in 1999–2004.

represent the fiscal circuit augmented by the policy forces of 1999–2004. The arrows numbered from 1 to 8 encompass the self-contained and circular system of aggregate third-party billing. They retrace the eight steps summarized in Box 1. Arrows 9–11 add the policy reversal in 1999–2004, to which the discussion turns below. The arrows numbered in brown, from 1 to 7, incorporate a simplified transmission to real output. Plus and minus signs on the side of the arrows indicate positive and negative relationships between variables.

In the beginning, enterprises maximize receivables subject to the expected subsidy. They index invoices with price surcharges to fiscal expectations. Invoices outgrow payments and—arrow 1, the plus sign—their balances end up in aged receivables. This creates the payment jam and may render net cash flow negative and halt operations across the economy. Under the payment jam—arrow 2, the plus sign—enterprises endeavour non-remittance of taxes withheld from workers and collected from consumers. The government engages in the game of chicken to enforce tax remittance and—arrow 3, the plus sign—has to securitize tax non-remittance, issue bonds. To minimize and limit tax non-remittance and delay the default of on the ever-growing debt the government is forced to monetize additional tax remittance (arrow 4, the plus sign, from tax non-remittance to the money supply and arrow 5, the minus sign, from the money supply to tax non-remittance). Monetization multiplied and transmitted through the banking system to enterprises—arrow 6, the minus sign—dissipates payment arrears and aged receivables in the short run. In the long run, both monetization—arrow 7, the plus sign—and tax non-remittance—arrow 8, the plus sign—as the complementary embodiment of fulfilled fiscal expectations, stimulate surcharged invoices and maximization of receivables.

The entire system of aggregate third-party billing sketched in Box 4 is circular, self-enforceable, and self-reinforcing. It had met its match in the policy introduced by the Central Bank of Russia in September–December 1998.

The Reversal of Powers and the Fall of the Freedom to Charge

This is a story of an accident of history with systemic consequences. It is a story of how a peripheral policy of the Central Bank, control of capital outflows aimed at accumulation of foreign exchange reserves, hit the fiscal feedback loop at the core.

In late 1998, the Central Bank of Russia mandated repatriation and domestic sale of foreign exchange revenues. Its principal objective was to accumulate foreign exchange reserves. The Russian government needed them desperately. By a sheer extraneous coincidence, interest and principal payments on the external debt of the Russian government came due in September 1998 and thereafter. This debt was rescheduled several times over seven years and the day of reckoning had arrived. The moment could not have been worse. On 17 August 1998, Russia defaulted on its domestic, ruble-denominated bonds and devalued its currency. Less than a month later, a bankrupt and illiquid government had to purchase billions of dollars with devalued rubles. It could not, and there were several technical defaults on external debt service. The government appealed to the Central Bank as the lender of last resort **of foreign exchange**. The Central Bank extended the government a foreign exchange loan in the amount of USD 6.7 billion in exchange for a dollar-denominated Russian bond. This nearly depleted the foreign exchange reserves of the Central Bank and rendered its net international reserves (net of IMF loans) negative.[1] More payments on external debt were coming due and the Central Bank could expect more borrowing from the government.

Rapid, indeed swift, accumulation of foreign exchange reserves had become the top priority of the Central Bank. On 16 September 1998, it enacted a seemingly minor and innocuous, procedural regulatory adjustment[2] which might have changed the course of recent Russian history. There was a long-standing regulation, with the legal force of a bylaw, that Russian enterprises were obligated to sell 50 per cent of their export revenues in foreign exchange for rubles at the market exchange rate. This foreign exchange could be sold through the Russian banking system. On 16 September 1998, the Central Bank issued a legally binding instruction that this mandated sale of 50 per cent of foreign exchange revenues had to be conducted solely through the designated currency exchanges. These were the Moscow Inter-Bank Currency Exchange and seven regional exchanges. Sales through the banking system and inter-bank sales of foreign exchange revenues were halted completely.

What is the difference? To put it simply, from 16 September 1998, foreign exchange revenues of Russian enterprises had to be sold **inside** Russia. Foreign exchange had to be brought and wired to Russia to be sold. The new rule meant **mandated repatriation** of foreign exchange revenues, indeed

[1] For the balance sheet and discussion, see our 'How Big Are Russia's Foreign Exchange Reserves?' at http://www.russianeconomy.org/comments/091100.pdf.
[2] The legal and institutional part of the story is reconstructed by bits and pieces from various Central Bank instructions and explanations. All bylaws and regulations of the Central Bank of Russia are published in its official circular, *The Circular of the Bank of Russia* (*Vestnik Banka Rossii*). See issues no. 66 (321), September 16 1998; no. 69 (324), October 1, 1998; no. 85 (340), December 9, 1998; no. 86 (341), December 18, 1998; and no. 1 (345), January 12, 1999.

forced repatriation and forced exchange of export revenues. This was an imposition of capital controls on the outflow side of the capital account.

Before 16 September 1998, foreign exchange revenues of Russian enterprises could be sold outside of Russia through correspondent accounts of various Russian banks abroad. They could be sold to subsidiaries of exporters themselves. Exporters could repurchase dollars at the cost of a banking transaction fee and deposit dollars abroad. They sold for rubles, but rubles did not enter their bank accounts in Russia. The preexisting rule mandated 50 per cent sale of foreign exchange revenues, not 50 per cent repatriation and deposit of ruble-denominated proceeds in enterprise accounts with Russian banks. The preexisting rule could not address capital outflow. Most importantly, while foreign exchange revenues of Russian exporters, either sold to subsidiaries or repurchased, were deposited abroad, their money balances with Russian banks remained at low levels. Enterprises could amass billions of dollars abroad and continue tax non-remittance in Russia. The government could not enforce tax remittance and had to monetize it due to low money balances of enterprises and the payment jam.

What was the true rate of foreign exchange sales before 16 September 1998, when the mandated rate was 50 per cent of export revenues? It could have been zero except when exporting enterprises needed rubles to reduce payroll arrears and pay wages. The instruction of 16 September 1998, raised it from nearly zero to 25 or 30 per cent initially, when enforcement was incomplete, to close to 50 per cent when enforcement strengthened. The Central Bank actually enforced its rule strictly by matching foreign trade accounts with physical volume and world prices against resulting repatriation and sale of foreign exchange. From 16 September 1998, the new rule was in place. Dollars and other foreign exchange came to Russia, were sold for rubles, and rubles stayed in Russia. They entered enterprise bank accounts and suddenly raised enterprise money balances and enabled the government to enforce tax payments.

This was not an aim or an intention of the Central Bank. It did not intend to run fiscal policy, to become the fiscal authority in lieu of the Finance Ministry. All that the Central Bank wanted was to bring dollars to Russia so that it could purchase them for reserves accumulation. To that end, the Central Bank issued the second instruction on 1 October 1998. Foreign exchange revenues had to be sold first at special trade sessions of the Moscow Inter-Bank Currency Exchange. This gave the Central Bank the right of first refusal at those sales. At the same time, it tightened enforcement of mandated repatriation. Finally, on 31 December 1998, the Central Bank raised the rate of mandated repatriation of foreign exchange revenues to 75 per cent of receipts. Later on, this rate was reduced from 75 to 50 to 30 to 25 per cent as the terms of trade for Russian exports improved, especially with the rise of world oil prices.[1] Over the course of 1999–2004, the Central Bank fulfilled its objective and increased its foreign exchange reserves from almost zero to USD125 billion (and to about USD150 billion by September 2005). However, the unintended fiscal consequences and real economic effects on output went much beyond that. The Central Bank printed rubles when it purchased foreign exchange reserves, that is, it expanded the monetary base (see also Chapter 6). Three implications followed in turn:

(1) Enterprise money balances in bank accounts expanded. This reduced the balances of payables and receivables, thereby dissipating the payment jam. This process continued through the flow of funds across enterprises and industries, reversing the chain reaction of payment arrears and ageing of receivables.

(2) **Enterprise export earnings started to monetize tax remittances**. The government could enforce tax remittance. The balances of tax arrears slowed down in 1999–2001 and declined significantly since October 2001. Figure 4.8 and Table 4.3 document this trend in detail. This implies that the flow of tax non-remittance started to decline since 1999, that is, tax remittance increased, and since October 2001 enterprises started to pay off past tax arrears. Government fiscal accounts reversed from deficits to surpluses.

(3) The link between monetization and the tax subsidy was weakened. Expansion of the monetary base was, to a significant extent, no longer a subsidy. It did not stimulate maximization of receivables.

These effects reduced the actual tax subsidy and fiscal expectations. Accumulation of receivables slowed down, surcharged invoicing slowed down, inflationary expectations subsided. Real money balances started to recover and real output followed suit.

The top row and blue arrows 9 to 11 in Box 4, 'The Mechanism of Enterprise Network Socialism,' incorporate these effects into the prior framework. They show a new loop through which the reversal of policy shifted the outcomes. Figure 4.10 presents the data to explore the new developments and

---

[1] It follows that no level of and no increase in world oil prices would have mattered if effective repatriation of foreign exchange revenues was zero. At the same time, the effect of mandated repatriation of foreign exchange revenues was strong already in 1999 even though an increase in world oil prices was modest. This effect strengthened in 2001 and 2002—the balances of tax non-remittance started to decline, see Figure 4.8—even though world oil prices declined (see Figure 4.1). These considerations are consistent with the data in Figures 4.1 and 4.2 which led us to conclude on page 56 that the connection between world oil prices and Russian economic recovery in 1999–2004 is specious if one abstracts from the economic system and policy.

Figure 4.10 Panels 1–3. Tax non-remittance, Money Stock, and Receivables, in Billion Rubles, Monthly Data, Russia, 1992–2005

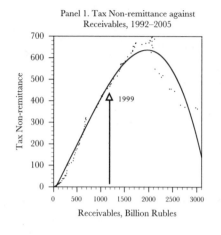

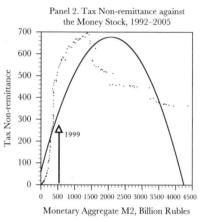

Panel 3. Receivables against the Money Stock, 1992–2005

Sources: Receivables and tax non-remittance: Rosstat.
Money: Central Bank of Russia.

reversed relationships. It extends bivariate regressions in Figure 4.7 from 1992–mid-1999 to the entire period 1992–2004. Panels 1 to 3 show that all principal bivariate relationships reversed from positive to negative some time after 1999. Their curves are non-monotonic concave and decreasing.

In panel 1, the balances of tax non-remittance and receivables were positively related before 1999 and some time thereafter, they slowed down together soon after 1999, and tax arrears started to decline thereafter (in October 2001, says Figure 4.8), their relationship with receivables turned negative. The relationship between tax non-remittance and monetization also turned from positive to negative some time after 1999 in panel 2 of Figure 4.10. The quadratic regression in panel 2 implies that monetization started to work to dissipate tax non-remittance. This suggests that forced repatriation of foreign exchange earnings indeed started to monetize tax remittance.

The relationship between the money balances and the balances of receivables in panel 3 of Figure 4.10 became ambiguous. Notice in panel 3 of Figure 4.10 as well as in Figure 4.8 that both the money balances (obviously) and the balances of receivables (not necessarily obviously) continued to grow in 1999–2004. However, the growth of receivables slowed down significantly relative to money growth. Monetization does not significantly stimulate amassment of receivables any more and may even discourage it in the future.

Judging from the data in Figures 4.6 and 4.10, a symbiotic relationship between the enterprise network and the government remains in place, but the positions of power have reversed. The Central Bank snatched fiscal power from the enterprise network. In effect, it started to run fiscal policy and delegated its execution, tax remittance, to the government. The latter started to reinforce its executive capacity to enforce tax remittance by additional crackdowns on the enterprise network, including partial and exemplary de-privatization and renationalization. The Central Bank also started to run an independent monetary policy—independent, that is, from the enterprise network. This was a major reversal of powers. The enterprise network continues to maximize the tax subsidy, subject to fiscal expectations, but its power to do so significantly diminished. It was no longer as free to charge the government and the public at large in 1999–2004 as it was in 1992–98.

Output Suppression and Recovery

Recall Figure 4.6 and call Figure 4.11 to the witness stand. They reveal what happens to the supply side in the world of aggregate third-party billing. Incentives are mixed. They combine maximization of real profit from production and maximization of redistributed income, specifically maximization of the tax subsidy from surcharged invoicing.

Given technological possibilities and existing capacity, production is bolstered by real profit, real spending, that is, mechanically, real money balances times their velocity of circulation. However, real money balances are not independent (exogenous) under Enterprise Network Socialism. Maximization of the tax subsidy operates through maximization of nominal receivables, subject to fiscal expectations. Figure 4.6 displays how growth of nominal receivables (the balances of invoices in excess of payments) aligns with price increases. Surcharged invoices automatically increase the price level. Fiscal expectations materialize as self-fulfilling inflationary expectations bypassing monetary

Figure 4.11 Indices of GDP (1991 = 100) and of the Ratio of M2 to Receivables (Year-End) (1991 = 100), Russia, 1991–2004

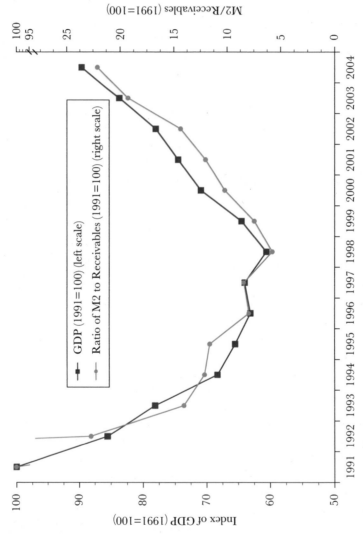

Note: The break in the right scale truncates the index of the ratio of M2 to receivables between 1991 and 1992, which truncates its sharp decline in 1992. Figure 4.12 presents the full scale.

Sources: GDP and enterprise receivables: Rosstat.
The monetary aggregate M2: Central Bank of Russia.
The data are reproduced in Table 4.1.

policy. They contract real money balances. The converse is also true. When fiscal expectations are lowered by aggressive government policy of subsidy cutting (i.e., suppressing enterprise freedom to charge, enforcing tax remittance), real money balances can grow.

One can view the index of the ratio of money balances M2 to receivables in Figure 4.11, as well as in Figure 4.12, as a proxy for the index of real money balances. This proxy curve of the index of money balances to receivables in Figure 4.11 shows the pendulum of real money balances on the downward path from 1991 through 1998 and on the upward path from 1998 through 2004. This pendulum corresponds to contraction of real money balances in 1992–98 when receivables outgrew nominal money balances and to recovery of real money balances in 1999–2004 when the course reversed and nominal money balances outgrew receivables.

The movement of this proxy curve of the index of real money balances in Figure 4.11 matches closely the index of real output (GDP) in 1992–2004 starting in 1991 as the benchmark 100 for both indices. Contraction of real money balances in 1992–98 matches the contraction path of real GDP during that period. Recovery of real money balances in 1999–2004 matches closely partial economic recovery since 1999. Minor annual fluctuations of real GDP upward and downward in 1996–98 also match annual movements of real money balances.

A uniform empirical relationship holds consistently for both contraction and recovery. When the outstanding balances of receivables outgrow nominal money balances, the economy contracts. When nominal money balances outgrow the balances of receivables, the economy recovers. **It is important, in our view, that this is a uniform and unified empirical regularity, with a unified mechanical and systemic explanation behind it.** Nothing is left to *ad hoc* reasoning. Notice, however, that nothing in the discussion above suggests that this relationship should hold for economic growth beyond recovery from a great contraction under aggregate third-party billing. Indeed, the above mechanics and systemic dissection are idiosyncratic and specific to the unique system of Enterprise Network Socialism.

Figure 4.11 and all prior discussion focused on the impact of subsidy maximization by surcharged invoicing on the real money balances. For simplicity, we abstracted from the independent impact of velocity of money circulation on overall spending in 1992–2004. There were already too many complicated variables to consider and to plot, and velocity (the inverse of the money demand) is one of the most difficult analytical issues which only specialists in that field can handle. But it is, in fact, real spending (money times its velocity), not just real money balances, that is approximated empirically in Figure 4.11.

Figure 4.12 Indices of GDP (1991 = 100) and of the Ratio of M2 to Receivables (Year-End) (1991 = 100), Russia, 1990–2004 (rescaled)

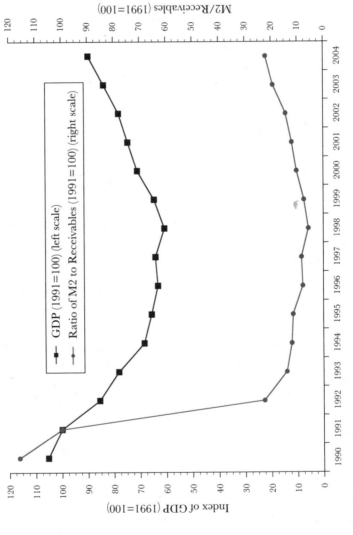

Sources: GDP and enterprise receivables: Rosstat.
The monetary aggregate M2: Central Bank of Russia.
The data are reproduced in Table 4.1.

In fact, another figure, Figure 4.12, separates real money balances and shows in full their collapse from 1991 to 1992 from which they never recovered throughout the period 1992–2004.

Only Figure 4.12 relays the meaning and the scope of the explosion of subsidy and inflationary expectations immediately after liberalization of January 1992 and shows how this brought down the real money balances in 1992 to about one-fifth of their level in 1991. Figure 4.12 plots the same data as Figure 4.11 plus it adds the year 1990 for reference. The difference is that Figure 4.12 uses the same full scale for both indices of real GDP and the ratio of money to receivables and does not truncate the scale for the latter index. Figure 4.11 truncated the index of the ratio of M2 to receivables between 1991 and 1992 and truncated the latter's scale accordingly. By doing so, Figure 4.11 in effect imitated a nearly fourfold increase in the velocity of money circulation in 1992 which did not let real GDP collapse by almost 80 per cent on par with the real money balances. Such a rapid increase in money velocity often accompanies episodes of high inflation when the real value of money balances depreciates and money holders reduce their money demand accordingly. Thus Figure 4.11 implicitly incorporates changes in velocity and compares the index of real GDP with a proxy for the index of real spending.

The left side of Box 4 summarizes the above discussed relationships between surcharged invoices, the price index, nominal money balances, the velocity, nominal spending, real spending, and, ultimately, real output. It incorporates this transmission mechanism with other mechanics of subsidy extraction under Enterprise Network Socialism.

The Ambivalence of Liberalization and Privatization

Russia's experience in 1992–2004 offers a quick reality check. It is the confluence of Figures 4.6 and 4.11. Figure 4.11 relates the pendulum of Russia's GDP in 1992–2004 to the index of the ratio of money balances to receivables. Figure 4.6 relates the index of receivables and the price index. Since the index of receivables merely embodies price surcharges in the balances of invoices in excess of payments, which makes the two indices match, the index of the ratio of money balances to receivables in Figure 4.11 acquires real-life meaning. It stands for the real money balances deflated by the price increases in excess invoicing, in pursuit of the subsidy. Fiscal expectations of the subsidy generate self-fulfilling inflationary expectations, namely surcharged invoices. They materialize in the outstanding balances of receivables in Figure 4.6, whence they are transplanted as the denominator in the index of the money balances to receivables in Figure 4.11.

Figure 4.11 relays how these inflationary expectations embodied in receivables interact with nominal spending (the money supply times the velocity of money circulation). They outgrow nominal spending and contract real money balances in 1992–98. When fiscal (and hence inflationary) expectations subside in 1999–2004 and the index of receivables decelerates, nominal spending outgrows receivables. Real money balances recovered in 1999–2004. When the real money balances contracted in 1992–98, real output (GDP) contracted in alignment. When the real money balances recovered in 1999–2004, real output (GDP) recovered in alignment, given the idle supply capacity after the great contraction and improved incentives. Less subsidy extraction, less socialism, more production.

Socialism from below, Enterprise Network Socialism, is just as ubiquitous and near-universal as socialism from above, central planning. Decontrolled transactions and privatized assets are not necessarily market prices and market assets. Freedom from government restriction is not necessarily freedom from income redistribution. Free socialism is still socialism, and free near-total socialism which redistributes the bulk of GDP is still near-total socialism. Socialism from below can be just as much socialism as from above. Freedom to charge is merely socialist devolution.

The Russian experience in 1992–2004 opens a new perspective on liberalization and privatization. Their peak in the 1990s coincided with the great contraction of GDP and their partial rollback in 1999–2004 coincided with partial economic recovery. The national assembly line inherited from central planning thwarted the expected positive effects of liberalization and privatization. This discussion suggests that liberalization and privatization are ambivalent. They can decrease efficiency as well as increase it. Government restriction is also ambivalent. It can increase or decrease efficiency. In Russia after September 1998, government restrictions reduced the freedom of enterprises to charge third parties and hence fostered production.

C. ECONOMIC POLICY ISSUES

5

SUSTAINING GROWTH IN A HYDROCARBON-BASED ECONOMY

Rudiger Ahrend[1]

Given its economic structure, Russia is bound to remain a heavily hydrocarbon-dependent economy for some time to come. This reality largely defines the two most important challenges facing Russian policy-makers as they seek to create a framework for sustained growth. These are managing a resource-based economy successfully and facilitating economic diversification over time. This chapter first looks at the policies and developments that have been underlying Russia's strong post-crisis growth performance, before setting out the policies that Russia—as a resource based economy—would have to follow in order to sustain high growth rates.

The Policies and Developments Underlying Growth

The most important economic policy choice underlying the expansion since 1998 was the adoption of a prudent fiscal stance—in sharp contrast to the pre-crisis period. From 2000 to 2004, federal budgets were drafted to aim for surpluses based on conservative oil price assumptions. This approach not only delivered sizeable surpluses but also a budget that was balanced over the oil price cycle. Simulations show that the federal budget would have remained in

[1] This chapter partly draws on material originally produced for the fifth OECD *Economic Survey* of the Russian Federation published in September 2004. The views expressed in this chapter are nonetheless those of the author and do not necessarily reflect those of the OECD or its member states. The author is indebted to Svetlana Arkina, Andrew Dean, Vladimir Drebentsov, Evsey Gurvich, Val Koromzay, Silvana Malle, Isabel Murray, Douglas Sutherland and William Tompson, as well as to many colleagues in the OECD Economics Department for helpful comments and discussions. Special thanks go to Corinne Chanteloup and Anne Legendre for technical assistance. Responsibility for any errors of fact or judgement that remain in the chapter rest, of course, entirely with the author.

rough balance even with oil prices unchanged at USD 19/bl (Urals) throughout the period. Indeed, there would have been only a relatively moderate deficit, not exceeding 2 per cent of GDP, if oil prices had fallen to very low levels (Kwon 2003, Ahrend 2004a). To be sure, fiscal responsibility was facilitated by growing revenues due to favourable terms of trade and strong growth. However, the government largely resisted the temptation to spend this windfall, instead using a significant part of it to repay debt and accumulate some reserves. Parts of these reserves were used to set up a stabilization fund.

Tight fiscal policy was also instrumental in sterilizing part of the foreign exchange inflows resulting from large external surpluses. These would otherwise have resulted in a sharper appreciation of the ruble or even faster monetary expansion. Fiscal sterilization was mainly achieved via budget surpluses. A limited share of fiscal sterilization was also realized by shifting hard-currency denominated sovereign debt into ruble-denominated debt, reflecting the financial markets' renewed interest in such instruments.[1]

Tax reform also played an important role in sustaining the recovery.[2] Greater simplicity increased the efficiency of taxation while decreasing distortions to economic activity. Many tax rates were significantly reduced, while tax bases were broadened. This diminished both incentives and opportunities for tax evasion. Moreover, the tax system was also oriented towards capturing a larger share of natural resource rents, especially windfall profits from high oil prices. This, together with a reduction in the profit tax rate and the introduction of a simplified unified social tax (UST; regrouping several social payments), was also a first step towards decreasing general tax pressure on the whole of the productive sector, while increasing taxation of the resource sector.

There were also very deep structural cuts on the expenditure side. General government expenditures (including all levels of government and social funds) in 1999–2005 were about 10 percentage points of GDP lower than before the crisis, while revenues relative to GDP remained at roughly their pre-crisis levels.[3] There was also a 'virtuous cycle' with respect to debt, as debt repayment from

---

[1] Internal government debt was roughly constant between 1999 and 2001 and increased by Rb144bn (ca. €4.8bn/USD 4.6bn) in 2002. In 2003, new issuance of domestic debt (OFZ-AD) increased significantly, to around Rb333bn (ca. €9.6bn/USD 10.8bn), but there was almost no net effect on outstanding internal debt, as the bulk of the OFZs issued in the rescheduling of the pre-crisis GKOs (OFZ-PD) fell due.

[2] For an overview of tax changes in 2000–01 see OECD (2002), for 2002–04 see OECD (2004), Box 1.4.

[3] This reduction in the spending-to-GDP ratio has coincided with massive reductions in wage and pension arrears, and has not resulted in any substantial deterioration in the provision of public services. This suggests that the creation of a federal treasury, the reform of fiscal federal relations and the government's overall spending restraint have contributed to more efficient expenditure management.

budget surpluses and ruble appreciation have led to sharp falls in the ratio of debt service to GDP. Federal interest expenditures fell from 3.4 per cent of GDP in 1999 to around 1 per cent in 2005. Lower levels of government expenditure also gave Russia room to reduce the tax burden, which has been an additional stimulus for private investment and consumption, and hence economic growth.

Prudent fiscal policy and the resulting budget surpluses played a key role in reviving private investment. Pre-crisis government borrowing had been massively crowding out private investment.[1] After the crisis, however, fiscal discipline led to very limited new issuance of government bonds. This helped reduce spreads on Russian external debt and lower internal real interest rates, which was reflected in increasing private investment.[2]

Declining sovereign foreign debt levels, together with the improved perceptions of the Russian economy, helped large Russian companies to borrow increasingly from foreign banks and international markets. While increased corporate borrowing in foreign currencies carries some systemic risks and also complicated monetary policy, the positive effect of this was that Russian banks were being forced to begin lending to a wider range of corporate clients than before, as well as to consumers.

Macroeconomic stabilization also reduced economic uncertainty. This reduction in perceived risk was evident, for example, in the decline in the risk premia both on Russian sovereign and corporate foreign-currency debt, which was better than the average decline seen in emerging markets overall. This, together with the (at least until mid-2003) widespread impression that property rights had become more secure, contributed to a stock-market boom which saw the major stock index increasing by around 50 per cent per year during 2001–03.

Although a number of developments in late 2003 and 2004 raised new concerns with respect to property rights, the perception that property rights had become sufficiently secure was one of the factors contributing to the recovery of investment in 2000 and especially 2001, particularly in the oil sector.[3] Oil-sector investment jumped from roughly 25 per cent of industrial investment before the crisis to around 35 per cent from 2000 onwards. Strikingly, the growth of oil-sector investment was led by companies controlled by the state or by oil industry insiders: by 2000, their investment was already 70 per cent above 1998 levels.

---

[1] From 1990 to 1998 real investment fell continuously. After 1995, this was to a great extent because large government deficits and correspondingly large borrowing requirements pushed real yields on government paper into double and even triple digits (see, e.g., Ahrend 1999).

[2] While interest rates for private borrowing mattered little immediately after the crisis (non-related-party lending was almost non-existent), this has markedly changed in recent years.

[3] Clearly, high oil prices were another major factor.

Table 5.1 Oil Sector Investment (as a percentage of 1998 figures)

	Upstream capital spending					
	1999	2000	2001	2002	2003	2004
Total	65	148	215	167	194	206
Financial group owned	48	117	188	160	185	171
of which 3 largest	35	122	225	202	260	226
Oil industry insider owned	80	169	229	174	198	244
State controlled	73	173	244	169	206	204

Source: Ministry of Energy, InfoTEK, Rennaissance Capital estimates, RIATEC, author's calculations.

Figure 5.1 Russian Oil Companies: Relative Performance
Growth 2001–2004 inclusive

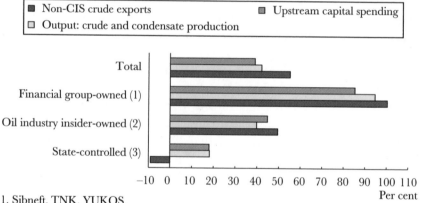

1. Sibneft, TNK, YUKOS.
2. LUKOIL, Surgutneftegaz.
3. Bashneft, Rosneft, Tatneft.

Source: Ministry of Energy, InfoTEK, Rennaissance Capital estimates, RIATEC, author's calculations.

By contrast, oil companies owned by major financial groups (whose owners' property rights were perceived as less secure) were investing only marginally more than in 1998 (Table 5.1, Figure 5.1).[1] In 2001, however, as perceptions of the security of property rights further improved, the latter group of companies began rapidly increasing investment, soon reaching levels comparable with the former group. This investment led to a sharp increase in oil production and exports in the following years. Output growth, however, was uneven. From 2000 to 2004 both insider-controlled and financial group-controlled companies

[1] See also Ahrend (2004a), Annex, Tables A3–5.

increased output, by roughly 40 per cent and 65 per cent respectively, with the output of the three largest oil companies owned by financial groups up by 95 per cent. State-controlled companies increased output only marginally. The picture with respect to exports is even more extreme. While there was a decline in the exports of state-controlled companies, exports were up by 50 per cent in the insider-controlled companies and 85 per cent in the financial group-controlled companies (around 100 per cent in the three largest).

Since 2000, the importance of the private oil companies' performance for the economy as a whole has been enormous. Industry accounted for slightly below half of GDP growth in 2000–04 and the oil sector for somewhat below half of industrial growth.[1] Since the state-owned companies barely grew, this means that Russia's private oil companies directly accounted for somewhere between one fifth and one quarter of GDP growth.[2] Taking into account the knock-on effects from oil-sector procurement and wages on domestic demand, the actual contribution of the private oil companies to economic growth was probably greater still. Moreover, the private oil companies played a crucial role in keeping Russia's external balance in surplus, and thus in allowing the consumption boom to unfold. It is unlikely that Russia would have been able to grow at anything like the rates it has experienced in 2002–04 had the private oil companies not raised investment, output and exports very rapidly. Moreover, the examples of the state-controlled oil companies and of other important state-controlled companies[3] would appear to suggest that Russia's leading private oil companies would not have achieved the growth performance of the last few years if they had remained under state control.

Russia's export structure is still dominated by commodities and basic manufactures, which account for over three-quarters of exports. More than half of exports are hydrocarbons, with the oil sector alone accounting for 40 per cent. Russia, as a large commodity exporter, benefited from healthy terms of trade from 2000 to 2005. The current account surplus, however, was not driven by high oil and commodity prices alone. Export volumes increased by roughly 50 per cent during 2000–05 (Figure 5.2). This increase was overwhelmingly driven by the oil sector, which increased export volumes by more than 80 per cent. The other major export sectors (ferrous and non-ferrous metals) contributed little to overall export growth, as their export volumes increased by

---

[1] Using adjusted sectoral weights. Contributions to industrial growth are calculated on the assumption that the share of value added in production has been roughly constant in the short term.

[2] See Ahrend (2004a). This corresponds closely to the conclusions reached by Gurvich (2004) who—using a different methodology—estimates that for the 2000–03 period, the oil sector as a whole directly accounted for 24.8 per cent of GDP growth.

[3] See Ahrend (2004b), Ahrend and Tompson (2005) and Tompson (2004).

Figure 5.2 Export Performance of Main Sectors

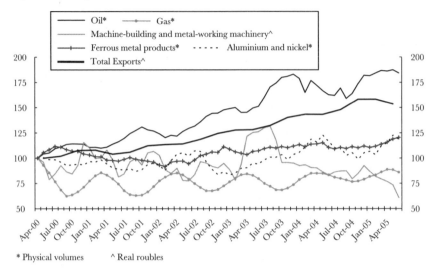

* Physical volumes　　　^ Real roubles

Source: Rosstat, author's calculations and estimates.

only around 20 per cent during the period,[1] the export volumes of the gas sector decreased somewhat, and machine building exports fell significantly.[2]

Given that import volumes increased by an average of almost 20 per cent per year between 2000 and 2004, both strong oil prices and sharply increasing oil export volumes have been vital in keeping the current account in surplus. Exports in 2000 were almost double the value of imports, which has allowed import growth to outstrip export growth for several years without pushing the current account into deficit. While import levels in 2005 were still significantly below those of exports, differences in growth rates between exports, which grew at an average annual rate just below 9 per cent during 2000–05, and imports will have to converge in coming years if Russia wants to keep a sustainable external balance.

While the current account surplus has been consistently large, the net outflow of private sector capital decreased steadily between 2001 and mid-2003 as the situation in Russia was perceived to normalize.[3] Since 2002, this trend

[1] According to official statements, the armaments sector increased export volumes, but there are no official published statistics. In any case it is unlikely that these increases would have influenced total export performance substantially as the share of arms in exports is relatively small, probably somewhere around 5 per cent.

[2] Gas export volumes to non-CIS countries, which are widely reported, actually increased over the period. Total gas export volumes (including to CIS countries) fell, however.

[3] Net private outflows, however, increased again as the so-called 'Yukos affair' unfolded.

was increasingly driven by corporate borrowing abroad. At the same time, unrecorded capital outflows continued unabated, doubtless reflecting what is often referred to as 'capital flight' or 'asset diversification', but also to some degree financing un- or under-reported imports.

Monetary policy in 2001–05 was dominated by the pursuit of conflicting policy goals, and was *de facto* very loose. The Central Bank of Russia (CBR) followed a policy aimed at gradually reducing inflation while limiting the real appreciation of the ruble in order not to endanger the competitiveness of Russian industry, with some degree of priority given to the latter goal (Vdovichenko 2004). Given the large current account surpluses and decreasing net capital outflows, this determination to prevent the ruble from appreciating too rapidly increasingly compelled the CBR to intervene on the foreign exchange market. Until 2002, the CBR's task was made easier by significant net private capital outflows, and fiscal sterilization was also able to absorb a large amount of the current account pressure, reducing the need for CBR intervention. Fiscal sterilization, however, declined in 2003, and would probably have become overburdened anyway, as net private capital outflows decreased sharply in early 2003. The policy of restraining the nominal and real appreciation of the ruble was therefore increasingly pursued via large-scale foreign currency purchases by the CBR. As a result, CBR reserves have reached levels that, if expressed as a share of GDP or exports, are very high by international standards. However, in the absence of efficient large-scale sterilization tools[1] the accumulation of reserves led to very strong monetary expansion. This loose monetary stance also meant that rates for ruble lending to enterprises and individuals were very low starting mid-2000, and real interest rates on deposits or government bonds were actually negative. In spite of a loose monetary stance, the CBR, aided by rapid growth in money demand, was nonetheless able to keep inflation on a downward path.

Consolidation in the industrial sector continued at a rapid pace in the aftermath of the crisis. The industrial structure that emerged was dominated by a relatively small number of large industrial groups, most of which were founded around some commodity exporting business, and which have in recent years mainly pursued strategies of vertical integration. The privately held industrial groups—usually tightly controlled by a small number of core shareholders—have generally restructured the businesses they owned or acquired in recent years and most of them are fairly well managed. The productivity of many private industrial groups' enterprises has been increasing briskly.[2] Since 2004,

---

[1] Large-scale, longer-term monetary sterilization was impossible until 2004, as the CBR could not issue its own debt.

[2] See also Boone and Rodionov (2002).

Figure 5.3 Income, Consumption and Imports

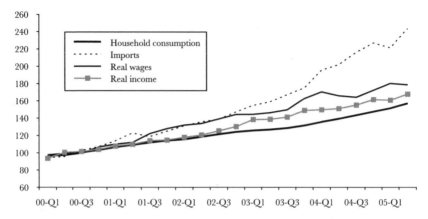

Source: Rosstat, author's calculations.

however, there has been a tendency for increasing state involvement and ownership in key economic sectors, which is likely to lead to decreasing economic efficiency.

The Challenge of Sustaining Growth: Managing a Resource-based Economy

Imports in recent years have tended to increase at least in line with disposable incomes (see Figure 5.3). Since one of the main aims and consequences of economic growth is to raise living standards, high growth rates will almost certainly imply a continuation of strongly increasing import demand. Russian industry is still unable to compete with imports of many sought-after consumer goods. Moreover, the continued real appreciation of the ruble will further increase demand for imported goods, for both consumption and investment.[1] This rise in imports may be somewhat dampened by further import substitution.[2] Nonetheless, it would be very surprising if imports did not continue to grow strongly.

To sustain such a situation, Russia must continue to increase exports. While the large current account surplus of recent years could be taken to mean that Russia has ample space for increasing imports without a corresponding increase in exports, this is not a sustainable situation. If oil prices went back to long-term historical averages the current account surplus would evaporate

[1] Short-term real appreciation will be driven by the current account surplus, medium-to-long term appreciation by the Balassa–Samuelson effect.
[2] Production increases in import-competing sectors would also contribute to a welcome diversification of the economy.

Figure 5.4 Structure of Exports (2003)

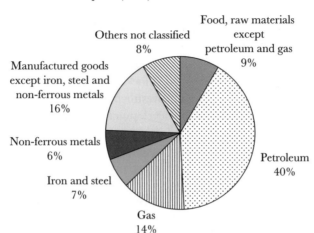

Source: United Nations, *Commodity Trade Statistics Database* (*COMTRADE* SITC Rev 3).

instantly. Even if oil prices stay at historically high levels, very strong import growth means that the current account surplus is bound to decline very rapidly in the absence of strong growth in export volumes. Given continued capital flight, Russia would become structurally dependent on importing foreign capital even when oil prices were relatively high. Given the country's vulnerability to terms-of-trade shocks, this would be a highly dangerous situation, especially in the absence of strong, stable FDI inflows. In short, if Russia wants to sustain high growth, it will have to be able to sustain rapid export growth.

While the Russian authorities would understandably—and rightly—prefer a more diversified export structure, Russia's revealed comparative advantage (RCA) in recent years has been in natural resources, especially hydrocarbons, and energy-intensive basic manufactures (steel, aluminium, nickel, fertilizer), plus some other commodities.[1] Moreover, the RCA in oil has been growing strongly in recent years (Ahrend 2004b), as the oil sector has increased exports much faster than any other important sector (Figure 5.2). In any case, more than 50 per cent of Russian exports consist of oil, oil products and gas (Figure 5.4). Even if Russia managed sharply to increase exports of more sophisticated manufactures,[2] their contribution to total export growth would remain modest for some years to come, given their small share in current exports. Basic manufacturing in energy-intensive sectors may also be able to make some contribution to future export growth, although part of their

[1] Russia also seems to have a comparative advantage in arms production.
[2] There is little scope to compete in labour-intensive basic manufactures with countries like China, which have much lower wage levels than Russia and almost unlimited surplus labour.

competitive advantage will be eroded by necessary increases in domestic energy prices and by exchange-rate appreciation. In any case, recent experience suggests that potential export growth in these sectors may be constrained by the threat of protectionist measures on the part of Russia's trade partners.[1]

Robust export growth in the short-to-medium term will probably not be possible without further increases in mineral, and especially hydrocarbon, exports. This, in turn, will necessitate investment in the pipeline infrastructure, as well as at some point in time the development of new fields. Therefore, if Russia is to maintain reasonable oil-sector growth beyond the end of the decade, it will be vital to ensure that fiscal and regulatory policies encourage the development of new oil fields to replace production from those currently in decline. While Russian oil companies appear to consider current fiscal terms attractive enough to invest in short-term projects, enhancing production from existing fields, it is not clear that this regime will be equally attractive when it comes to making large, up-front investments in the development of new fields. Any changes in oil-sector taxation should be sensitive to this problem, and there is an urgent need to streamline government decision-making with respect to new field development and to reduce the existing, very considerable bureaucratic barriers that currently impede such activity. In this connection, it will also be important to ensure that property rights are clearly assigned and secure, lest asset-control contests damage the sector's ability to finance new investment. Moreover, it should be borne in mind that, as recent strong performance of the oil sector has been overwhelmingly driven by private companies, any important further shift away from the existing model of the oil sector towards more state ownership and control will in all likelihood significantly further dampen the growth potential of the sector.

In the longer term, oil exports probably cannot remain the chief driver of export growth. Russian oil reserves are comparatively limited.[2] The obvious candidate to take the lead as oil export growth slows would be gas. Russia has the world's largest proven gas reserves. While many of them are in areas that are difficult to develop, Russia's gas monopolist OAO Gazprom, as well as its smaller gas producers, has exhibited real technical excellence in extracting them. Gas has the added advantages that world demand for it will probably continue to increase and Russia's gas reserves mean that it probably faces no threat of a price war if it increases exports. Unfortunately the gas sector in its

[1] According to the Ministry of Economic Development and Trade, Russian exporters in early 2004 faced 93 different restrictions on access to foreign markets, including 57 anti-dumping measures of various kinds. Roughly 60 per cent of these applied to steel exports, with a further 25 per cent affecting the chemicals sector.

[2] At least those for which development is commercially viable at current technology levels.

current highly monopolized and heavily regulated configuration is unlikely to deliver sustained output and export growth. This underlines the importance of gas-sector reform from a macroeconomic point of view. The oil sector has shown that with the correct incentive structures—including multiple privately owned production companies and fair access to export infrastructure— production increases on a totally unexpected scale have been possible. In all likelihood the same would hold for a reformed gas sector.

The service sector could be another driver of long-term growth. With Russia becoming a richer country, demand for services will increase. As the service sector is still largely underdeveloped (once the statistical effect of transfer pricing in export sectors is stripped out), there is ample scope for catch-up growth in services.[1] The service sector, however, will not develop very strongly in the absence of a general increase in living standards: in other words, services growth may well outpace overall GDP growth but it must be accompanied by increases in goods production and exports.

A strategy of further developing resource-sector exports is not without risks, but these should remain manageable. Moreover, this is the course Russia has been following for several years now and it is difficult to see how it could change in the short to medium term without causing major disruptions. Even if policies favouring economic diversification are highly successful, Russia's performance will continue to depend on its resource sectors for quite some time to come. In a resource-exporting economy there are, however, three important types of potential risk that policy-makers need to address: external vulnerability, Dutch disease and institutional pathologies that appear to be associated with resource-driven development.

Given its industrial and export structure, the crucial importance of good fiscal and monetary policy for the Russian economy can hardly be overstated. It will also be important to continue developing institutions that enhance the sustainability and political feasibility of responsible macroeconomic policies. On the fiscal side, given that revenues are extremely sensitive to oil prices, this translates into a need for prudent fiscal policy based on conservative oil price assumptions and a large Stabilization Fund. If Russia continues to adhere to the fiscal conservatism of recent years, the negative impact of a sharp fall in oil prices would be substantially mitigated. If not, effects would be magnified, as the government would have to run extremely restrictive (pro-cyclical) fiscal policies during periods of low oil prices, because external borrowing in such circumstances would probably be prohibitively expensive, if available at all on the necessary scale.

---

[1] Part of the increasing weight of services in GDP will also come from a shift in relative prices. Domestic prices for non-tradables will be increasing faster than for tradables with the Russian currency appreciating.

The Stabilization Fund established in 2004 could continue to play a crucial role in using fiscal policy as a stabilization tool over the oil price cycle. If the fund is indeed to serve its purpose, it must be ensured that it remains large enough to insure the budget against several years of below-average oil prices. This cannot be taken as a given due to the fact that only the first 500 billion rubles have strong legal protection against being spent for non-stabilization purposes. Once the Stabilization Fund reaches a level at which the budget is adequately insured against oil-price drops, it is advisable to use additional surplus revenues in the first instance for early debt repayment. Though there may be some discussion as to whether the size of the Stabilization Fund was already above its optimal level, Russia pursued early debt repayments very actively in 2005. Especially in a situation where there may be some fear that accumulated money may eventually be spent in a pro-cyclical fashion, this appears a reasonable approach from a political-economy perspective. Moreover, early debt payments have the advantage that they allow for sustainable higher government non-interest spending or lower taxation levels in subsequent years. The authorities might also wish to consider accumulating additional oil windfalls in the fully funded pillar of the state pension system. This would be a macro-economically responsible way of distributing the windfall to the population,[1] and would help in particular to enhance the pensions of those citizens who, owing to age or income, will otherwise have little or no direct involvement in the fully funded scheme. The authorities should resist the temptation to use windfall revenues accruing after the fund has grown to the required level to finance tax cuts or higher current spending that in all likelihood would turn out to be unsustainable and strongly pro-cyclical (and would thus counteract the purpose of stabilization), since oil prices are likely to be relatively high when the fund achieves whatever planned level is set for it.

Keeping external debt low can also help to reduce external vulnerability, both by decreasing the risk of currency crises and by limiting the economic fall-out from such crises if they occur. This applies to both sovereign and private external debt, so it will be important to prevent the private sector's external borrowing from reaching dangerous proportions. Recent empirical work undertaken at the IMF suggests that external debt above a certain level has a negative impact on growth. This research suggests that the optimal external debt level for Russia is probably somewhere below 40 per cent of GDP.[2] The reduction in

[1] Assuming obviously that this money gets invested in non-ruble assets, as otherwise this would not serve the purpose of stabilization.

[2] Empirical work by Patillo et al. (2002) argues that, for developing and emerging countries, the average impact of external debt on growth becomes negative at about 35–40 per cent of GDP or about 160–170 per cent of exports. The marginal impact of debt would start being negative at about half of these values. This would suggest that, for Russia, optimal external debt levels would be somewhere in the range of 15–40 per cent of GDP.

external sovereign debt in recent years is thus a welcome development, as is the shift from external to internal sovereign debt issues, although this has so far been on a small scale. Ideally, sovereign debt should be predominantly in domestic currency, or at least oil-price indexed, so that debt service would fall when oil prices were low. Hitherto, commodity-price-indexed bonds have principally been employed by companies or in the context of sovereign debt restructurings, but there is no obvious reason why they could not be used more widely for sovereign issues.[1] Such paper could be attractive to individuals, companies or countries needing a hedge against an oil price rise.

On the monetary side, given the large share of exports that are subject to large price fluctuations (a share that may further increase in the short-to-medium term), exchange-rate flexibility is needed to accommodate terms-of-trade shocks, especially negative ones. Exchange-rate corrections following terms-of-trade shocks are especially painful if the exchange rate has become fundamentally overvalued beforehand. In this respect, there may be some scope for efforts to avoid excessive exchange-rate appreciation, especially when oil prices are high and there are major short-term capital inflows. However, the pursuit of such exchange-rate goals with the monetary policy tools currently available (mainly unsterilized exchange-rate intervention) incurs significant costs in terms of inflation. While it may be both desirable and necessary to accept relatively gradual disinflation in order to support growth and manage the exchange rate, it is important to ensure that inflation does remain on a downward path, to avoid a shift of expectations from declining to increasing inflation. Such a shift would make fighting inflation much harder and costlier in the future. Continued disinflation should thus be a priority even if it meant a somewhat stronger nominal appreciation of the ruble.

It should be possible to make the inflation/ruble appreciation trade-off somewhat less acute by giving the CBR an especially large capacity for monetary sterilization.[2] First and foremost this means that Russia should have a large market in ruble-denominated government debt. In this respect it is also useful that since 2004 the CBR can issue securities.[3] More generally, dollarization (or euro-ization) of the economy as such should be avoided or reduced, with prices and contracts being in local currency as far as possible. Such a structural shift would further reduce the economy's vulnerability to exchange-rate fluctuations. This shift will not happen overnight. It will require further bolstering the

[1] See UNCTAD (1998:41–5).

[2] In recent years sterilization may have been difficult because of limited demand for ruble debt instruments. This is no longer the case, as witnessed by the fact that interest rates on ruble instruments are very low and often negative in real terms.

[3] The primary legislation needed to do this has been in force for some time, but the secondary legislation has been slow to emerge.

confidence of business and the public in the ruble, above all by maintaining sound fiscal policies and achieving stable low inflation.

Further increasing the importance of the mineral sector in the economy also increases the risk of 'Dutch disease'. This term usually refers to a situation in which a country suddenly discovers large natural resources, the extraction of which increases the equilibrium exchange rate and thereby puts pressure on the competitiveness of the other tradable sectors in the economy.[1] In the Russian context, the discovery of natural resources as such is not the source of the problem. Rather, it is the fact that their full weight in the economy made itself felt only at the start of the transition, when the relative prices of primary raw materials, which had been held at artificially low levels under central planning, soared, as did resource exports. This exposed large differences in productivity between sectors in Russia. Whereas the export-oriented energy sector is highly competitive and profitable, and would be so even at a stronger exchange rate, many enterprises, especially in the manufacturing sector, are already barely competitive at current wage and exchange-rate levels. The fact that some manufacturing enterprises are located in places with unfavourable climatic conditions, which increases operating costs, does not help (Mikhailova 2003).

The strength of the resource sector allows—indeed, compels—Russia to have a relatively strong exchange rate, while high wages in the resource sector put upward pressure on wages in the rest of the economy. This is not all bad news. It increases living standards and boosts production in the non-tradable sector. However, it makes life much harder for other tradable sectors. Given the structure of the Russian economy, this is unavoidable. The non-resource tradable sector must therefore increase productivity and restrain unit labour costs sufficiently to stay competitive in order either to export or at least to withstand import competition. In this context, positive developments with respect to productivity in most sectors, and to some degree also unit labour costs, are encouraging (Ahrend 2004b). This improvement must be sustained if Russia wants to maintain high growth rates and achieve a more diversified industrial structure in the longer term. Ironically, Russia's otherwise problematic industrial inheritance has so far made it easier for processing industries to cope with the effects of rising wage levels and an appreciating real exchange rate: the inefficiency of former Soviet industrial enterprises meant that there was often a great deal of scope for relatively easy productivity gains—not least by means of 'passive' restructuring (i.e., labour-shedding). However, there are limits to how far such passive restructuring can go. Further *active* industrial

---

[1] The name 'Dutch disease' is in fact rather unfortunate, as the Netherlands actually handled such a situation comparatively well.

restructuring, including private investment to modernize production capacities, is thus the *sine qua non* for continuing strong growth.

Dutch disease may also, however, affect equilibrium employment levels. To the extent that the strength of the resource sector (which provides relatively little employment) necessitates relatively high levels of labour productivity in other industrial sectors, it also risks contributing to reductions in industrial employment. Decreasing industrial employment would not necessarily be a problem in itself if employment in the service sector could compensate for lost industrial jobs. The problem, however, is that a lot of the potential employment opportunities in the service sector are of rather low productivity, which would imply comparatively low wages. To the degree that large wage inequality may be socially and politically unacceptable, these potential employment opportunities in services may not arise.

There are, however, policy measures that can help limit the potential negative impact of the natural resource sector on the economy and ease the adjustment process for the tradable non-resource sector, while trying to avoid a low employment trap. While real exchange-rate appreciation in itself is not only desirable, but also unavoidable over the long term, attempts should be made to avoid sharp movements in relatively short time-spans. This is yet another reason for a fiscal policy that is to some degree countercyclical to the oil price, a substantial Stabilization Fund and a wider range of monetary sterilization mechanisms.

The tax system is also an important lever that can be used simultaneously to avoid 'Dutch disease' and assist the development of the non-resource sector. The guiding principle in both cases is to make extensive use of taxes that specifically target the resource sectors, which in turn allows low general tax rates. As such a tax system could also substantially contribute to further the diversification of the economy, we discuss it in detail in the following section on diversification.

Many of the potential macroeconomic problems arising from resource dependence can be resolved or at least substantially mitigated by the right macroeconomic policies and related structural reforms. The potential political economy implications may therefore be the toughest challenge. The literature suggests a number of reasons why resource orientation may complicate economic development. First, it has been shown that a larger share of natural resources in exports is related to more corruption (da Cunha Leite and Weidmann 1999), which is associated with slower long-term growth (Mauro 1995). Second, a higher natural resource share in the economy is often accompanied by greater inequality of incomes, which has also been shown to undermine long-term growth performance. Third, it has been argued that the allocation of talent in natural resource economies is biased in favour of the resource sector. Highly capable individuals may focus on securing resource rents rather than building successful businesses in sectors with more potential for innovation.[1] Fourth, resource wealth may favour the development of political and economic institutions which likewise favour rent-seeking over entrepreneurship, thereby reinforcing the structure of incentives faced by individuals.[2]

To the extent that inequality in Russian society is mainly driven by the fact that those active in natural resource sectors (owners, managers and workers alike) get their share of the resource rent, and hence are usually doing far better than those in similar positions in other sectors, the solution is to tax away a larger part of the resource rents in a relatively corruption-proof way and to reduce general tax levels for the economy as a whole. This is essentially what the Russian authorities are committed to doing. Some increase in targeted social transfers would also play a role. A large reduction in resource rents going to individuals instead of the state would also help solve the problem of potential misallocation of talent to resource sectors. The main obstacle to achieving this is that it requires a fairly efficient and non-corrupt administration. Hence the second and third concerns, regarding income inequality and the allocation of talent, basically reinforce the importance of the first, namely low levels of corruption.

There are various measures that can be taken to limit corruption. The first step is to create more corruption-resistant structures. Rules, if necessary at all, should be simple, transparent and standardized, with few exceptions and as little reliance as possible on bureaucratic discretion. Many recent legislative changes seem to be at least partly motivated by this kind of reasoning, including changes to fiscal federal relations and measures to curb bureaucratic interference in commercial activity by, for example, curtailing officials' inspection powers, simplifying business registration and reducing the range of activities subject to licensing requirements. In this context, recent proposals to vary effective tax rates in the oil sector on the basis of the quality of deposits exploited should be viewed with caution. Such an approach would in theory be more efficient, as it would not only favour the exploration of less profitable fields but would also prolong the life of declining fields beyond what would be commercially viable under the current tax system. However, it will be critical to ensure that any such system of taxation relies on a small number of variables that are easily collected and monitored and that it is implemented in a manner which does

---

[1] See Acemoglu and Verdier (1998) for a related point.

[2] Countries that are highly dependent on natural resource exports are also more likely to experience large-scale rebellions and civil wars. This point, however, seems not particularly relevant for Russia.

not give much discretion to bureaucrats. In Alberta, for example, the royalty system takes into account three basic variables—the age of the field, the depth of the oil and the flow rate—all of which are easy to monitor. Though the adoption of such a relatively simple system may be advisable in the medium term, given widespread corruption and transfer pricing in the sector, it probably makes more sense at present to tax natural resources mainly through excise and similar taxes, as well as export taxes.

While drafting corruption resilient legislation is important, it will not be sufficient on its own to reduce corruption levels as long as corruption goes largely unpunished because of a lack of monitoring. Cross-country research shows that both the efficiency of the rule of law and the development of civil society are strongly and negatively correlated with corruption levels (Brunetti and Weder 1999). The evidence also suggests that a lack of press freedom causes corruption (Ahrend 2002). It would thus be in Russia's economic interest not only to strengthen the judicial system, but also to foster the development of civil society and press freedom. Strengthening the rule of law and increasing the accountability of officialdom are particularly important in creating an institutional environment more conducive to entrepreneurship and wealth creation rather than rent-seeking.[1]

The Challenge of Sustaining Growth: Achieving Successful Diversification

Developing a successful modern economy based on natural resource exports is—in principle—feasible, given the right institutions and policies, as the examples of OECD countries such as Canada, Australia or the Scandinavian countries demonstrate. As stated above, there are, however, dangers, such as external vulnerability, associated with being highly dependent on a limited number of resource-based sectors. Therefore, a more diversified economic structure is something that in principle is desirable. Moreover, for a significant part of the Russian political elite—given the global ambitions they see for the Russian state—a resource-based development path is politically unacceptable. Hence Russia should—and will—pursue policies to foster diversification in coming years. It will, however, be important not to lose sight of what diversification policies can and cannot achieve. First, it must be clear that there is no miracle recipe to achieve diversification overnight. Fostering diversification will be a long drawn out process, and should hence be seen as a long-term

---

[1] Interestingly, all resource-based economies that have developed successfully had strong civil societies, relatively well-functioning and independent judicial systems, high levels of press freedom and relatively low levels of corruption, whereas resource economies that failed to achieve adequate economic progress usually lacked most of these features.

goal. Second, there is no shortage of examples of failed diversification policies, and economists know fairly well on the basis of international experience what does not work. Fiscal irresponsibility as well as large-scale state investment in pet industrial projects and sectors ('picking winners') rank at the top of the list of what should be avoided in Russia. Unfortunately, there is less agreement among economists about what *does* work, as policies that work well in one place often fail dramatically elsewhere. Indeed, failures have been so common (and sometimes so spectacular) that, in recent years, economists have often preferred not to give any advice at all with respect to diversification policies.

Nevertheless, there are some policies that are helpful in fostering diversification that should be fairly uncontroversial. Broadly speaking they consist of getting framework conditions for entrepreneurship right, making sure that the business environment is generally competitive, and that there are sufficient incentives to invest in non-resource sectors. As such they involve a large number of structural reforms typically advocated by mainstream economics. However, some economists have expressed doubts as to whether these policies would turn out to be sufficient to achieve the stated goal of diversification in a reasonable time span (Drebentsov 2004). While acknowledging the need for establishing good framework conditions for business as a *sine qua non*, they advocate the pursuit of 'new style' industrial policies as a supplement to the structural reform agenda. The discussion that follows considers first our own recommendations for achieving diversification, which we regard as fairly conservative and conventional, before reporting some of the more innovative, but less proven, ideas that have been floated recently.

The most obvious conventional measure is to use the tax system to assist the development of the non-resource sector. The abolition of turnover taxes in Russia since 2000 represents an important step in this direction, since such taxes weigh particularly heavily on processing industries.[1] Increasing direct taxation of the natural resource sector (not only the oil sector) via excise, extraction or export taxes should be used to lower overall tax levels in the economy and in particular to cut the UST, thereby reducing non-wage labour costs. Such a cut might in some sectors be partially or even wholly offset by wage increases, but it should certainly lead to lower total labour costs in sectors with low productivity. Since a cut in the UST would cause shortfalls for the Pension Fund, it might be desirable to earmark a certain portion of price-independent resource taxes to make up these losses. However, any increase in taxation of resource-extraction industries must ensure that these sectors, which are critical to growth, remain sufficiently profitable to allow for their

---

[1] See OECD (2004), Box 1.4.

further development. Steps undertaken in recent years to increase the tax burden on the oil sector, especially under favourable oil prices, while closing tax loopholes at the same time, were hence a move in the right direction. However, it would be unwise to focus solely on the taxation of the oil industry. There should also be attempts to increase taxation of other resource or related sectors. Taxing a larger part of the resource rent away should also lead to relatively lower wages in the resource sector and hence diminish the pressure on wages in other sectors. To the degree that this would allow the paying of lower wages for activities with lower productivity, it would help to preserve employment that would otherwise be lost (or facilitate the creation of jobs that might not otherwise exist).

In addition to tax policy, there is also a large list of structural reforms, including financial sector and administrative reform that would be particularly important for facilitating the diversification of economic activity. Despite recent rapid growth in lending to the private sector, mechanisms for efficiently allocating investment resources across—and not merely within—economic sectors remain underdeveloped in Russia. Further reform of the banking sector, in particular, is thus a key priority. Facilitating the emergence of a venture capital industry would also be helpful, especially for assisting start-ups in sectors at the technological frontier. At the same time, there is a crucial need to improve basic framework conditions for business, particularly small and medium enterprises (SMEs). Further reducing the burdens imposed by heavy regulation and an often corrupt bureaucracy, in addition to strengthening the financial system, would help to create a more level playing field and decrease barriers to entry. In this respect, a more active competition policy would also be needed. This is especially true for sectors such as natural gas and electricity, where large, state-controlled monopolies should be restructured, while creating legal and regulatory frameworks that combine robust competition with effective regulation. Finally, streamlining burdensome custom procedures could be helpful for potential Russian exporters (especially for SMEs) by facilitating their access to international markets. However, none of the above can be achieved without substantial improvements in the probity, efficiency and accountability of the courts, the bureaucracy and other state institutions.

On the less conventional side, advocates of 'new-style interventions' recommend the creation of programmes that would directly improve the productivity and competitiveness of selected enterprises, which would to some degree serve as an example for other entrepreneurs. The guiding features of such policies usually include that they be highly transparent, that participation in these programmes be determined by private sector representatives, and that the period during which any single enterprise can participate in such a programme be strictly limited. Programmes should not involve significant transfers of resources to participating enterprises, but rather focus on the transfer of knowledge or skills, such as new production, management or marketing techniques, or the dissemination of specific information (e.g., about potential export markets). Another important feature of such programmes could be to establish links and networks. In this spirit, it has, for example, been suggested to create research parks and technology transfer centers attached to the leading educational and research facilities (Kim 2004). An extensive discussion of 'new style' industrial policy, and a survey of various international experiences in this field is beyond the scope of this chapter, but can for example be found in Rodrik (2004) and Drebentsov (2004).

Conclusion

Diversification is an important long-term goal, but, even if diversification policies are relatively successful, the main structural changes in the composition of the Russian economy in the coming years will probably first and foremost consist of an increase in the relative weight of the service sector, as well as some increase in import substitution industries. Any major diversification in the export structure is unlikely except in the long term. Hence, for the foreseeable future, Russia is almost certain to remain highly dependent on natural resource exports. While natural resources are sometimes seen as a 'curse' for long-term economic development (Sachs and Warner 2001), many of the potential problems can be avoided, or at least significantly mitigated by good macroeconomic policies and a sound institutional framework. Moreover, it has recently been argued that it is not resources as such, but rather the fact that most resource-based economies have relied heavily on state ownership and intervention that has been responsible for their disappointing economic performance (Aslund 2004, Ross 1999). The examples of economies with strong private entrepreneurship in resource sectors, such as Canada, Australia or the Scandinavian countries, demonstrate that, given the right institutions and policies, developing a successful modern economy based on natural resource exports is feasible. Until diversification has borne significant fruit—that is for quite some time to come—Russia should therefore make sure that while avoiding the pitfalls so often associated with resource-dependent growth, it follows policies that will allow it to make the best of its resource endowments.

Bibliography

Acemoglu, D, and Verdier, T, 1998, Property rights, corruption, and the allocation of talent: a general equilibrium approach, *Economic Journal*, 108, pp. 1381–1401.

Ahrend, R, 1999, Russia's Post-Stabilisation Economic Decline, its Crash, and Finally its Revival. Don't Just Blame the Corruption—It's the Exchange Rate, Stupid!, *Russian Economic Trends*, 8:3.

Ahrend, R, 2002, Press freedom, human capital and corruption, *DELTA Working Paper* 2002–11, February.

Ahrend, R, 2004a, Accounting for Russia's post-crisis growth, *OECD Economics Department Working Paper*, No. 404, October.

Ahrend, R, 2004b, Russian industrial restructuring: trends in productivity, competitiveness and comparative advantage, *OECD Economics Department Working Paper*, No. 408, October.

Ahrend, R and Tompson, W, 2005, Unnatural monopoly: the endless wait for gas-sector reform in Russia, *Europe–Asia Studies*, Vol. 57, No. 6, pp. 801–21.

Aslund, A, 2004, Russia's 'curse', *The Moscow Times*, January 16.

Boone, P and Rodionov D, 2002, Sustaining growth, *Brunswick USB Warburg Russia Equity Research*, September.

Brunetti, A, and Weder, B, 2003, A free press is bad news for corruption, *Journal of Public Economics*, 87, pp. 1801–24.

Drebentsov, V, 2004, Diversifying Russia's economy—key to sustainable growth, The World Bank, mimeo, Moscow.

Gurvich, E T, 2004, Makroekonomicheskaya otsenka roli Rossiiskogo neftegazovogo sektora, *Voprosy ekonomiki*, No. 10.

Kim, A, 2004, Why Google Is not a Russian company, *The Moscow Times*, August 23.

Kwon, G, 2003, Post-crisis fiscal revenue developments in Russia: from an oil perspective, *Public Finance and Management*, 3:4 pp. 505–30.

da Cunha Leite, C A and Weidmann, J, (1999), Does Mother nature corrupt? Natural resources, corruption, and economic growth, *IMF Working Paper* No. 99/85, June.

Mauro, P, 1995, Corruption and growth, *Quarterly Journal of Economics* 110, 3, August.

Mikhailova, T, 2003, The cost of the cold, *mimeo*, Pennsylvania State University.

OECD, 2002, *OECD Economic Surveys: Russian Federation*, Paris, February.

OECD, 2004, *OECD Economic Surveys: Russian Federation*, Paris, September.

Patillo, C, Poirson, H and Ricci, L, 2002, External debt and growth, *IMF Working Paper* WP/02/69, April.

Rodrik, D, 2004, Industrial policy for the twenty-first century, *KSG Faculty Research Working Paper 04–047*, Harvard University.

Ross, M, 1999, The political economy of the resource curse, *World Politics*, January.

Sachs, J and Warner, A, 2001, Natural resources and economic development: the curse of natural resources, *European Economic Review*, 45, pp. 827–38.

Tompson, W, 2004, Restructuring Russia's electricity sector: towards effective competition or *faux* liberalization?, *OECD Economics Department Working Paper*, No. 403, September.

UNCTAD, 1998, A survey of commodity risk management instruments, Report by the UNCTAD Secretariat (mimeo, Geneva, 6 April).

Vdovichenko, A, 2004, Monetary policy rules and their application in Russia, Moscow, Economic Expert Group.

6

THE ROAD TO SPONTANEOUS DIVERSIFICATION

Evgeny Gavrilenkov

Background

Russia's economy has made a clear and remarkably speedy recovery since the doldrums of 1998, having averaged growth of 6.8 per cent per year. As a result, in 1999–2005 the Russian economy grew by 57 per cent. In spite of the fact that the rate of growth slowed in mid-2004 and early 2005, largely due to a negative change in economic policy, growth numbers remained relatively strong (if not as high as they could be).

So, Russia continues to demonstrate a healthier macroeconomic performance than many other countries. Equally important, is the fact that Russia financed this growth mainly from its own sources, i.e., without any massive inflow of FDI or external borrowing (albeit the latter did increase substantially in 2003 and has kept growing since then). Russia for decades was a country that exported capital. Capital flight was not a phenomenon only of the 1990s. It also took place in earlier decades, although for different reasons and through different channels. From the macroeconomic point of view, continuous support of communist regimes all over the world can be treated as capital flight legitimized by the government. It also means that once Russia starts attracting more FDI, which will finance particular projects, growth rates may be high even in the absence of domestic financing. That said, the well-known task of doubling the GDP in 10 years, as was suggested by the Russian president in 2003, in principle looks achievable. Obviously, higher volumes of FDI cannot be considered as the only sufficient condition for sustainable and high growth rates. Some of the well-known structural impediments should be removed. In particular, one may point to the need for the long-awaited restructuring of the financial system, removing red tape and restructuring of the natural monopolies.

Not only have the growth numbers looked impressive in recent years. More important was that some structural changes took place. The macroeconomic performance already in 2002 clearly indicated that the country could no longer rely on the advantages of 'easy' growth and that a repeat of the same growth pattern, which emerged after the 1998 crisis and which was based on the possibility of higher utilization of existed capacities, would be impossible. Not surprisingly GDP growth in 2002 (4.7 per cent) slowed considerably compared to an average annual 7.2 per cent rate of growth in 1999–2001.

Growth slowed in 2002, as increased domestic demand saw consumer preferences shift toward more expensive higher quality goods, a sector in which Russian manufacturers are unable to compete with imports. The food industry provides a clear example of how growing incomes have transformed consumer demand. In 1999–2000, when incomes were low, production of cheap foodstuffs (such as vegetable oil, bread, etc.) grew rapidly. In 2001, as real incomes increased, production of those foodstuffs stopped growing and the focus shifted to more expensive high-protein foods. In 2002 and in the early 2003, growth in the Russian food industry slowed further from 11.4 per cent and 8.4 per cent in 2000 and 2002, respectively, to around 5 per cent in 2003. Since demand for food was almost entirely saturated, consumer demand shifted toward higher quality more expensive foodstuffs, consumer durables and services.

Domestic manufacturers throughout the market therefore realized that to compete with imports, they needed to offer better (and possibly more expensive) products, which means they need to invest in new productive capacities. Thus increased investment activity was one of the major growth drivers since 2003 and is expected to remain so in the years to come. In 2003 and 2004, annual growth exceeded 7 per cent largely as a result of higher investment activity.

Various other factors were also behind the growth acceleration in 2003 and early 2004, notably: higher oil prices (which caused the money supply to surge), low interest rates and a rapid increase in domestic demand as a result. The latter, as has been pointed out, was largely driven by greater investment activity, which was needed to resuscitate the exhausted growth mechanism that had emerged from the 1998 crisis and was based on increased capacity utilization.

As a result of the changing growth model, investment activity in 2003 rose across the board, not only in the oil and gas sector, as had previously been the case. Moreover, medium-size companies oriented toward the domestic consumer market set their sights on more aggressive growth. On the back of the liquidity surge in the financial system and low real interest rates, they sought to raise funds by issuing ruble corporate bonds and borrowing directly from domestic banks. According to the Central Bank, the money supply in 2003 expanded by more than 50 per cent. Meanwhile, nominal lending rates in 2003 dropped to around 12 per cent, the level of inflation reported for the year. Thanks to the zero real interest rates, bank loans to the private sector swelled by around 45 per cent and the ruble corporate bond market by over 90 per cent (the ruble corporate bond market kept expanding in 2004–05 and in three years grew from an almost zero level to nearly USD20 billion). The year 2003 was a clear example of the beginning of spontaneous diversification of the Russian economy.

Bigger companies with access to global financial markets raised funds there. In 2003, domestic non-financial institutions borrowed some USD16.5 billion on world markets, versus the financial sector's USD10.6 billion. In 2004 the non-financial sector borrowed already around USD18 billion externally and in the first half of 2005 this part of Russia's foreign debt rose by another USD14 billion. As a result, the foreign debt of Russia's non-financial institutions approached USD80 billion and became comparable with the country's public foreign debt (after Russia prepaid USD15 billion to Paris club in mid-2005), which is no real cause for serious concern given that economic growth continues and the ruble keeps appreciating in real terms. However, the rapid increase in the so-called quasi-sovereign debt may bring more problems in the future as state-owned quasi-sovereign borrowers (such as Gazprom or Rosneft) demonstrate relatively poor performance.

Overall, investment grew by 12.8 per cent in 2003 and by 10.8 per cent in 2004. Meanwhile, high oil prices and increased physical volumes of exports bumped up the current account surplus to nearly USD60 billion in 2004, which was twice as high as in the previous years. The current account surplus widened in 2005 even more. This enabled the Central Bank to accumulate more than USD 180 billion in international reserves by the end of 2005 and expand the money supply considerably. As a result, the monetization of the economy has steadily increased since 1999. The same pattern of economic development can be expected until the current account weakens.

Due to increased foreign borrowing, Russia's dependence on the oil price has fallen slightly since the end of 2002, but is still strong, as export revenues remain a catalyst for economic growth (as analysed in Chapter 4). It also goes without saying that high commodity prices have helped the government maintain macroeconomic stability and at the same time stimulated economic growth occurring on the back of extremely strong current account and cheap money, which will not last indefinitely.

Increased taxation of the oil industry since mid-2004 also contributed to a weakening of the ties between the current account and growth. As a result, in spite of the significantly increased oil price and increased exports, the rate of

economic growth slowed in 2004–05 (Figure 6.1). Government attempts to
stimulate diversification of the economy through increased taxation of the oil
industry and attempts to reallocate more capital through the budget have only
contributed to a deceleration of growth and relatively high inflation of the
annual rate of which remained at around 12 per cent for almost three years
since 2003.

As already said, some positive structural changes took place in 2003. One
important feature of industrial growth since 2003 is that it did not originate
from increased activity in the export-oriented sectors only. Both the manufacturing and the construction materials sectors grew more rapidly than the oil
and gas industry, largely thanks to the increased investment demand. And
despite the temporary slowdown of both industrial growth and investment
activity caused by the Yukos affair, the GDP continued to rise. This, in particular, also indicates that the Yukos affair had less of an effect on the service
sector. Demand for market services continued to rise in line with the steady
growth in real incomes that the high oil prices brought about. So the rapid
expansion of the market services sector reflects the ongoing structural
changes in the domestic economy, which could be linked to the mentioned
above changes in consumer demand.

Russia's economic policy switched course in mid-2004 (see Chapter 1). The
developments in the Yukos affair, a mini banking crisis and determined
government rhetoric on the need for a strong state presence in the social
and economic life of the country (by which time there was already no going
back) stayed the appetite for investment. Investment decisions are no mean
feat when you cannot be sure exactly what sort of economic system is emerging.

Figure 6.1 Growth Decelerated in Spite of Increased Oil Price

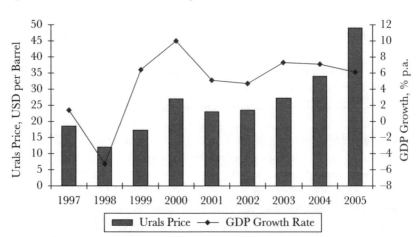

Figure 6.2 Output of the Five Basic Sectors (Seasonally Adjusted)

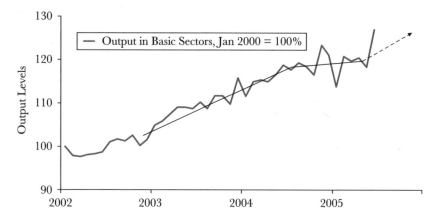

Economic policy has either dried up altogether or turned aside from its liberal course, assumed a repressive mien and gone in search of a curtailment of economic growth.

However, some improvements could be seen more recently: it looks as if in early 2005 the Kremlin realized the need to tread a more cautious line with business. As a result economic activity increased in mid-2005 and will probably remain relatively high in 2006 and beyond (Figure 6.2). Meanwhile, in spite of the improvements in economic policy in the short run, more fundamental changes can be expected in a couple of years, which will be discussed below.

Economic Policy and Diversification

For a couple of years the external environment has remained extremely favorable for Russia, the Urals oil price beating all earlier expectations. Not surprisingly, Russia grew faster than the rest of the world: an average of nearly 7 per cent a year since 1999. A reasonable macroeconomic policy has contributed to the economic performance. The government has a strong commitment to maintain macroeconomic stability, which secured a relatively high rate of economic growth in 2005 (in spite of the slow structural reforms). The ruble is strengthening, but this is largely a result of economic growth and is thus natural: the gap between PPP and the market exchange rate is narrowing. By the end of 2005 the real ruble exchange rate will have returned to the pre-crisis 1997–98 level (Figure 6.3). In spite of the ongoing real currency appreciation the economy keeps growing, unlike the situation in the pre-crisis period. This growth occurs on the back of some restructuring at the micro level and a higher efficiency of production.

Figure 6.3 The Real Ruble has Returned to the 1998 Level

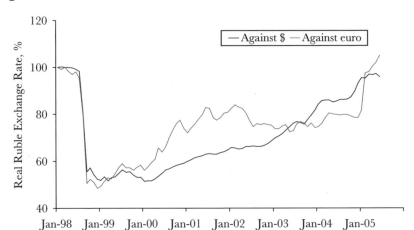

Figure 6.4 GDP in Real Terms, Nominal Dollars and Euros

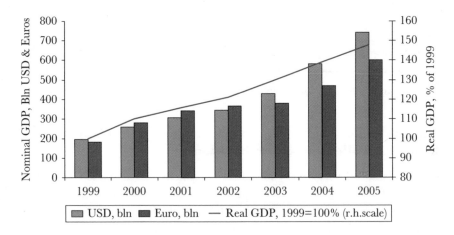

As a result of the real appreciation of the ruble, Russia's GDP in dollars (or in euros) has grown even faster than in real terms (Figure 6.4).

In spite of the fact that economic growth depends largely on export revenues, this growth is balanced: consumption and investment are both growing fast. Export revenues are a catalyst for economic growth and diversification. External borrowing, FDI and the domestic financial system are playing an increasingly important role in economic diversification. Remonetization (faster growth of the real money supply than of aggregate output) is happening on the back of growing incomes and incentives to save money domestically, which reduces the velocity of circulation. Growth in the economy and in the market is liquidity-driven and will continue to be so in the future.

Meanwhile, Russia is still an economy with a low level of monetization (having developed 'capitalism without capital'), so that the money supply to GDP ratio (a bit below 30 per cent) is much smaller than in most other countries. Lack of accumulated capital is reflected in the fact that loan maturities are very short in Russia (on average around one year). It goes without saying that monetization cannot be increased overnight. It grew from around 15 per cent of GDP to slightly below 30 per cent in five years. Growth in monetization is associated with economic growth, and incentives to save and invest money in Russia. This implies that the real money supply in the long run should also grow faster than GDP. The country needs to accumulate capital, which is a long-term evolutionary process. Gradual accumulation of capital will enable the financial system to develop and play a more and more important role in economic growth.

Unlike most of the Central European Economies, which had clear geopolitical objectives from the very beginning of transformation, Russia has had no such goal. Building institutions in accordance with European standards contributed to a high predictability of economic performance and social evolution in Eastern Europe. Given that Russia's long-term geopolitical objective has never been clearly announced, Russia's future is much less predicable, both with respect to economic performance and to the evolution of the social and political systems. Thus Russia is not on a 'balanced growth path', it remains 'path dependent': the future largely depends on the decisions to be taken each year. Given that market institutions in Russia are weak, the role of economic policy is particularly important as it determines the direction and intensity of capital flows: in or out of Russia, and how much.

It looks as if uncertainty increased significantly due to the recent attempts to reconstruct the political system and revise economic strategy. The ongoing transformation of the political system, such as abandoning elections for governors, replacing mixed voting (proportional and majority) by proportional voting alone, and the expected increase in the threshold needed for political parties to enter the Duma, may contribute to an even greater concentration of power in the Kremlin. Entry for the new politicians into the political system will be substantially complicated. Since such a political system may lack the flexibility necessary to react to possible external and internal changes, it may be relatively short-lived. At the same time, the risk of a loss of control over the parliament by the pro-Kremlin forces will increase if social conditions deteriorate, as the pro-Kremlin party could face a low turnout and lukewarm response at the polls. It could lose out to the Communist Party, 'Rodina' (Motherland) party with its so-called 'patriotic' origins and Vladimir

Zhirinovsky's Liberal Democratic Party of Russia, all of which have an active grassroots membership eager to catch the floating voter.

There is growing consensus among political analysts that the emerging political system will contradict the 1993 Constitution in certain aspects, such as the proclaimed division of powers. Strategic decision-making lacks transparency and may be even less transparent in the future due to the already high concentration of power in the Kremlin and the large majority of the pro-Kremlin party in the Duma which enables basic legislation to be revised easily.

That said, it appears that the Kremlin plans to establish a relatively liberal economic environment in the non-strategic sectors of the economy (which, however, have never been clearly specified) accompanied by tight political controls. At the same time the state is supposed to play a much greater role in the 'strategic' sectors and 'manage' the diversification of the economy. This is an obvious change relative to the system which emerged in the 1990s. It is unclear, however, if the new model will work well in the long run in Russia. An Asian-type economic model may not work in Russia due to a number of reasons (such as the declining and ageing population, an already largely urbanized population, etc.). Will it be a peculiar mix of the Asian and Latin American types of economic systems? Not necessarily. If that is the case, then one may expect that fundamental changes in the social and political environment may take place again sometime in the future.

The government (or the administration in a broader sense) is not homogeneous and consists of a variety of groups with different interests. Thus when analysing strategic decision-making on the top level, it makes more sense to consider it in terms of game theory (rather than as an implementation of some clearly defined strategy): there are several players with different objectives, they make moves one after another, the situation changes and the outcome of the game is unclear. Especially when the rules of the game are also subject to change.

The Russian government does have the clear objective to secure high rates of economic growth, which is impossible without economic diversification. So-called 'managed' diversification can scarcely be successful given the well-known inefficiency of the Russian government. According to Transparency International Russia has been and remains at the bottom of the list of least corrupt countries, and no progress in improving the situation has been observed in recent years. Spontaneous diversification as was happening in 2003 to early 2004 has more chances for success.

At the same time the oil sector is and will be important for Russia as a source of the financial resources needed to finance economic growth for a quite prolonged period. In this regard oil should be considered as a catalyst for growth in the entire economy. However, high growth rates in the non-energy sectors can be attained only if the investment climate remains attractive and economic policy is clear.

Obviously structural reforms have slowed recently. This is yet one more indication of the fact that Russia's future is less certain now than in Putin's first term. The Russian economy is influenced both by strong fundamentals originating from an extremely favorable external environment and by inconsistent economic policies. The former push the economy upwards, while the latter contribute to excessive volatility of the system and often pull it down. Nevertheless in the long run the fundamentals should dominate.

Unlike the lack of success in structural reforms, macroeconomic policy has been relatively reasonable. The government has a long-term commitment to maintain macroeconomic stability, reduce inflation and keep the budget balanced. Tax policy is aimed at a gradual reduction of the tax burden in nominal terms. This policy was, and most likely will be successful, so that the effective tax rates are not supposed to decline. Relatively low taxes, an obvious competitive advantage for Russia, may compensate for inefficiencies originating from the inadequate administrative system. However, in 2005 even macroeconomic policy was threatened by the pressure on the Finance Ministry to increase spending and start using the Stabilization Fund for domestic purposes. With elections ahead, this pressure can only keep growing.

As stated, the government has strong ambitions: doubling GDP in ten years implies that the annual growth rate should be around 7.3 per cent. Unlike China or India with their growing population and ongoing urbanization, it will be more difficult for Russia to grow as fast as the Asian countries. The population is going to decline steadily, which will inevitably decelerate growth already in the coming years. To secure high growth rates on such a vast territory as Russia, the country will be forced to liberalize its migration policy. The country does not look ready for such a decision: on the contrary recently migration control was significantly tightened.

As said, investment began to drive economic growth since 2003, which substantially contributed to an acceleration of economic growth and its diversification. It then slowed in the second half of 2004, due to the above-mentioned problems, which in general may be characterized as a 'crisis of confidence', in particular affecting the banking system. The economy, however, carried on expanding apace, as people saved less and spent more and export revenues continued to pour in. While consumer demand remains an important driver of economic growth in Russia, it is less significant than in many other countries: household consumption as a percentage of GDP in Russia is 46 per cent, well below the nearly 70 per cent in the US, for example. At the same time, changes in exports (and net exports, as defined by the SNA method) influence economic growth much more on a relative basis: the export of goods to GDP ratio remains a fairly high 31 per cent and net exports account for around 15 per cent of GDP.

So, due to this change of the growth model the economy since 2003 became more dependent on investment activity than ever before and became more sensitive to changes in economic policy. Thus deceleration of investment activity in mid-2004 negatively affected the growth rate of the GDP. It is also important to mention that growing consumer demand on its own cannot secure high rates of growth: if no new productive capacities are added then it can only stimulate imports or inflation.

It is not a surprise that the acceleration in inflation since mid-2004 was the result of a relatively weak economic performance as high inflation is actually a reflection of the growing inability of suppliers to meet demand. It can be shown that there is no direct correlation between growth in the money supply and inflation, whatever the supposed lag between them. Highly unstable velocity of money circulation is one of the major reasons for that. Indeed, the deceleration in inflation in mid-2005 coincided with an acceleration in the money supply (Figure 6.5).

What is clear is that inter-bank rates have been negative in real terms, despite the changes in demand for money and the money supply. This is not surprising. With the money stock low (less than 30 per cent of GDP) and inflows strong (the current account surplus was equal to more than 10 per cent of GDP in recent years), the supply of foreign currency has been far higher than the demand for it. The Central Bank has thus been forced to buy up the bulk of export revenues, generating a significant increase in the money

Figure 6.5 Inflation Increases on Back of Slowing Production (in %, y-o-y)

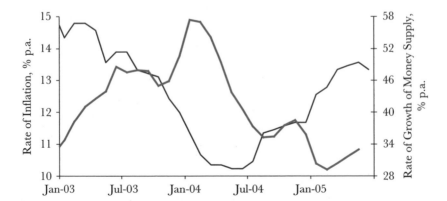

supply (see Chapter 4). That said, Russian monetary policy involves little more than conversion of the current account (plus or minus the net flow of capital through the capital account) by the Central Bank into ruble liquidity through the buildup of international reserves (Figure 6.6). Part of this ruble liquidity is sterilized as a result of the fiscal surplus being channeled into the stabilization fund. Since the inflow of liquidity has been quite strong relative to the stock of money, interest rates on money markets have remained low, money has been cheap and there has been no need for a refinancing mechanism (i.e., banks have had no need to borrow from the Central Bank at its much higher refinancing rate, still 13 per cent).

It needs to be borne in mind that Russia's growth story since 1999 has come about largely on the back of cheap money, and this will not be available indefinitely. The financial system has yet to face the test of positive real interest rates, which make money more expensive. This test may not be long in coming.

Interest rates could rise for any number of reasons. Demand for money could rocket as a result of a rapid expansion in economic activity, for example, or from the government sector, as was the case in the 1990s. At that time, the government was unable to achieve a budget surplus and covered the fiscal deficit by sucking the bulk of the liquidity from the market at very high interest rates, the outcome of which is still fresh in many memories. Interest rates may also rise as a result of a tightening in monetary policy, i.e., if the net inflow of foreign currency (from current and capital accounts) decreases as a percentage of GDP (or of money stocks). What is unlikely is that the Central Bank will halt the buildup of international reserves, in view of the strong balance of payments.

Figure 6.6 Accumulation of Gross International Reserves is Major Driver of Money Supply

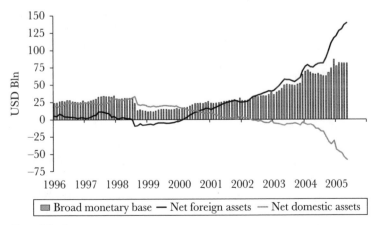

Source: Central Bank.

Following this logic, remonetization of the economy and the ongoing growth in ruble liquidity will inevitably lead to a deceleration in the growth of the money supply, if it is assumed that this will continue to depend on the Central Bank's foreign exchange policy. At the same time, interest rates on the inter-bank market should eventually drift back into positive figures and reach a level that will prompt banks to switch their borrowings to the Central Bank. In turn, more expensive money will inevitably force a restructuring of the banking sector. This may, in fact, only be a year or two down the road from now. If for instance, the current account surplus falls to 5–6 per cent of GDP in 2006–07, and the money supply reaches 30 per cent of GDP, then growth in the money supply could well, as a result of reserve accumulation, decelerate to 16–17 per cent, from 32 to 36 per cent in 2004–05. If inflation in 2006–07 holds at around 10 per cent, and the economy is growing by around 5 per cent a year, then the money supply would need to expand at a rate of at least 16 per cent p.a. just to maintain a stable money stock to GDP ratio, assuming that the velocity of circulation remains stable. In fact, this velocity will continue to decelerate, requiring that the money supply grow even faster.

Most likely inevitable changes in Russia's economic growth model are going to take place in the near future. Due to capacity limitations, growth in exports (in real terms) will start to decelerate, while imports will continue to grow. If commodity prices stop growing, net exports will shrink in nominal terms and as a share of GDP. This will hurt the accumulation of gross international reserves, and the expansion in the money supply, which will push interest rates upwards. This looks to be the most likely scenario, which will be analysed in the last part of this chapter.

Theoretically, the Central Bank could increase liquidity in the domestic banking system by lowering the refinancing rate and encouraging borrowing. However, the government is intent on reducing inflation to single digits, so that the lending rate is unlikely to drop to a negative real rate. This could well unleash a liquidity shortage on the money markets that may lead to a major restructuring of the banking sector and possible rapid disinflation. This may allow the Central Bank to reduce the refinancing rate further, but keep it positive in real terms (Figure 6.7).

One possible barrier to disinflation is fiscal; fiscal policy can be an effective antidisinflationary tool. However, this is not a major threat in the medium term. The government's new medium-term financial plan suggests that it is looking to implement a balanced, cautious fiscal policy, despite the announced increase in social spending in 2005 and beyond. In 2005 federal expenditures have been raised 13 per cent from 3,048 billion ruble(USD109 billion) to 3,454 billion ruble(USD123 billion), a figure expected to be close to 17 per cent of GDP. Although spending will be higher in 2005 than in 2004 (16.2 per cent

Figure 6.7 Central Bank Tries to Keep Real Refinancing Rate Positive

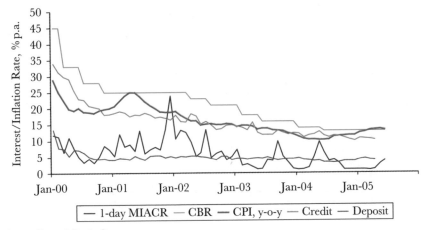

Source: Central Bank, Rosstat.

Figure 6.8 Spending will be Higher than Originally Planned, but Bearable

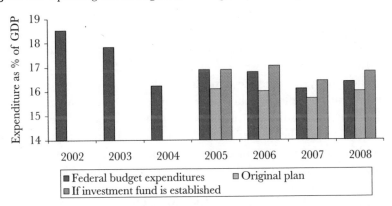

Source: Finance Ministry.

of GDP), the announced figure is less than in 2002 (18.5 per cent) and 2003 (17.8 per cent).

In 2006, federal budget spending will be almost unchanged. And the government has announced that it will be lower as a percentage of GDP in 2007 and 2008 (Figure 6.8). Given that Russians will be electing a new Duma in December 2007, though, and a new president in March 2008, these promises should be treated with caution; it is more than likely that spending will again be increased.

Discussions within the government on the need for a budgetary investment fund and for greater investment in infrastructure than has thus far been budgeted

Table 6.1 Federal Budget Expenditures by Items, % of GDP

	2005E	2006F	2007F	2008F
Expenditures	*16.9*	*16.8*	*16.1*	*16.4*
Interest	1.1	0.9	0.8	0.7
Non-interest	15.8	15.9	15.3	15.7
Transfers to the regional budgets	5.8	5.5	5.3	5.6
Transfers to the off-budgetary funds	3.6	3.8	3.9	4.3
Capital expenditures	1.6	1.6	1.5	1.4
Others (including salaries)	4.7	5.0	4.6	4.4
Old expenditures	*16.1*	*16.0*	*15.7*	*16.0*
Expenditures if the investment fund is established	*16.9*	*17.1*	*16.4*	*16.8*

Source: Finance Ministry. E indicates an estimate and F a forecast.

for may also be a cause for concern. Economics Minister German Gref has suggested that such a fund be established in 2006. It would be created in much the same way as the stabilization fund, receiving additional revenues from oil export duties and the oil production tax, if the price of (Urals) oil is above a certain level. The ministry estimates that the fund could receive revenues of 60 billion rubles in 2006, 120 billion rubles in 2007 and 120 billion rubles in 2008 (Table 6.1). This, however, would be achieved at the expense of the stabilization fund, reducing the sterilization effect.

It is unclear how effective these investments will be and whether they can contribute to a diversification of the economy and support a growth rate at reasonable levels. The procedures for selecting investment projects look unclear, introducing the possibility of corruption, but the size of the proposed investment fund rules out any threat to Russia's macroeconomic stability.

Medium-term Trends: More Changes Ahead

While investment decelerated in mid-2004, the gross national savings ratio changed little, remaining at over 30 per cent of GDP for much of the period. Given that the gross investment to GDP ratio (i.e., in both capacity and inventory) is around 21 per cent, the chances of investment and economic growth increasing seem decent, at least in theory.

As mentioned above, investment in capacity and modernization will remain a key driver of economic growth for some time. Due to well-documented demographic problems, Russia's labor force will not expand over the coming decades. In fact, it will probably start shrinking very soon if not boosted by a steady inflow of immigrant workers, which does not look likely. Greater labor productivity is therefore vital if the economy is to expand at a steady rate.

Given the depreciation and obsolescence of fixed capital, investment may continue to rise more rapidly than GDP, at least for a couple of years.

The main source of investment financing is private savings. By definition, national savings are associated with the sum of fixed capital investments, investments in stocks and the current account surplus (excluding interest payments). If eventually, say, from 2006, the current account surplus starts shrinking in both nominal terms and as a percentage of GDP, then savings could fall also. A drop in savings will not necessarily bring down investment, however. The main victim will be the state sector, while the private sector will most probably see its savings (as a percentage of GDP) remain flat.

This assertion is reinforced by the fact that the 2006–08 fiscal plan forecasts a drop in the federal budget surplus from the current 5 per cent to 1–1.5 per cent of GDP on the back of lower oil prices. In addition, the level at which additional revenues from oil export duties and the crude oil production tax are transferred to the stabilization fund is to be increased from USD20/barrel to USD27/barrel of Urals blend, which will also reduce the surplus and thus the contributions to the reserve. The drop in the surplus is expected to bring down the overall government savings to GDP ratio.

In recent years Russia's balance of payments has been remarkably strong: the current account surplus climbed from USD24.6 billion in 1999 to USD59.9 billion in 2004. The main catalyst of this rapid turnaround has been exports, which rose from USD75.6 billion in 1999 to USD182 billion in 2004. In 2005, with the average price of oil and other commodities expected to remain buoyant, exports are likely to approach USD240 billion, which is three times as much as in the first post-crisis year and would mean an increase in the inflow of foreign currency.

As official statistics show (Figure 6.9), the share of commodities in total exports has changed little in recent years. The share of minerals, metals, chemicals and timber has hovered around 85 per cent.

As already mentioned, Russia remains an economy with a low level of monetization, with a money supply to GDP ratio of less than 30 per cent, and rapid GDP growth requires greater liquidity. Moreover, the real money supply needs to expand more rapidly than the economy; income is highly concentrated among only a handful of sectors, regions and groups of people, and the highest earners have a greater propensity to save. As seen in 1999–2004, a surge in deposits helps to remonetize the economy and reduces the velocity of circulation, while an increase in bank assets stimulates GDP growth, as banks intermediate more between saving and investment. These factors in turn increase the length of loans and deposit maturity terms.

Relative fast money supply growth is thus a precondition for economic expansion. And as Russia's monetary policy centers on the Central Bank creating

Figure 6.9 Export Structure Remains Unchanged

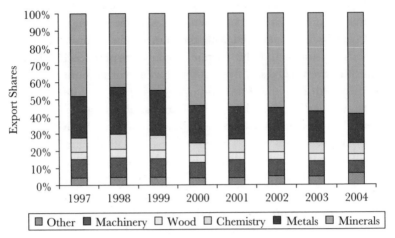

Source: State Customs Committee.

ruble liquidity by converting funds in the current account surplus (and some of the inflow into the capital account), commodity exports have always been a major catalyst of the country's economic growth.

Greater export volumes have caused certain sectors to swell in recent years. More importantly, however, export revenues, primarily from the metals and the oil and gas industries, have been redistributed throughout the economy by the financial system, which has driven up domestic demand. As it is well known, prices of oil and other commodities, export revenues and GDP growth rates correlated closely until 2004, when their relationship deteriorated for two reasons. First, investment activity waned as hardliners within the government ratcheted up the pressure on business. Second, taxation of the oil sector was increased, which drained liquidity out of the private financial system. While this enabled the Finance Ministry to accumulate tens of billions of dollars in the Stabilization Fund, it also stifled growth in the banking system's capitalization, thus reducing the potential for economic expansion. As a result, GDP growth slowed despite a rise in exports, both gross and net (Figure 6.10).

The growth in export revenues may dwindle considerably in the medium term as neither state-controlled nor private firms in the export-oriented sectors have injected the vast amounts of capital expenditures needed to secure high rates of growth. In the oil and gas industry, the state's widely discussed drive to secure a grip on 'strategic' assets will most likely reduce efficiency (see also Chapter 2). To date in Russia, state-backed oil and gas companies have delivered much poorer production and financial results than private ones, and there are no indications that this will change in the years ahead.

Figure 6.10 Rise in Exports Stimulated Growth Until Mid-2004

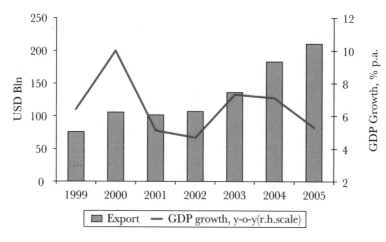

Table 6.2 Capacity Utilization

	1990	1998	2003	2004E
Oil refining (%)	87	60	76	78
Iron ore (%)	98	81	93	95
Cast iron (%)	94	71	91	94
Steel (%)	94	63	84	88
Rolled ferrous metals (%)	92	59	82	87
Mineral fertilizers (%)	75	47	73	81
Timber (%)	69	29	44	43
Paper (%)	94	54	83	87

Source: Rosstat.

In 2004, capacity utilization rates in the main export-oriented sectors were close to the levels reached in 1990, the Soviet Union's peak year for production (Table 6.2 & Figure 6.11). Unsurprisingly, output of Russia's main commodities was also approaching the records set that year. In the last few years, however, production growth has been increasingly held back due to the lack of spare capacity.

Due to a lack of investment, no major new production facilities have been brought online in the capital-intensive oil and gas and metals industries, which account for the bulk of Russia's exports. For that same reason, non-commodity exports are highly unlikely to take off any time soon, so growth of export volumes may taper off or even stop in two or three years. If commodity prices also stop climbing (for example, if the dollar gains substantial ground against the euro, energy prices may even drop), Russia's total exports may level off at the 2005 level. Meanwhile, real ruble appreciation and the existing capacity

Figure 6.11 Production of Major Commodities Reaches 1990 Level

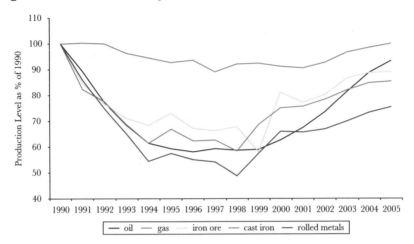

constraints in the industries supplying the domestic market will continue to drive up imports, albeit at a lower rate than in recent years. The current account surplus will thus start to shrink, although it will remain positive.

The slowdown in export growth should have both a direct and indirect impact on economic expansion: a fall in the current account surplus will limit the rise in the money supply, thus slowing the rate of remonetization and bank asset growth.

As a result of real ruble appreciation, Russia's GDP will increase more rapidly in dollar terms than in real rubles, meaning that the current account surplus as a percentage of GDP will decrease even faster in nominal terms. One may see the current account surplus drop to USD30 billion in 2007 and USD20 billion in 2008 (compared with nearly USD60 billion in 2004 and over USD90 billion expected in 2005), or to around 3 per cent of GDP (Figure 6.12). In this case, the growth of international reserves and thus the monetary base would slow.

Sluggish money supply expansion and the capacity constraints in the export-oriented sectors will inevitably change the economic growth model, possibly around 2007. And with the next presidential elections due to be held in 2008, these two years promise to be a period of crucial change in Russia. The greater need to invest in capacity will drive up foreign borrowing substantially, as growth firms will be unable to raise large amounts domestically. In 2006–08, companies and banks will be tapping over USD20 billion per year from the international market. Manufacturing may also mushroom in the years ahead, as investors may be interested in modernizing certain less capital-intensive segments where spare capacity still exists. Given that Russia's

Figure 6.12 Current Account Surplus will Shrink as Export Growth Slows

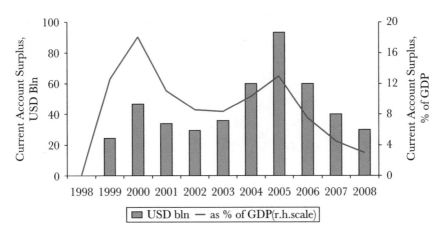

current account surplus and net exports as a percentage of GDP are likely to shrink in the years to come, gross investment and in particular consumption will see their percentage grow. All in all, the economy has a chance to diversify 'spontaneously' as it was happening in 2003.

There is also a need to lighten the tax burden on the oil sector, although this will be difficult to do without also reducing budget expenditures. As discussed above public spending remains a problematic issue, as the government needs to keep it moderate to secure macroeconomic stability on the one hand and to prevent social unrest on the other hand, especially in light of the events in Ukraine and Kyrgyzstan in 2004–05. In 2006, public spending, including transfers to the Russian Pension Fund, is expected to soar. Given the strong signal sent to the Kremlin by the pensioners' protests at the beginning of 2005, one should not be surprised to see annual non-interest spending in nominal terms rise by as much as one third.

Government investment should also climb in 2006, although that does not necessarily mean that one will see an improvement in the quality of public institutions, which seems to be an Achilles heel for Russia. Corruption in the country remains widespread and, as studies by Transparency International show, no progress in tackling the problem is being made. It therefore seems doubtful that government investment will result in more efficiency.

It looks as if the government recognizes (at least partially) the problem. In spite of a general deterioration in economic policy, fiscal policy remains reasonable. The government has strong commitments to maintain macroeconomic stability. In spite of enormous pressure on the Finance Ministry to start spending the Stabilization Fund (often without clear ideas and concrete business plans) the ministry was able to resist the pressure. From this point of view an

Figure 6.13 Government Spending as a Percentage of GDP will Remain Unchanged

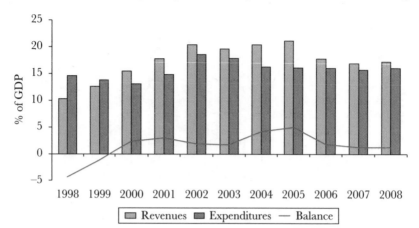

Source: Finance Ministry, Economics Ministry.

agreement with the Paris club to prepay USD15 billion of Russia's debt to the creditors ahead of schedule looks timely. Decreasing public debt may stimulate rating agencies to upgrade Russia more, which may create a better environment for external borrowing by the Russian corporate sector.

The numbers in the draft 2006–08 budget show that the compromise between the liberals and conservatives was achieved in an unusual way. Government spending as a percentage of GDP is to remain almost unchanged over 2004–08 (see Figure 6.13), as are growth rates (i.e., well below the target 7 per cent per annum), but the cutoff price above which oil revenues are transferred to the Stabilization Fund will be increased from the current USD20/barrel to USD27/barrel.

It is not the aim of this chapter to discuss how correct the Economics Ministry and the Finance Ministry assumptions and forecasts are, nor is there any point in guessing where the oil price will go next year and beyond. The reality may, and most likely will, be rather different from the ministries' predictions. What is important here is that the government has made a firm commitment to running a budget surplus and maintaining macroeconomic stability, despite all the internal wrangling within its ranks.

As was mentioned above, the most likely scenario is that the current account surplus (measured as a percentage of GDP and in nominal terms) will shrink over the next few years but remain positive. The government's medium-term fiscal plan also envisages a fiscal surplus in the years to come; thus, both the external and internal balances will remain in the black (see Figure 6.14).

Figure 6.14 Two Surpluses—Internal and External—Guarantee Macroeconomic Stability

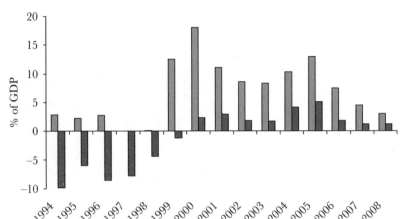

Source: Finance Ministry, Economics Ministry, own estimates.

In turn, this means that the ruble will continue to appreciate in real terms over the next few years, and the rate of its rise will largely depend on inflation. Inflation in modern Russia is not only a monetary phenomenon. Inflationary expectations, incentives to save money, confidence and other factors that are difficult to measure are also highly significant. If confidence is gradually restored and the investment climate improves enough to stimulate faster economic growth, then one could see quite rapid disinflation to single-digit levels on the back of higher demand for money. However, if uncertainty remains high and economic growth slow, then inflation will most likely stay above 10 per cent in the years to come.

As for debt, the government medium-term fiscal strategy does not envisage the state issuing Eurobonds in the foreseeable future. This is no surprise, given the expected current account and fiscal surpluses and overall macroeconomic outlook. The government is to continue borrowing internationally, however, albeit in limited amounts: foreign borrowing (including tied credits) will reach USD1 billion in 2006 and USD0.7–0.6 billion over 2007–08. If another agreement with the Paris Club is reached later on and Russia pays back step by step all its debt over 2006–07, then the country's public foreign debt could shrink from the current USD95 billion to USD40 billion by 2008.

In this situation, Russia stands a good chance of being upgraded by the rating agencies, which will improve the terms of borrowing for the Russian corporate sector, mainly for quasi-sovereign borrowers. As Figure 6.15 shows,

Figure 6.15 Public and Private Foreign Debt

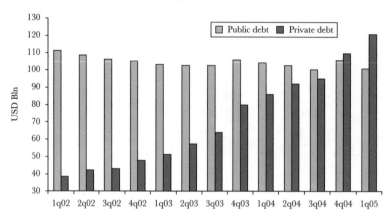

Source: Central Bank.

public foreign debt has already contracted over the past few years, while private foreign debt (which includes quasi-sovereign borrowers, such as Gazprom, Rosneft and Transneft) has expanded at a rapid pace. Thus, Russia's total foreign debt swelled by nearly 14 per cent in 2004 alone, but we do not yet consider this a threat: the total foreign debt to GDP ratio decreased from 43 per cent in 2003 to about 36 per cent in 2004. So in general foreign borrowing has supported economic growth.

What does give rise to concern for the future is quasi-sovereign borrowing. Of the total USD18.6 billion increase in the foreign debt of the non-financial sector in 2004, about USD11–12 billion was borrowed by Gazprom and Rosneft; the latter raised funds to acquire Yuganskneftegaz, which made no contribution to economic growth or higher productivity at all. Alarm bells will sound if these quasi-sovereign borrowers continue to raise funds aggressively on global markets without a substantial increase in productivity, and this cannot be ruled out. While formally Russia's sovereign debt fell slightly in 2004, total sovereign plus quasi-sovereign debt actually rose over the year.

The government's debt strategy envisages total public debt (foreign and domestic) gradually falling from 23.5 per cent of GDP as of end 2004 to 16.4 per cent by end 2006, 13.9 per cent by end 2007 and 12.42 per cent by end 2008. Domestic public debt will continue to increase but is expected to rise no higher than 5.3 per cent of GDP by end 2008. This once again confirms that the government is strongly committed to maintaining macroeconomic stability, and moderate expansion of the domestic debt market should be treated as a positive trend, as more financial instruments will be on offer. Should this become true continuous spontaneous diversification of the economy

Table 6.3 Sources of Investment Financing: Own Funds Predominate, although Companies Borrow More

	2004	2003	2002	2001
Total	100.0	100.0	100.0	100.0
Own funds (%)	46.8	45.6	45.0	49.4
Bank loans (%)	7.3	6.4	5.9	4.4
Loans from other enterprises (%)	7.0	6.8	6.5	4.9
Budget (%)	17.4	19.6	19.9	20.4
Off-budget funds (%)	0.8	0.9	2.4	2.6
Other (%)	20.7	21.1	20.3	28.3

Source: Rosstat.

becomes increasingly possible, and this process will take place on the back of economic growth.

The dependence on commodity exports, which developed and gathered strength over decades, will not go away overnight. To break it, massive and efficient investment in non-energy sectors is required. Russia has not yet seen such investment on a large scale, although some investment in non-energy sectors has taken place recently. The breakdown of investment by source of finance (see Table 6.3) shows that enterprises have continued to rely mainly on their own funds. The share of borrowed money (bank loans and loans from other enterprises) increased in 2003 and in the first half of 2004 compared to previous years indicating that the financial system is becoming more and more important for Russia's growth.

That own funds were the single biggest source of fixed investment means that money stayed mostly in those sectors where it was generated, contributing little to economic diversification. The share of borrowings (bank loans and loans from other enterprises), although increasing (especially in 2003), remains relatively low. Generally, the higher this share, the greater the economy's opportunities for diversification (provided that the borrowings are allocated to non-energy sectors). It is expected that the share of borrowed money will increase further, although one can scarcely expect borrowings to make a much higher share of Russian investment in the very near future. Cashflows are concentrated in a few export-oriented industries, while the financial system is still too weak to reallocate capital to other sectors. Its 'weakness', however, does not stem only from the inadequacy of financial institutions themselves. There are other, macroeconomic reasons, such as a low monetization rate.

So, the expectation is that total consumption will grow as a percentage of GDP in the long run and do this on the back of a shrinking current account surplus and falling net exports. One would not expect this to be achieved via rapid expansion of the public sector. On the contrary, it is private consumption that will be picking up pace. Plans afoot for reform of housing, education and healthcare suggest that people will have to pay more for these services, while the proportion of unpaid services will decline. The recent move toward monetization of benefits went in this direction. As a result, the services sector will grow faster than manufacturing, as was also the case in recent years.

7

ECONOMIC GROWTH
AND THE MOBILIZATION MODEL

Gregory Khanin

Introduction

The evaluation of the current situation and prospects of the contemporary Russian economy in the Russian and Western economic literature and in the activities of the international economic organizations is complicated by two factors. First, Russian economic statistics remain unreliable. Second, the over-whelming majority of researchers make forecasts of Russian long-term economic development based on the results of the last few years, at the most of the past 10–20 years. Furthermore, these forecasts are based on purely economic factors, without taking account of the human potential and moral condition of the society.

My goal is to evaluate the prospects for Russian economic development on the basis of reliable economic statistics and on the main features of its economic development over the past three hundred years, for which period there are more or less reliable macroeconomic statistics. In the economic development of Russia in this period one can observe some regularities that enable one to forecast the future development of Russia and its economic policy. I attempt also, to the extent that is possible, to take account of the human potential and moral condition of contemporary Russian society.

Contemporary Russian Macroeconomic Statistics and the Need for Alternative Estimates of the State of the Russian Economy

Despite the fact that the Russian statistical service since the beginning of the 1990s has declared its transition to international statistical standards, Russian macroeconomic statistics remain unreliable. The reasons for this unreliability are connected both with the general defects of the Russian state apparatus and public administration as a whole (incompetence, lying, irresponsibility) and also with the general chaos in the economy in the post-Soviet period, and the huge growth of the shadow economy, the size of which is difficult to determine. For these reasons, the need for alternative estimates of the state of the Russian economy is just as urgent now as in Soviet times.

Our research has shown that the greatest distortions in the post-Soviet period concern the value of fixed and working capital, profitability and net investment. Hence the statistical distortions in the post-Soviet period differ from those in the Soviet period when the biggest distortions concerned the growth of GDP and of specific sectors of the economy. Moreover, and this also differs from the Soviet period, official statistics now understate some economic indices. For example, according to our calculations GDP in current prices is now significantly understated as a result of a significant (about 20 per cent) understatement of personal consumption and of investment in some service sectors (e.g., according to our calculations investment in retail trade is actually about 16 times greater than the data given in official statistics), of the value of fixed and working capital, and of the profitability and output of certain industries. If we confine ourselves just to the GDP, then this is understated by approximately 10–15 per cent.

In the 1970s and 1980s, I made alternative estimates of the dynamics of the Soviet economy in 1928–87. These were most detailed for 1955–87.[1] These estimates were largely based on indirect indices of economic activity and were made using several methods (for example, in the case of industry six). As a result it was possible to give a much more objective estimate of the development of the Soviet economy than was given by the official Soviet statistical bodies.

Beginning in 1996, I renewed my calculations of alternative estimates of the state of the Russian economy together with my colleagues: at first N.I. Suslov and then with O.I. Polosova, D.A. Fomin and N.V. Ivanchenko, students and graduate students at Novosibirsk universities. For the period 1996–2003 we were able not only to make alternative annual estimates of the growth of the Russian economy and its sectors but also, for the first time, for some years also to estimate the real value of fixed and working capital for the goods sector and some of its branches and for retail trade. Using these estimates, we estimated the profitability of production and capital employed

---

[1] The fullest version of these calculations was published in Khanin, G I, 1991, *Dinamika ekonomicheskogo razvitiya SSSR* (Novosibirsk).

for a number of branches of the goods sector and for retail trade. In connection with alterations in the collection of official statistical data in the post-Soviet period, we used some new methods for the estimation of the growth of the economy.[1]

Preliminary Estimates of the Growth of the Russian GDP in 1999–2004

I will set out the results we have obtained for the period 1999–2004 which are the most important from the point of view of estimating the prospects for the Russian economy. It is necessary to point out that estimates have varying degrees of detail. The most detailed are the calculations for 1999–2000.[2] For 2001–03 they are less detailed. The estimates for 2004 are preliminary. The degree of detail also differs for the different economic variables. They are most detailed for the goods sectors and some of its branches, and less so for the services sector. The estimates of profitability and replacement value of fixed capital are only for certain years. The estimate of the growth of fixed capital in particular is only a rough estimate. Here we used also the estimates of I.B. Voskoboinikov.[3] Due to space limitations, in this chapter several intermediate stages in the calculations are omitted.

Our estimates confirm the conclusion of official statistics, that the period 1999–2004, unlike the previous crisis period, was a period of fairly fast economic growth. However, our calculations indicate that this growth was considerably lower than the rates published in official statistics. For 1999–2003 the growth of GDP was 23 per cent rather than the official 38 per cent. In other words, the official estimates on average in this period exaggerate the rate of growth by about 3 per cent p.a. Furthermore, it is possible that our estimates of growth for this period are too high. After making these calculations, we discovered that for 1996–2003, the official statistics for the

---

[1] Our main results were published in Khanin, G I, Polosova, O I and Ivanchenko, N V, 2002, Promyshlennoe proizvodstvo v Rossii v 1996–1999 gody: al'ternativnaya otsenka, *EKO*, No. 1; Khanin, G I, Polesova, O I, and Ivanchenko, N V, 2002, Stroitel'stvo v Rossii v 1996–2000 gody: al'ternativnaya otsenka tempov razvitiya, *Voprosy statistiki*, No. 12; Khanin, G I, Polosova, O I and Ivanchenko, N V, 2004, Rossiiskaya ekonomika v 1996–2000 gody: al'ternativnaya otsenka, *EKO*, No. 2; Khanin, G I, Polosova, O I, and Fomin, D A, 2005, Dinamika produktsii promyshlennosti RF v 2001–2003 g : al'ternativnaya otsenka, *EKO*, No. 2; Khanin, G.I., 2005, Za vernuyu tsifru, *Voprosy statistiki*, No.3.

[2] Khanin, G I, and Polosova, O I, 2004, Ekonomika Rossii. Rossii v 1996–2000 gody: alternativnaya otsenka, *EKO*, No. 2.

[3] Voskoboinikov, I B, 2004, O korrektirovke dinamiki osnovnykh fondov v rossiiskoi ekonomike, *Ekonomicheskii zhurnal VshE*, No. 1.

output of some agricultural products and for agricultural production as a whole, which we used in our calculations, are exaggerated.[1] I present also an estimate of the growth of GDP in 2004, although this is very preliminary. It is based on extending to 2004 the relationship between the growth of GDP and domestic fuel consumption which existed in 2001–03.

Calculating an index for output in 2001–03 has two parts. First calculating an index for the output of goods and then an index for the output of services. The index for the production of goods was calculated using three methods.

The first method for calculating the output of goods is based on indices for the output of the various branches of this sector using the share of these branches in the value added of this sector. The results of this calculation are presented in Table 7.1.

The second method of calculation is based on the growth of domestic consumption of fuel. The results of this calculation are presented in Table 7.2.

The third method is based on the growth of freight transport. The results of this calculation are set out in Table 7.3.

Using these three methods we arrived at the final estimate of the growth of the goods sector. The results are set out in Table 7.4.

The estimate of the growth of services was made using data on employment in this sector and on labour productivity. The growth of labour productivity in this sector was calculated starting from the growth of labour productivity in the goods sector and the relationship between the growth of labour productivity

Table 7.1 Growth of the Output of the Goods Sector According to the First Method (% p.a.)

Branch	2001	2002	2003
Industry[a]	3.4	1.3	4.2
Agriculture[b]	7.5	1.5	1.5
Construction[c]	3.4	2.9	3.7
Total	4.01	1.61	4.05

Notes:
[a] See Khanin, G I, Polosova, O I, and Fomin, D A, 2005, Dinamika produktsii promyshlennosti RF v 2001–03 gody: alternativnaya otsenka, *EKO*, No.2 p. 17.
[b] The Rosstat data.
[c] Based on calculations by O.I. Polosova.

[1] The exaggeration of the output levels of some agricultural products was revealed by comparing their volumes of production and consumption, and of their rates of growth using alternative methods for calculating them. See Khanin, G I, and Fomin, D A, 2005, Dinamika proizvodstva produktsii sel'skogo khozyaistva v 1999–2003 godakh: al'ternativnaya otsenka. *Voprosy statistiki*, No. 10.

Table 7.2 Growth of the Output of the Goods Sector According to the Second Method (% p.a.)

	2001	2002	2003
Domestic consumption of fuel	4.4	−1.3	4.9
Production of goods	5.2	−0.5	5.7

Notes:
(1) Domestic consumption of fuel is calculated as the difference between the production of fuel and its export.
(2) The relationship between fuel consumption and goods production was calculated using the relationship for this which existed in the USA in 1970–75 (when the latter exceeded the former by 0.8% p.a.).

Table 7.3 Growth of the Output of the Goods Sector According to the Third Method (% p.a.)

	2001	2002	2003
Public freight transport	3.2	5.8	7.9
Production of goods	2.6	5.2	7.3

Note: The relationship between public freight transport and the production of goods was taken from this relationship for the USA in 1970–75 (the latter was 0.6 per cent p.a. less than the former). Possibly it would have been desirable to use data for the transport of goods, but I could not find this data for the USA.

Table 7.4 Final Estimate of the Growth of the Goods Sector (% p.a.)

Method	2001	2002	2003
First method	4.01	1.61	4.05
Second method	5.2	−0.5	5.7
Third method	2.6	5.1	7.3
Final estimate (arithmetic mean)	3.9	2.1	5.7

in the goods sector and the services sector in 1996–2000. In this period labour productivity growth p.a. in the goods sector was 3.9 percentage points greater than in the services sector.[1] The results of this calculation are set out in Table 7.5.

To calculate the growth of Russia's GDP for 2001–03, the growth of output of goods and services derived from the calculations presented above, are

[1] Calculated by the author from data concerning alternative estimates of output and employment in these sectors, which is not presented here as a result of space limitations.

Table 7.5 Growth of Service Sector Output, 2001–03 (% p.a.)

	2001	2002	2003
Growth of output of goods	3.9	2.1	5.7
Growth of employment in the goods sector[a]	−0.7	−1.8	−2.6
Growth of labour productivity in the goods sector	4.6	4.0	8.5
Growth of labour productivity in the services sector	0.7	0.1	4.6
Growth of employment in the services sector	1.6	3.2	1.5
Growth of output of services	2.3	3.3	6.1

Note: [a] Calculated from data on employment in industry, construction and agriculture.

Table 7.6 Alternative Estimates of the Growth of GDP in 2001–03

	2001	2002	2003
Growth of output of goods and services	3.14	2.62	5.91
Growth of GDP	3.44	2.92	6.21
Rosstat's estimate of GDP growth	5.1	4.7	7.3
Difference between Rosstat estimate and alternative estimate	1.66	1.78	1.09

Table 7.7 Official and Alternative Estimates of the Growth of GDP in 1999–2003 (% p.a.)

	1999[a]	2000[a]	2001	2002	2003	1998–2003
Alternative estimate	1.2	7.6	3.4	2.9	6.2	23.0
Official (i.e., Rosstat) estimate	6.4	10.0	5.1	4.7	7.3	38.0
Difference	5.2	2.4	1.7	1.8	1.1	15.0

Note: [a] The data for 1999–2000 come from Khanin, G I, and Polosova, O I, 2004, Ekonomika Rossii v 1996–2000 gody: al'ternativnaya otsenka, *EKO*, No. 2.

weighted by the share of goods and services in GDP in 2003, adjusted by the World Bank estimate of the exaggeration of the share of the trade sector, and corrected by the decline in material intensity of the GDP in 1996–2000 (0.3 percentage points p.a.). This produces estimates of GDP growth in 2001–03 which can be compared with those of Rosstat (Table 7.6).

A comparison between the Rosstat estimates and the alternative estimates for 1999–2003 is set out in Table 7.7.

On average, the official data exceeded the alternative estimates by about three per cent a year, with the biggest differences being in 1999–2000.

For a very preliminary estimate of GDP growth in 2004, I used the relationship between the growth of domestic consumption of fuel in 2001–03 and the alternative estimate of GDP growth, which was extended to 2004. In 2001–03 domestic consumption of fuel increased by 8.1 per cent (Table 7.2) while GDP increased by 11.9 per cent. This means that the growth of the former exceeded that of the latter by 3.8 percentage points or 1.3 percentage points a year. In 2004, (apparent) domestic consumption of fuel rose by 1.3 per cent.[1] Hence, using this method, the GDP rose by 2.6 per cent instead of the 7.2 per cent calculated by Rosstat, which is a difference of more than 4 per cent. This result agrees with other indicators, for example the production of electricity, which increased in 2004 by only 1.6 per cent.[2] In addition, the volume of freight transport increased by only 2.4 per cent.[3] Hence all three indirect indicators of economic development give similar results.

It is significant that deflating the volume of industrial output in 2004 by the price index for industrial production in 2004 (December on December) gives an increase of industrial production of 3.2 per cent instead of the official 6.1 per cent. This confirms the huge overstatement of growth in the official statistics for 2004.

If one uses the sufficiently reliable indirect indicators of economic growth, a sharp decline in economic growth took place in 2004. And this was at a time of record world prices for oil. Furthermore, at the end of 2004 and the beginning of 2005 the growth of GDP even according to official data sharply declined. Bearing in mind the distortions in the official 2004 data, this may signify the end of economic growth in 2005 and even the beginning of economic decline. Whether this has happened, will of course require confirmation by calculations for 2005. At the moment of writing, for 2005 there is only the Rosstat data about the domestic market for oil products in the first half, which are evidence of the complete halt in the growth of this indicator in comparison with the comparable period for 2004. In addition, domestic consumption of gas declined. Furthermore, the rate of growth of freight transport fell by almost two-thirds.

In this period net disinvestment continued. Taking account of shadow incomes, the only profitable sectors were the extractive industries, the preliminary processing of raw materials (ferrous and non-ferrous metallurgy), the food industry, and the majority of market services. Almost all branches of manufacturing, agriculture, and transport, remained loss-making.

Analysis of the Economic Development of Russia in 1999–2004

Undoubtedly, the period 1999–2004 differs radically from the previous period (1990–98) which was a period of deep economic decline. As a result, many

---

[1] Calculated from data in *Sotsial'no-ekonomicheskoe polozhenie Rossii 2004g* (Moscow 2005) p. 105.
[2] Ibid p. 21.
[3] Ibid p. 80.

Table 7.8 Growth of Labour Productivity in Russia in 1999–2004 (% p.a.)

	1999	2000	2001	2002	2003	2004
1. Growth of GDP	1.2	7.6	3.4	3.0	6.2	2.9
2. Growth of number employed	0.0	0.6	0.6	1.0	0.5	0.4
3. Growth of labour productivity (2–1)	1.2	7.0	2.8	2.0	5.7	2.5

Russian and Western economists conclude that the Russian economy has already overcome its chief difficulties and created the conditions for stable economic growth in the future. To determine the perspectives for Russian economic development it is essential to analyse the causes of the economic growth in 1999–2004. I will begin this task with an analysis of the growth of labour productivity and of the labour force (Table 7.8). Labour productivity is calculated per year, because data on the number of hours worked is given in the statistical publications only for industry, is unsystematic, and not very reliable.

As Table 7.8 makes clear, economic growth—using labour productivity as the indicator—had a definite intensive character. Labour productivity growth for the whole period 1999–2004 significantly exceeded the growth in the number employed. The growth rate of hourly labour productivity was somewhat lower because the available data indicates a growth in the number of hours worked by approximately 1 per cent p.a.

It is much more complicated to determine what happened to the level and rate of change of the efficiency of fixed capital. The calculations of the dynamics of fixed capital, carried out by I.B. Voskoboinikov, myself and my colleagues, are very rough. They do not provide the possibility of calculating the year to year changes. The only thing that is clear is that in this period there continued, though at a slower rate than in the previous period, a reduction in fixed capital, especially in machines and equipment. This is confirmed by the data on the total availability of certain types of equipment, the reduction in productive capacity for various products and the increase in the average life of machinery in industry. Therefore, one can say with confidence that in this period there occurred an improved utilization of fixed capital in general and of machinery in particular.

An increase in labour productivity and an improvement in the utilization of fixed capital are characteristic features of a recovery period in the economy, i.e., a recovery from war or economic crisis.[1] At the beginning of a recovery

[1] E.G. Gaidar in his book *Dolgoe vremya* published in 2005, in a very knowledgeable analysis which takes account of the analogous NEP period in Soviet economic development, drew attention to this specific feature of the economic development of contemporary Russia.

period there are large unutilized reserves of labour and productive capacity. In the light of this specific factor (which has been neglected by many economists), neither the real rates of economic growth nor the improvement in the utilization of the factors of production are very impressive. They lag a long way behind the recovery periods in the USSR and in foreign countries after a war and (for capitalist countries) economic crises. Nevertheless, I certainly do not deny that there has been an important improvement in the economic mechanism of Russia since the financial crisis of 1998. There has been a significant growth in the professionalism of Russian entrepreneurs, which till then was on an extremely low level.

In the period considered, there has also been an improvement in the structure of the economy. As a result of the depreciation of the ruble and the growth of productivity and of consumer demand, there have been increases in the share of manufacturing and some science-intensive branches of the economy in GDP and in exports (measured in physical units), the share of expenditures on science in the GDP has grown, and the rate of investment has increased. However, the basic structural weaknesses of the Russian economy in the 1990s (the hypertrophied raw material and trading sectors, the low rates of investment and R&D, etc.) remained.

Usually completion of the recovery period is related to the achievement of the pre-crisis (or pre-war) level of output. I agree with the point of view of E.T. Gaidar (though not with his reasons for it) that in post-Soviet Russia the recovery period may end even before the achievement of the pre-crisis level of GDP. The point is that in the past the pre-crisis level of output and of fixed capital were reached simultaneously. The peculiarity of the economy of post-Soviet Russia is that there has been a significant decline in fixed capital, and especially machinery and equipment, compared with the pre-crisis level. It is this which leads to the recovery period in contemporary Russia ending before the pre-crisis level of GDP has been reached. This, possibly, happened at the end of 2004 and the beginning of 2005.

Perspectives for the Russian Economy: The Inertial Scenario

My evaluation of the perspectives for the Russian economy is based on an alternative estimate of the dynamics of its development over a long preceding period and its structure at the present time, the state of the moral and human potential of Russian society, and the specific features of Russian economic development in the past three to three and a half centuries.

There are two possible scenarios for the development of the Russian economy in the coming 10–15 years, the inertial and mobilization. In evaluating their possibilities it is necessary to bear in mind that the Russian economy at the present time faces colossal difficulties, which may be insurmountable. They are, the extreme ageing and rapid decline of fixed capital, the rapid diminution of reserves of raw materials, the huge reduction in intellectual potential as a result of the brain drain, the worsening in the quality of education and the cuts in the post-Soviet period in the scientific-intellectual sphere. The economic upswing of 1999–2004, as was pointed out in the previous section, was of a recovery type and as a result of the completion of recovery has practically ended. Moreover, it was assisted by a huge growth in the world price of fuel, which cannot carry on indefinitely.

The inertial scenario means the preservation of the socio-economic and political mechanism which has existed for the past 15 years. The current Russian socio-economic and political mechanisms are nonviable and extremely inefficient. This has been shown by myself and by a number of competent Russian economists, sociologists and political scientists (L. Shevtsova, I. Klyamkin, D. Furman, V. Solovei and a number of others) and by the actual situation of the Russian economy in the past 15 years. With respect to the economy they quickly improved after 1998, but their current situation is such, it seems to me, that their economic maturity, relying on the weak intellectual and management resources available, would require decades. This is shown by the experience of other countries and the analogous problems in pre-revolutionary Russia. Just look at the state of corporate governance, the bank and insurance system and the securities market. Possible improvements in this system, undertaken on the initiative of the state and using state pressure, can only lead to a quantitative but not qualitative improvement in their efficiency. This is what has happened in the past 15 years. The most effective method of such an improvement is the intensified attraction of foreign capital, which was the main factor in the economic upswing in many countries of Eastern Europe. However, the barriers to the attraction of foreign capital to Russia are much greater than in those countries. The reasons for this are too well known to need repeating here.

Possible attempts to stimulate economic growth by Keynesian methods, it seems to me, can give only a limited result. This is because the basic barriers to economic growth in contemporary Russia are not on the demand side but on the supply side, which is poorly reflected in official statistics (this concerns not just fixed capital but also labour and natural resources).

In evaluating the prospects for the inertial model, it is necessary to take account of the human and moral state of Russian society. It is difficult to give them a statistical value, but they are reflected in productivity, and also in the learning activity of the members of society. Judging by its manifestation in various spheres of social life, this potential has been continuously worsening in recent decades. This is demonstrated by the passive attitude of the overwhelming majority of the population to the disintegration of society in the concluding stage of stagnation; the unimpeded theft of national wealth in the perestroika and post-Soviet period; the shoving aside—even more so in the post-Soviet than in the Soviet period—of the best people, in a professional and moral sense, from the management of society and particular social organizations; and the dying away of constructive social activity in the post-Soviet period. The emigration in the Soviet and post-Soviet periods of the most talented and energetic members of society, and the sharp worsening of the quality of education, in particular higher education, contributed to the degradation of human potential.

In the best, and improbable (as a result of the intellectual and administrative weakness of the state and of domestic entrepreneurship) case the inertial variant may prevent a reduction in the GDP in the coming 10–15 years. However, this is absolutely inadequate for resolving the serious socio-economic and geopolitical problems of Russia. More likely is a reduction of GDP in the coming 10–15 years by 20–30 per cent as a result of the reduction in fixed capital (the volume of machinery and equipment used in the goods sector is currently declining, according to our rough calculations, by 2–3 per cent p.a.) combined with the absence of a radical change in the share of investment in GDP, which most likely will lead to a social and political explosion.

In evaluating the state of fixed capital, it is necessary to bear in mind that its obsolescence, which is very high even according to official statistics, is understated. This is because the value of old fixed capital with high rates of obsolescence in the total value of fixed capital is understated because it has not been revalued according to its replacement cost. According to calculations for the electricity generation sector carried out by D.A. Fomin, the understatement of the obsolescence of fixed capital is more than ten percentage points. With such large obsolescence of fixed capital it is practically inevitable that there will be some technological catastrophes.

The Historical Experience of Russia in Overcoming Economic Backwardness

The economic lag of Russia behind the developed countries, which began already in the 1970s–1980s, acquired particularly serious dimensions in the post-Soviet period. One might wonder whether it will ever be possible to reduce this gap somewhat. However, three times in its history Russia has been in an analogous position: at the end of the seventeenth century, in the middle of the nineteenth century, and at the end of the 1920s. Study of Russian economic development in these three periods is therefore of special interest. I will set out here in brief the conclusions of my earlier research on this experience and the lessons to be drawn from it.[1]

Of the three attempts to overcome economic backwardness two were successful, the period of Peter the Great and his successors and the period of the classical command economy model (in the 1930s–1950s of the twentieth century). The attempt to overcome economic backwardness after the abolition of serfdom was unsuccessful, despite significant progress by the Russian economy in this period. Similarly, the attempt to overcome economic backwardness by means of the New Economic Policy of the 1920s (NEP) was also unsuccessful, hence the need for the transition to the command economy.[2] The lag behind the developed countries increased with the transition from the classical model of the command economy to the liberal model in the 1960s–1980s and still more in the 1990s of the twentieth century.

What unites the successful and unsuccessful attempts to overcome economic backwardness? The successful attempts were linked to a mobilization model of the economy and an authoritarian political regime. The unsuccessful, with the development of market relations in the economy and a liberal political system. The conclusion, it would seem, is obvious. An authoritarian political system is necessary, which is able to use force to mobilize the immense resources necessary for overcoming economic backwardness. However, things are not so simple. It proved impossible to continue the successful beginning of a catch-up process. Fifty or sixty years after the economic leap, carried out by an authoritarian regime, a period of economic stagnation set in. The suppression of civil and political rights and economic initiatives in the period of the leap did not permit the creation of the mechanism of a self-regulating economy. In this the situation differed from that in Western countries. The inevitability under these conditions of a slowing down of economic growth and hence the necessity of a certain democratization of society and decentralization of the economy was understood even by Stalin at the end of his life.[3]

Another specific feature of Russian economic development, as can be seen from what has already been said, consists of development by leaps, from stagnation to rapid growth, followed by new stagnation and new rapid growth. Of course, uneven economic growth in the long-run took place also in Western countries. However, nowhere has it been as significant as in Russia. A number of Russian authors (e.g., A.A. Prokhorov) have connected this

[1] For further details see my article, Teoriya ryvka i opyt Rossii po preodoleniyu ekonomicheskoi otstalosti, *EKO*, 2004, No. 9.

[2] Khanin, G I, 1989, Pochemu i kogda pogib NEP, *EKO*, No. 11.

[3] Khanin, G I, 2005, Stalin initsiator perestroiki i liberalizatsii? (gipoteza) *EKO*, No. 9.

peculiarity of Russian economic development with the national character of the Russian people, formed by agricultural production characterized by a switch between intense work in the summer and relaxation in the winter. A deeper explanation was offered more than forty years ago by the outstanding American economist Alexander Gerschenkron, '... a period of rapid development was very likely to give way to prolonged stagnation, because the great effort had been pushed beyond the physical endurance of the population.'[1]

Despite the harmful effects of the development of the economy by leaps, in the current miserable situation of the Russian economy such a past gives hope for a new leap, which will once more allow the beginning of a process of overcoming Russian economic backwardness.

The Technology of an Economic Leap in Russia

Study of the previous successful economic leaps permits the singling out of a number of socio-economic and political elements necessary for implementing an economic leap.[2] First, obviously, is a sharp increase in the share of investment in the GDP or national income. Such an increase is necessary for a rapid increase in the capital stock. The share of investment in the national income of the USSR at the beginning of the 1930s, taking account of the underpricing of investment goods, was 40–45 per cent, a threefold increase in just a few years. Second, a buildup in human capital by big investments in education and science, and the invitation of foreign specialists. Third, an increase in the motivation of skilled work by a sharp differentiation in wages and salaries depending on qualifications and raising the social prestige of skilled work. Fourth, putting forward an attractive national idea, which can inspire the population and justify the inevitable sacrifices during the economic leap. Fifth, the leading role of the state in implementing the leap as a result of the weakness of domestic private capital. Sixth, a renewal of the governing stratum. This is dictated by the fact that the old ruling stratum was formed during the economic decline, or in the most favourable case, stagnation. In these periods energetic, talented and honest people are not needed. Seventh, the existence of wise and strong rulers. Up till now, sad to relate, this was always linked to the establishment in Russia of a strict authoritarian regime, implemented by dictators with strategic goals, a high organizational capacity, and the ability to select officials for the resolution of the problems confronting the country.

[1] Quoted from Hedlund, S, 2003, Can they go back and fix it?, *Acta Slavica Japonica* Vol. 20 (Slavic Research Center, Hokkaido University), pp. 52–53.
[2] For further details see my article, Tekhnologiya ekonomicheskogo ryvka v Rossii, *EKO*, 2004, No. 10.

Eighth, the sensible utilization of foreign economic relations for economic development.

Even if we ignore the large number of victims of such a policy, and hence its desirability, this technology for overcoming economic backwardness, tried and tested in the past, may not be successful in the new economic and technological conditions of the economy of the twenty-first century. Hence, naturally, it will require serious modification.

A Mobilization Scenario for the Contemporary Russian Economy

Analysis of the previous periods of implementation of a mobilization scenario allows one to pick out the following components of a mobilization scenario for the economic development of Russia relevant for current conditions.

First, a sharp increase in the share of investment in fixed capital compared to the current level which—taking account of the real purchasing power of the ruble in various sectors of final use of the GDP according to international comparisons—is 10 per cent[1] at the present time, to 35–40 per cent. This should be achieved by a sharp reduction in household consumption, in particular the consumption of the better-off households. In view of its exceptional importance I consider it necessary to discuss this component of the mobilization scenario in the greatest detail.

It is required by the need, given the almost full utilization of the current productive capacity (according to the calculations of myself and my colleagues and also of I.B. Voskoboinikov) for a growth of the capital stock by about 6–7 per cent per year for the next 15 years to overcome the economic backwardness of Russia, which arose in the post-Soviet period, and provide a further stable growth of the economy. Such a growth of the capital stock requires an approximately threefold (allowing for investment in the shadow economy) increase in the share of investment in the economy, [2] with the predominant share of the investment in the goods sector. It should be noted that the need for a radical increase in the share of investment in the GDP has also been argued by other Russian economists. The first was K.K. Val'tukh already in 1997. He was followed by V.M. Simchera and F. Klotsvog. Their

[1] The Japanese economist Professor Tabata in several works has drawn attention to the importance of recalculating the official statistics on the share of investment in the GDP. See, for example, Tabata, S, 1997, The investment crisis in Russia, *Post-Soviet Geography and Economics*, Vol. 38, No. 9, p. 562.

[2] For the derivation of this estimate see Khanin, G I, Tekhnologiya ekonomicheskogo ryvka, p. 168. However, this article does not take account of investment in the shadow economy, especially in services.

calculations of the necessary increase in investment were similar to mine. However, these authors did not suggest a way to achieve this increase.

We now have relatively reliable data on the distribution of income by decile group.[1] This enables one to determine the reduction in the incomes of the population necessary to mobilize the financial resources for investment and also for an increase in the incomes of the poorest sections of the population. Taking account of the possibility of mobilizing the excessive positive foreign trade balance, the amount by which it is necessary to reduce total personal incomes is approximately one third. While raising the incomes of the poorest sections of the population, the incomes of the middle strata could be left as they were. The resulting increase in the incomes of the poor will be fairly modest (50–100 per cent). Hence about 10 per cent of the population would lose out from the proposed income redistribution. About 20 per cent would gain. The decile ratio would fall from the current 26:1 to 5:1, which is the level of several East European countries and of the pre-reform USSR. There would persist a huge difference in the ownership of wealth between households, which the richest—though with some difficulty—could turn into current income. Calculations of the proposed income redistribution are set out in Table 7.9.

As a result of this income redistribution, household consumption would fall by 2.6 trillion rubles. Investment needs to increase by 4 trillion rubles. The difference could be obtained by reducing the positive foreign trade balance from its current 2.1 trillion rubles (11.2 per cent of GDP) to 0.3–0.4 trillion rubles (2 per cent of GDP), a more normal level by international standards. This would enable 1.8 trillion rubles to be directed towards investment and leave something over for the improvement of human capital (e.g., science, education, medical care). This may require a few extra percent of the GDP, which could be mobilized by using the huge resources of the Stabilization Fund, of the gold and foreign exchange reserves of the central bank, and the return of part of the capital stolen from Russia.

The redistribution of income would sharply alter the real financial situation in Russia. At the present time this is very distorted by the huge undervaluation

---

[1] Previously, as a result of a justifiable lack of confidence in official data about income distribution, I used for calculating the size of the redistribution the data of a 1997 survey carried out by the Institute for Socio-Economic Problems of the Population of the Russian Academy of Sciences. It is now apparent that this exaggerated the extent of income differentiation. The data I currently use comes from a large survey (15,000 people in 408 places) carried out in the autumn of 2004 by the Institute of Social Planning and the company Romir Monitoring which was published in *Ekspert*, 2005, No. 19. The reliability of this research is confirmed by the coincidence of incomes, calculated on the basis of this research, with the total incomes of the Russian population according to the SNA, and the most plausible estimates of the distribution of income in Russia (A.Yu. Shevyakov, S.A. Aivazyan).

Table 7.9 The Redistribution of Incomes in Russia in 2007–08 (2004 Prices & Incomes)

No. of groups	Annual average income per person (thousand rubles)	No. of people (million)	Annual income before redistribution (billion rubles)	% of income remaining after redistribution	Annual income after redistribution (billion rubles)
1	2	3	4	5	6
1[a]	4500.0	0.4	1800.0	16.6	298.9
2	300.0	2.64	792.0	40.0	316.8
3	180.0	3.82	687.6	40.0	275.0
4	120.0	8.08	969.6	40.0	387.8
5	96.0	7.94	762.2	100.0	766.2
6	67.2	30.6	2056.3	100.0	2056.3
7	42.0	14.7	617.4	100.0	617.4
8	27.6	45.6	1258.6	100.0	1258.6
9	25.2	7.3	184.0	150.0	276.0
10	18.0	7.1	127.8	200.0	255.6
11	9.6	14.3	137.3	200.0	274.6
Total		142.8	9693.0		6806.1

Note: [a] Approximate.
Source: Calculated from *Ekspert*, 2005, No.19 p.35. The total of column 3 does not coincide with the total Russian population because the percentage distribution given in the article is less than 100%.

of fixed capital, which according to our calculations, which are based on the calculations of the replacement cost of capital using the investment output ratio, is more than tenfold.[1] Hence the level of depreciation is underestimated and the share of net profit in the economy is exaggerated. To determine the real level of depreciation it is necessary to correct the official estimates for this underestimate. However, to increase it by the amount of the underestimation (i.e., tenfold) would be wrong because the rate of depreciation—as is shown by a comparison of its level in 2001 according to the System of National Accounts (SNA) (this was the last year for which this data has been published)—greatly exceeds (by about two and a half times) real obsolescence in the majority

[1] See the following articles:Khanin, G I, and Ivanchenko, N V, 2003, Al'ternativnaya otsenka material'nykh fondov i rentabel'nosti v proizvodstvennoi sfere rossiiskoi ekonomiki, *Voprosy statistiki*, No. 9; Khanin, G I, and Fomin, D A, 2004, Al'ternativnaya otsenka rentabel'nosti rossiiskogo sel'skogo khozyaistva v 2001 godu, *Voprosy statistiki*, No. 2; Khanin, G I, and Fomin, D A, 2005, Tsena torgovli, *EKO*, No. 6; Khanin, G I, and Fomin, D A, 2005, Prodovol'stvennyi kompleks Rossii: al'ternativnaya otsenka finansogo-ekonomicheskikh pokazatelei, *Problemy prognozirovaniya*, No. 3.

Table 7.10 The Structure of GDP by Primary Incomes Before and After the Redistribution of Incomes in 2007–08 (Trillions of Rubles, 2004 Prices)

Type of income	Before redistribution	After redistribution
Wages and salaries	8.2	5.7
Net taxes on production and imports	2.8	2.8
Depreciation	5.1	5.1
Net profits and mixed incomes	1.2	3.7
Total	17.3	17.3
Share of net profits and mixed incomes in GDP (%)	7.0	21.3
Net profit and mixed incomes as % of fixed assets	2.2	6.8

Notes:

(1) This table compares the structure of primary incomes as it was in 2004 and as it would have been had the hypothetical income redistribution of 2007-08 been implemented in 2004.

(2) The data on the 2004 allocation of primary incomes (with the exception of depreciation) are from the Rosstat website.

(3) The data for depreciation is an estimate of mine based on the Rosstat data for depreciation in 2001 and the relationship between replacement costs and balance sheet values. Replacement costs were calculated by me on the basis of data on the relationship between replacement costs and balance sheet values for a number of sectors of the Russian economy at the beginning of the twenty-first century and are approximate.

(4) A large share of net mixed incomes and net profit is comprised of personal incomes (dividends and the profits of unincorporated businesses).

of sectors and in the economy as a whole. This is probably a result of the use of excessive depreciation rates by many enterprises to compensate for the underestimate of the value of fixed assets. Therefore, I raised the volume of depreciation fourfold, which most likely underestimates it. Table 7.10 gives the distribution of the GDP before the redistribution of personal income (but with the recalculated share of depreciation) and after the redistribution.

The result of the redistribution of income is significantly to increase the absolute size and share of profits and net mixed incomes, which combined with the fourfold increase in depreciation, provides the financial resources for the growth of fixed capital and of human capital. In this way, the current excessive personal incomes of proprietors and top-managers, directly or indirectly raising production costs and reducing profits, could be used as a source of economic growth.

The realization of other components of the mobilization model, which were discussed in the previous section, are just as urgent as in the time of Peter the Great and Stalin. I have in mind, strengthening the motivation of highly qualified personnel, undermined in the stagnation and post-Soviet periods; a very substantial renewal of the rotten and incompetent ruling stratum; the formation of a strong and wise state instead of the current weak and stupid one; the sensible utilization of foreign economic relations, combining the advantages of the international division of labour and attracting foreign capital and technical and managerial experience, with the defence and support of promising domestic production; and promoting the modernization of the economy as the national idea of Russia. This last point requires more detailed explanation.

The reduction in the standard of living of a large and very active part of the population could obtain, if not support, then at any rate understanding, if it were justified by the patriotic idea of national salvation, which is what the idea of economic modernization is. In this connection, it is important that the burden of implementing the economic modernization is borne not only by ordinary people, which was always the case in Russia in the past, but also by the ruling stratum, which today has unreasonably enriched itself. The income redistribution should begin with the incomes of the richest sections of the population, so as to justify the absence of redistribution towards the middle sections of the population and the modest number of beneficiaries from the income redistribution.

It is obvious that the realization of the mobilization strategy means very substantial alterations in the structure of the Russian economy. The aim of these alterations is to create a more diversified and competitive (on the internal and external markets) economy, which is able in the future to provide the rapid and stable development of the Russian economy. To achieve these goals it is necessary to create an economy which relies not just on the raw material sectors, as at the present time, but also on many others, several branches of manufacturing industry re-equipped on new technological bases, agriculture, a modern housing-utilities sector, transport and communications, roads, etc. Particular attention should be paid to infrastructure sectors which are in a difficult situation because of the obsolescence of their capital stock, e.g., electrical generation, railway transport and housing-utilities. The choice of concrete priority sectors requires an inventarization of the Russian economy and a careful economic analysis of their economic and technological condition both at the national level and at the level of big firms and groups of firms.

In this connection it should be noted that the current actual loss-making situation of a large part of Russian manufacturing is not a result of a fatal inability of Russia to produce competitive manufactured products, but of the outdated nature of its productive capacities, resulting from the inadequate attention to this sector in the Soviet and post-Soviet periods, and the excessive incomes of the owners and top-managers in the post-Soviet period who in effect have often played havoc with their enterprises. It is only possible here to outline other possible changes. Currently the share in the economy of market services, primarily oriented to meeting the needs of the rich, and as shown by our calculations relatively profitable, on the level of the oil and natural gas industries,[1] is hypertrophied. With the proposed reduction in household incomes of one third, this sector would inevitably be sharply squeezed. This might create a crisis in the loan-financed retail property sector, which is also oriented to the demand of the well-off part of the population, and often serves as an attractive investment for surplus funds.

The approximate three-fold increase of investment in the economy will require a huge increase in the output of the engineering and construction sectors and of the building materials industry. Partly this might be possible by utilizing existing capacity, since there still exists some unused capacity, partly it would require substantial expansion of existing capacities and the development of green-field plants using the latest technologies. The resources unavailable internally should be imported, as a result of which the import of equipment would rise sharply at the cost of the import of consumer goods. For a number of years, till the coming on stream of the new and expanded plants, these imports would be the main source of investment goods and occupy the main place in Russia's imports, as was the case in the first five-year plan. A major obstacle to the expansion of the output of engineering is the lack of skilled workers and of engineering-technical personnel, and the extreme weakness of the design and development organizations. These sectors require great efforts for their regeneration and development.

At the same time the light and food industries, which are oriented to the cheap segments of the domestic market, might grow, despite the reduction in aggregate consumer demand. The volume and structure of foreign trade would change substantially. The volume of exports would fall sharply, because many kinds of output, currently oriented to the foreign market because of the limited domestic market, would substantially increase deliveries to the growing internal market for intermediate and investment goods (for example, ferrous and non-ferrous metals, the fuel industry).

One could anticipate also a considerable change in the income differences between the biggest cities, currently flourishing, largely as a result of the large incomes of the trading sector and from corruption (in particular Moscow and St. Petersburg) and the remaining regions and rural areas.

What institutional conditions are required for implementing the mobilization strategy? Theoretically one can imagine the modernization strategy being implemented within the framework of the existing socio-economic system. Private

---

[1] Khanin, G I, and Fomin, D A, 2005, Tsena torgovli, *EKO*, No. 6.

entrepreneurs in order to increase their competitiveness might on their own reduce the incomes of their employees (particularly the highly paid ones) and owners. In this connection it should be noted that recently a general meeting of the shareholders of RAO UES (the national electricity generating company) reduced by three quarters the pay of the members of the Board of Directors. However, the low level of social and professional culture of the overwhelming majority to Russian entrepreneurs makes this possibility, in my opinion, highly unlikely. Furthermore, with the existing organization of the Russian economy it is difficult to take seriously the possibility of mobilizing the immense financial resources of private entrepreneurs for the reconstruction of whole branches of manufacturing industry. The new generation of Russian entrepreneurs has prospered in services. Production, especially manufacturing, requires much greater technical and organizational abilities. Here at the moment only foreign entrepreneurs are flourishing (e.g., in the motor car industry).

In this system one can imagine an active role for the state in altering the structure of the economy, for example with the help of a flexible system of taxes to help priority sectors of the economy and increased taxation of currently hypertrophied sectors such as trade. Also other instruments of industrial policy used in market economies could be employed. However, there is no assurance that these methods of state regulation which have worked in other countries would work in Russia. The difference between the behaviour and professional qualities of entrepreneurs and officials in these countries and in Russia is huge.

Hence it is most likely that the main subject for the modernization of the Russian economy will be the state, possibly in partnership with private capital. The state will have to apply massive efforts to achieve the redistribution of incomes. This would require either strict supervision of the owners of financial resources or the nationalization of the most profitable sectors of the economy. Furthermore, it would be necessary to use all the instruments of income redistribution known from international experience (high tax rates on the income of the wealthy, wealth taxes on the rich, high indirect taxes on luxuries, etc.).

Could an Economic Leap be Successful in Today's Russia?

The fact that in the past a mobilization strategy was successful in overcoming economic backwardness does not give any assurance that these achievements (which were at the cost of large numbers of victims) could be repeated at the present time. The mechanical application of past experience might be fruitless. There is a great difference between the character of the economy in the past and now. Now what is particularly important is the creation of the conditions for the development of the initiative and creativity of the population. However, I see the biggest problem as the low level of the political leadership of Russia and the degradation of the human and moral potential of the country. Whether it is possible to resolve this difficult question is outside the competence of an economist. However, the achievement of an average growth rate of GDP of 3–4 per cent p.a., although it would be difficult, is an entirely realistic task. A higher growth rate of 6–7 per cent p.a. would require colossal effort and its achievement would seem almost impossible. Still, sometimes Russia has been able to do the almost impossible.

8

THE IMPORTANCE OF GEOGRAPHY

Vladimir Kontorovich[1]

Entrepreneurship and geography are both important factors of economic development. Both have been recognized as posing problems for the long-run growth of the Russian economy. This chapter looks at a possible connection between these two factors.

Stunted Entrepreneurship

Theoretical arguments about the importance of new business creation for economic growth are usually traced back to Josef Schumpeter, and have been further developed in the last 25 years in the context of models of industry evolution. Empirical evidence in support of this proposition has long remained fragmentary, as in Audretsch (2002, pp. 17–27). Comprehensive data on firm dynamics across many countries now make it possible to estimate the contribution of firm births and deaths to the growth of labor productivity, which turns out to be significant (Bartelsman, *et al.* 2004, pp. 32–44). Unlike the mature market economies, where the annual number of firm births closely matches that of deaths, the more successful Eastern European economies have seen explosive growth in the number of new firms in the 1990s (Bartelsman *et al.* 2004, pp. 15–17). Indeed, it is argued that their success was, in large part, a result of this growth (McMillan and Woodruff 2002).

Data on firm births and deaths in Russia are not available, and published data on the total number of firms appear to be deeply flawed (Kontorovich 2005, pp. 243–4). Net new business creation can be approximated by the change in the number of small firms, since most firms are born small, and at any moment in time the vast majority of existing firms are also small (Audretsch 2002, p. 20; Bartelsman *et al.* 2004, p. 18). In this chapter, data on

[1] I thank Gregory Brock, Julian Cooper, Wolfram Schrettl, and Shinichiro Tabata for helpful suggestions.

the number of small businesses are used as an indicator of the process of creative destruction. There is a strain of literature that argues that small businesses possess special virtues and therefore deserve preferential treatment (reviewed in Beck, *et al.* 2005). This is not my concern here.

Russia experienced a short growth spurt in its total number of small firms in 1992–93 followed by a ten-year period of stagnation (Iasin, *et al.* 2004, pp. 22–7).[1] The lull in net new business formation has outlasted the depressed conditions of the 1990s, the shock of 1998, and at least five years of the subsequent recovery.[2] This leaves the number of small businesses per capita in Russia at a level several times lower than in the European Union (Ministerstvo 2001). The anemic state of entrepreneurship, as evidenced by the apparent dearth of net new business formation, is a potential constraint on the country's long-term growth prospects.

The data on the number of small firms, on which the diagnosis of an entrepreneurship gap is based and which are used throughout this paper, overstate the number of active businesses. This happens because some firms which ceased operation or never got off the ground are not eliminated from the state register in a timely fashion. The national census of small businesses in 2000–01 shed light on the dimensions of this data problem, which is not unique to Russia. Only three quarters of the more than 833,300 firms targeted by the census responded to the mailed questionnaire, with non-responders being a mix of currently inactive firms, firms in the process of shutting down and others.[3] In the period considered here, tax law contained hardly any real concessions for small firms (Iasin *et al.* 2004, pp. 66–9). The very stability of the number of small firms suggests that the use of this legal status for tax evasion purposes was not a significant problem, unlike with that of individual entrepreneur (PBOIuL).[4] Data on employment and sales of the small firms, while illuminating the development of this sector *per se*, are less relevant to the issue at hand—new business creation—and are subject to distortions of their own.

Since the Russian entrepreneurship gap was first noticed in the mid-1990s, two types of studies related to it have appeared: rankings of various burdens on existing small businesses in the country and comparative international measures of barriers to entrepreneurship. The latter studies are better positioned to explain stagnation in the number of small businesses, but so far have not

---

[1] I discuss how the data on the number of small businesses are compiled, and the possible benign interpretations of that number's stagnation in Kontorovich (1999) and Kontorovich (2005, pp. 243–8, 261–2).

[2] A 7 per cent jump in the number of small businesses in 2004 may signal the end of stagnation (Rosstat 2005, p. 166).

[3] 'Osnovnye ....', p. 6. See also 'O khode ....' 2001, p. 17.

[4] Among others, top officials of Yukos were using this status to reduce their personal taxes.

produced any strong conclusions. Russia ranks high on some of Djankov *et al.*'s (2002) indicators of regulatory entry barriers for limited liability companies in 85 countries, and falls in the middle range for others. Johnson *et al.* (2002) found that in 1997, Russia lagged significantly behind Poland, Slovakia and Romania in the frequency of extortion by government and non-government actors, tax burden and effectiveness of courts in enforcing contracts. They found that secure property rights are both necessary and sufficient for investment by small firms in these countries. Blanchflower *et al.* (2001) report on subjective attitudes towards being self-employed vs. an employee across 25 countries, with a third of Russians preferring the former, as compared to 50 per cent of Hungarians, 58 per cent of Slovenians and 80 per cent of Poles.

Regional Disparities in the Number of Small Businesses

Another approach to investigating the entrepreneurship gap would be to exploit variations in the number of small firms by region. Since the early 1990s, the distribution of small businesses across the country has been highly uneven, with a massive concentration in the cities of Moscow and St. Petersburg (Iasin *et al.* 2004, p. 25). In 2002, these two cities accounted for more than 30 per cent of all small businesses in the country. Moscow and St. Petersburg also had the highest number of firms per 1,000 inhabitants, or small business density (18.3 and 19.2), among Russia's 79 regions. The average national density in 2002 was 6.1, the median 4.2 (Belgorod region) and the minimum 0.5 (Dagestan).[1]

The almost 40-fold gap between the maximum and minimum regional business density appears to be extraordinarily large. For comparison, in the United States in 2002, the highest density of employer firms (33.0, in Wyoming) was only twice as high as the lowest (16.7 in Missisippi). The range for the density of non-employer firms was similar, from 46.7 in West Virginia to 88.0 in Vermont.[2] This is in keeping with Hanson's (2005, p. 300) finding that regional disparities in post-Communist Russia are much greater than in the West. Note also that the density of small businesses in Russia's two capital cities is about the same as the national average density of employer businesses in the US, even though the latter is a broader concept than the former. The key to Russia's entrepreneurship deficit appears to lie in the provinces.

[1] Korotetskii (2004, p. 65) states, without indicating a source, that Moscow's share of individual entrepreneurs who do not set up legal entities is lower (170 thousand out of 4,630 thousand nationally) than its share of the nation's population. There are serious problems with statistics on this legal form (Kontorovich 2005, pp. 246–7), and their regional breakdown has not been published.
[2] US business densities calculated using SBA1 and SBA2 data on the number of firms and US Census (2003, p. 21) data on population.

Presently observed firm populations are the cumulative result of the births and deaths over the past 15 years. Since data on deaths are not available, the reduced form explanation has to be used, relating the number of firms directly to the factors impacting the costs and benefits of running a business.

In an earlier paper, I tested a number of variables for their ability to shed light on regional variation in small business density (Kontorovich 2005, pp. 254–8). With two exceptions, the variables were selected because of data availability (in the statistical yearbooks). I used per capita gross regional product and per capita personal income deflated by the cost of a fixed food basket as measures of market size; the murder rate and crime rate as proxies for safety of life and property; expert ratings of the regions' democratization and economic liberalization as proxies for regulatory climate; and distance from Moscow and average January temperature as factors of cost of doing business in the region. In regressions of small business density by region in 2001 on these variables in the same or previous year, many of the coefficients had the wrong sign, and most were not statistically significant at anywhere near the conventional levels.

The only variables that were statistically significant and had the correct sign were the share of urban population in the region, its population density and a seaport dummy. These three variables alone explained more than two thirds of the variation in small business density across 79 regions. The usually discussed barriers to new business creation—the cost of regulation, safety of property rights and access to capital—were not investigated for lack of data (they are not part of the regular statistical reporting system). Studies that have investigated these barriers (Djankov *et al.* 2002; Simon and McMillan 2002) used data sets specifically developed for the purpose. To the degree that access to capital and regulatory burdens matter for the differential rates of birth and survival of Russian small businesses, the estimates with the three geographic variables are likely to be biased.

Barriers to New Business Formation Across Regions

In recent years, several data sets relevant to barriers to new business formation were compiled for some of Russia's regions. These can be combined with the three geographic variables in a more plausible specification of the small business density equation.

Transparency International (2002) studied several aspects of official corruption in 40 regions of Russia, based on a survey of 1,838 small and medium entrepreneurs.[1] They published data on the number, average size and total amount of bribes given by the businessmen in a region; indexes of businessmen's

[1] The date of the survey is not indicated, but judging from dates on their online materials, it was probably early 2002.

confidence in federal, regional and local authorities, as well as in the executive, legislative and judicial branches and the police; indexes of the degree of corruption of these branches and levels of government; and indexes of three aspects of official corruption (extortion, capture of the state by business and official capture of business).

I regressed small business density in these 40 regions in 2001 on measures of corruption and the three geographic variables.[1] The number, size and total amount of bribes, as well as administrative extortions and business capture variables turned out not to be statistically significant. State capture was significant at the 10 per cent level, but had the wrong sign (positive). The port dummy was also not significant, with so many ports excluded from the sample. Population density and share of urban population were both highly statistically significant. Excluding the two capital cities (with their extraordinarily high values of the dependent variable) from the sample did not change the picture: corruption variables either lacked statistical significance, or had the wrong signs, or both. The same was true when growth in the number of small businesses in 1999–2002 was used as the dependent variable.

Since 2002, the Russian research organization CEFIR (Centre for Economic and Financial Research at the New Economic School, Moscow) has periodically monitored barriers to small business development based on interviews with businessmen in 20 regions. They derive the length of time needed to complete the process of entry, number of person-days spent on gaining entry and the ruble cost of the process. They also rank regions in terms of various aspects of the regulatory burden, such as the frequency of official inspections, cost of registration, licensing and certification. The ability of these data to account for regional disparities in small business density is thrown into doubt by examining the rankings produced by the first survey in the spring of 2002. Moscow ranked the worst in terms of frequency of inspections, required the longest wait and had the second highest cost of entry. It fell in the middle of the sample with respect to the other indicators, together with St. Petersburg, another champion in business density. In a regression of small business density in 2001 on these variables obtained in the spring of 2002 (CEFIR 2002), coefficients were either not statistically significant, or had the wrong signs. Eliminating the two capital cities from the sample did not help.

The available measures of business conditions in the regions focus on factors that are commonly believed to be important for successful entry and survival of small businesses (e.g., Iakovlev 2005, p. 25). Yet they fail to explain any variation in the number of businesses per capita. Of course, it may be that the measures themselves are not refined enough. Alternately, these measures

---

[1] Details of the estimations are available from the author.

represent a snapshot of current business conditions, whereas small business density is the result of the past trajectory of these conditions (which may have seen significant change). Yet another possibility is that the predominant influence on small business density in a region is geographic factors.[1]

Geography and Firm Density

I estimated a regression with small business density by region at the end of 2002 as the dependent variable and three independent variables. Population density (persons per square kilometer) and percentage share of urban population by region according to 9 October 2002 population census (Goskomstat 2003) stand for different aspects of agglomeration.[2] Seaport dummy represents easier access to maritime transportation.[3]

The estimates are presented in Table 8.1 (Equation 1). Both population density and the share of urban population are significant at the 0.1 per cent level. One percentage point increase in the share of urban population in the region drives small business density up by 1.7 per cent of its median level. A change in population density of 10 persons/km^2, as between the Riazan and Smolensk regions, changes the median level of small business density by 0.03 per cent. The port dummy is significant at the 1.5 per cent level. Having a seaport adds 1.5 small businesses per 1,000 of population in the region. This is a strong influence, if we remember that the average small business density in 2002 was 6.1 and the median 4.2.

There is a problem with interpreting Equation 1 as showing a significant effect of agglomeration on small business density. Our sample combines two great cities and 77 regions, which include settlements of different sizes as well as unpopulated areas. Population density of 10,400 per km^2 in Moscow and 7,700 in St. Petersburg reflects the degree of agglomeration, as commonly understood. However, population density of 1.8 in Khabarovsk *krai* does not mean that economic activity occurs there in places with a population 1,000 times more sparse than in Moscow. What it means is that there is no economic activity on much of the region's territory. The share of urban population is a somewhat better measure of agglomeration, which in a binary fashion separates greater—urban—concentrations of population from smaller ones.

---

[1] Clearly, this analysis cannot pick up the effects of barriers to new business creation that are uniformly higher throughout Russian regions compared to other countries.

[2] To calculate population density separately in the two capitals and the surrounding regions, I used data on the area of Moscow and St. Petersburg as of 1993 from Gorkin (1998, pp. 363, 501).

[3] Regions coded as having a seaport are: Arkhangel'sk, Kaliningrad, Leningrad obl., Murmansk, St. Petersburg, Krasnodar, Rostov, Primorskii, Kamchatka, Magadan and Sakhalin.

Table 8.1 Regression Results for Small Business Density by Region in 2002

Independent variables	Equation 1*	Equation 2*	Equation 3**	Equation 4**
URBAN POPULATION				
SHARE: coefficient	0.073		0.074	
Standard error	*0.018*		*0.018*	
POPULATION				
DENSITY: coefficient	0.00125		0.011	
Standard error	*0.00015*		*0.008*	
SEAPORT: coefficient	1.54	2.22	1.43	1.40
Standard error	*0.62*	*0.81*	*0.64*	*0.66*
POPULATION SHARE in cities with 100K inhab-				
itants or more: coefficient		0.14		0.076
Standard error		*0.021*		*0.019*
POPULATION SHARE in cities with less than 100K				
inhabitants: coefficient		0.08		0.074
Standard error		*0.026*		*0.02*
INTERCEPT	–0.85	–3.36	–1.14	–0.96
Standard error	*1.22*	*1.49*	*1.24*	*1.22*
F statistic	49.9	20.69	10.18	9.89
Adjusted R^2	0.65	0.43	0.27	0.26

* 79 observations.
** 77 observations (w/o Moscow and St. Petersburg).

Available data make it possible to refine somewhat this crude measure of agglomeration by calculating the share of people in cities with 100,000 or more inhabitants in the region's population and the share of urban dwellers in cities with less than 100,000 inhabitants. Instead of different city sizes or regional employment densities, which are common independent variables in the studies of agglomeration (cited below), we now have shares of population in two classes of cities across regions. Equation 2 is estimated with small business density by region regressed on the share of regional population in cities with more than 100,000 residents, share of the smaller cities and the port dummy. Population density is dropped in this specification. Equation 2 has an adjusted *R*-squared lower than Equation 1, but is still respectable at 0.43 (Table 8.1). All variables are significant at the 1 per cent level, and the coefficient for the share of population in larger cities is twice as large as that for the share of smaller cities.

The two population shares are closely correlated (–0.69), but the *t*-statistics are all high enough to suggest that the estimates make sense. As an alternative,

I estimate the same equation substituting the share of non-urban population for the share of population in smaller cities. The correlation between the former variable and the share of population in large cities is smaller (–0.5). The resulting equation has an *F*-statistic and *R*-squared very close to that of Equation 2, all variables are highly significant, and the coefficient at non-urban population share is –0.08, while it is 0.06 at large-city population share. The effect of a one percentage point change in the share of population in cities with 100,000 or more inhabitants on small business density is close in magnitude to that of change in the share of all urban population in Equation 1.

Another way to see if the results reported above are a byproduct of mixing cities and regions in one sample is to exclude Moscow and St. Petersburg from the sample, and run the same specifications as Equations 1 and 2 for 77 regions. Capital cities are outliers: they have the highest levels of the dependent variable since 100 per cent of their population is urban and their population density is orders of magnitude higher than elsewhere. One may also wonder if the strength of geographic variables in Equations 1 and 2 is solely due to these two outliers. On the other hand, the concentration of small businesses in the two largest cities is the most outstanding characteristic of their spatial distribution, the thing most in need of explanation, so excluding these two particular outliers robs the analysis of some of its purpose.

Equation 3 in Table 8.1 replicates the specification of Equation 1 without the capital cities. Their exclusion reduces the variance of the dependent variable by more than a factor of 2 (the sum of squares is 337 instead of 738). Of this reduced variation, the three independent variables now explain only 27 per cent. The *F*-statistic for the whole relationship is highly significant. Population density is no longer statistically significant, but port dummy is significant at the 3 per cent level, despite the loss of a port (St. Petersburg) with a record density of small businesses, and the share of urban population is significant at the 0.1 per cent level. Equation 4 replicates the specification of Equation 2, but is estimated without the capital cities. It has a smaller *R*-squared, a highly significant *F*-statistic, and highly statistically significant coefficients for population share variables. Without the capital cities, the magnitude of the effect of changes in the region's share of population in large and small cities on small business density is the same. Geographic variables have survived the exclusion of the capital cities from the sample.

Discussion of the Results

The main finding of the previous section is the apparent strength of the agglomeration effect on new business formation and survival. The agglomeration effect, or external economies of proximity to other producers, is defined in terms of productivity. When firms locate near each other, sharing inputs produced with internal economies of scale, access to a larger labor pool, benefits from knowledge produced by others, and other mechanisms shift each firm's production function upward (Rosenthal and Strange 2004, pp. 2121–4).[1] These external economies are stronger, the greater the territorial concentration of activity. Studies using city size as a measure of concentration found that productivity and wages are higher in cities with larger populations (ibid. pp. 2133, 2140; Glaeser and Mare 2001). Density of population or employment is another way to measure the concentration of economic activity. Thus, Ciccone and Hall (1996) found that more than half of the variance in labor productivity across states in the US can be explained by differences in employment density (i.e., number of workers per acre of territory) measured at county level. Ciccone (2002) found that greater employment density has a similar effect on labor productivity across regions in five European countries.[2]

The closest that studies of the effects of agglomeration have come to our subject is in considering geographic variation in the rate of firm births. Spatial concentration of economic activity may increase the number of firm births per capita if profit-maximizing entrepreneurs are disproportionately drawn to more productive locales, those where agglomeration economies operate, as noted by Rosenthal and Strange (2003). They find that employment at existing firms, especially small ones, has a positive effect on the number of new business births in the area. Armington and Acs (2002) show that the number of establishments per 1,000 population, along with other variables, helps explain variation in firm births per 1,000 labor force across 394 labor market areas in the US.

That areas with higher population density have higher firm birth rates is suggestive, but does not by itself explain a higher density of existing firms, the phenomenon that stood out in our study of Russian small business. It is plausible to argue that competition is sharper in regions with high concentrations of population, and the death rates of firms are higher, with the overall effect of population concentration on firm density being indeterminate.

A different argument can be made by referring to the proposition that division of labor is limited by the extent of the market.[3] Greater concentrations of population afford more latitude for specialization, which gets embodied

[1] The list of channels through which agglomeration economies operate is probably incomplete because its exact nature is only partially understood (Anas, et al. 1998, p. 1454).

[2] Territorial concentration of population is a powerful factor also tied to effects such as the increase in the number of hours worked by people in professional occupations (Rosenthal and Strange 2004, p. 2143) and increased earnings inequality (Wheeler 2004).

[3] This old theoretical proposition has been recently finding systematic empirical support (Arora et al. 2005).

in more firms.[1] Indeed, Holmes (1999) found that in US manufacturing, establishments located in an area where their industry is concentrated are less vertically integrated (i.e., they buy rather than make themselves a larger share of their inputs), compared to establishments situated outside of industry hubs. I do not know of systematic studies of business density in market economies, but it has been observed that in the US, 'the five largest metropolitan areas taken as a whole have more non-farm establishments per capita than the country as a whole.' (Glaeser and Mare 2001, p. 317).

The impact of agglomeration on small business density in Russia appears much stronger than it is in the West. I estimated an analog of Equation 1 for the US, using data on the number of employer firms per 1,000 of population by state.[2] Port dummy and share of urban population have low levels of statistical significance, and the adjusted R-squared is 0.07. Using the share of metropolitan instead of urban population does not improve the regression. Also, direct comparisons are impossible because of different specifications of equations, but it takes more independent variables to explain two thirds of variation in the studies of firm births cited above than it does in our regressions.

A stronger effect of urban concentration may just mean that the pattern of settlement in Russia is very different from that in the US and from other established market economies. Urban concentration in the USSR was lower than in Western Europe (Demko and Fuchs 1984, p. 59). Size distribution of Soviet cities deviated from that predicted by Zipf's law, a regularity that holds for most other times and places (Gabaix 1999, p. 129; Rosen and Resnick 1980, p. 167). Clayton and Richardson (1989, p. 162) found that major Soviet cities were smaller than predicted by Zipf's law, and Hill and Gaddy (2003, pp. 17–21) reached the same conclusion for Russian cities.[3]

The effect of the port dummy on the small business density is less surprising than that of population density and city size. Access to maritime transportation is a well-known natural advantage of locating at the seashore, overland carriage being around seven times more expensive than sea-borne transport for the same distance (Redding and Venables 2002, p. 96).

---

[1] Greater specialization in production of intermediate goods in denser markets in turn contributes to agglomeration economies by lowering the cost to local downstream producers (Krugman 1991, p. 49).

[2] The seaport dummy was set to unity for states opening on either the Atlantic or Pacific coast, and zero otherwise.

[3] On Soviet policies concerning the regulation of city size, see, e.g., Jensen 1984. Deichmann and Henderson (2000, pp. 4–5) cite a UN study which finds that in Poland and elsewhere in Eastern Europe and Central Asia the extent of urban concentration has been modest by world standards, suggesting this may be a common legacy of central planning.

Conclusion

The ancient idea that geographic conditions matter for economic performance, is new to the literature on the Russian economy. When students of the Soviet economy wrote about regional economics, they focused primarily on how central planning influenced industrial location and settlement. This was but a reflection of a general professional deformation: mainstream economics largely ignored space (Krugman 1991, pp. 2–4).[1]

In the 1990s, geography was reintegrated into economics, both on the theoretical (Krugman 1991) and empirical (Gallup, *et al.* 1998) level. At the same time, the collapse of the Soviet system made transparent that many settlements in the northern and eastern regions were economically unsustainable (Kontorovich 2000; 2001). The drag on Russia's resources of subsidizing these territories became a subject of domestic public discussion (Parshev 2000), illuminating the economic cost of cold and distance that had been imposed by Soviet-era planning decisions (Hill and Gaddy 2003).

This chapter suggests that a distorted size distribution of cities has real economic costs, just as settling people beyond the Arctic Circle does. These results have been obtained using crude data, and therefore should be treated with caution. To confirm the existence and more confidently estimate the strength of the relationship between the concentration of economic activity and the number of firms per capita, it would be necessary to use data on a sub-regional level. One way of doing this would be to combine data on the number of small businesses by city with the published information on city size.

With this qualification in mind, the results suggest that a significant part of the entrepreneurship gap in Russia may be attributable to geographic factors, in particular, to the pattern of settlement inherited from the Soviet era. Since the distribution of population across the territory is slow to change, its suspected effects on entrepreneurship may be considered as a durable factor retarding economic development in Russia.

Bibliography

Anas, A, Arnott, R and Small K, 1998, Urban spatial structure, *Journal of Economic Literature*, Vol. 36, September.

Armington, C and Acs, Z J, 2002, The determinants of regional variation in new firm formation, *Regional Studies*, Vol. 36, No. 1.

Arora, A, Vogt, W B and Yoon, J, 2005, Is the division of labor limited by the extent of the market? Evidence from chemical industry, *SSRN Working Papers Series*.

[1] This may have been a part of a general decline in interest in geography in the American academy after 1945 (Landes 1999, p. 4). Note, however, that Richard Pipes's history starts with the overview of Russia's climate (Pipes 1974, pp. 1–7).

184   RUSSIA'S OIL AND NATURAL GAS

Audretsch, D B, 2002, The dynamic role of small firms: evidence from the US, *Small Business Economics*, Vol. 18.

Bartelsman, E J, Haltiwanger, J and Scarpetta, S, 2004, Microeconomic evidence of creative destruction in industrial and developing countries, The World Bank, Policy Research Working Paper No, 3464, October.

Beck, T, Demircgu-Kunt, A and Levine, R, 2005, SMEs, growth, and poverty, *NBER Working Paper 11224*, March.

Blanchflower, D G, Oswald, A and Stutzer, A, 2001, Latent entrepreneurship across nations, *European Economic Review*, 45.

CEFIR, 2002, http://www.cefir.ru/p_dereg.html, visited in May 2005.

Ciccone, A, 2002, Agglomeration effects in Europe, *European Economic Review*, Vol. 46.

Ciccone, A and Hall, R E, 1996, Productivity and the density of economic activity, *American Economic Review*, Vol. 86, No. 1, March.

Clayton, E and Richardson, T, 1989, Soviet control of city size, *Economic Development and Cultural Change*, Vol. 38, No. 1, October.

Deichmann, U and Henderson, V, 2000, Urban and regional dynamics in Poland, *Policy Research Working Paper 2457*, The World Bank.

Demko, G J and Fuchs, R J 1984, Urban policy and settlement system change in the USSR, 1897–1979, In: George J D and Roland J F, eds, *Geographical Studies of the Soviet Union. Essays in Honor of Chauncy D. Harris.* Chicago, The University of Chicago Press.

Djankov, S, La Porta, R, Lopes-de-Silanes, F and Shleifer, A, 2002, The regulation of entry, *Quarterly Journal of Economics* 117, Issue 1 (February).

Gabaix, X, 1999, Zipf's law and the growth of cities, *American Economic Review*, Vol. 89, No. 2, May.

Gallup, J L, Sachs, J D and Mellinger, D A, 1998, *Geography and Economic Development.* Cambridge, MA, National Bureau of Economic Research, *Working paper series no. 6849*, December.

Glaeser, E L and Mare, D C, 2001 Cities and skills, *Journal of Labor Economics*, Vol. 19, No. 2.

Gorkin, A P, ed., 1998, *Geografiia Rossii. Entsyklopediia*, Moscow, Bol'shaia Rossiiskaia Entsyklopediia.

Goskomstat, 2003, *Rossiiskii Statisticheskii Iezhegodnik 2003*, Moscow.

Hanson, P, 2005, Federalism with a Russian face: regional inequality and regional budgets in Russia, In: Reddaway, P and Orttung R, eds, *The Dynamics of Russian Politics*, Vol. 2, Lanham, MD, Rowman & Littlefield.

Hill, F and Gaddy, C, 2003, *The Siberian Curse. How Communist Planners Left Russia Out in the Cold*, Washington, DC, Brookings Institution Press.

Holmes, T J, 1999, Localization of industry and vertical disintegration, *Review of Economics and Statistics*, Vol. 81, No. 2, May.

Iasin, Ie G, *et al.*, eds, 2004, *Maloe predprinimatel'stvo v Rossii: proshloe, nastoiashchee i budushchee*, Moscow, Novoe izdatel'stvo.

Iakovlev, A, 2005, Tirazhirovat' luchshuiu praktiku, *Ekspert*, No. 28, July, pp. 25–31.

Jensen, R G, 1984, The anti-metropolitan syndrome in Soviet urban policy, In: Demko, G J and Fuchs, R. J, eds, *Geographical Studies of the Soviet Union. Essays in Honor of Chauncy D. Harris*, Chicago, The University of Chicago Press.

Johnson, S, McMillan, J and Woodruff, C, 2002, Property rights and finance, *American Economic Review* 92, No. 5, December.

Kontorovich, V, 1999, Has new business creation in Russia come to a halt?, *Journal of Business Venturing* 14, 5–6, pp. 451–60.

Kontorovich, V, 2000, Can Russia resettle the Far East?, *Post-Communist Economies and Transformation* 12, 3:, pp. 65–84, September.

Kontorovich, V, 2001, Economic crisis in the Russian Far East: overdevelopment or colonial exploitation?, *Post-Soviet Geography and Economy* 42, 6, pp. 391–415.

Kontorovich, V, 2005, Small business and Putin's federal reform, In: Reddaway, P and Orttung, R W, eds, *The Dynamics of Russian Politics, Volume 2: Putin's Reform of Federal-Regional Relations*, Lanham, MD, Rowman and Littlefield.

Korotetskii, I, 2004, Bez litsa, *Ekspert*, No. 8, March, pp. 1–7.

Krugman, P, 1991, *Geography and Trade*. Cambridge, MA, MIT Press.

Landes, D S, 1999, *The Wealth and Poverty of Nations*, New York, W. W. Norton and Co.

McMillan, J and Woodruff, C, 2002, The central role of entrepreneurs in transition economies, *Journal of Economic Perspectives*, 16:3, Summer, pp. 153–70.

Ministerstvo Rossiiskoi Federatsii po antimonopol'noi politike i podderzhke predprinimatel'stva, 2001, Doklad o sostoianii i razvitii malogo predprinimatel'stva v Rossiiskoi Federatsii i merah po ego gosudarstvennoi podderzhke. Moscow. http://www.maprf.ru/ru/support_predpr/State_reports/195/ last visited 5/27/2005.

O khode provedeniia sploshnogo obsledovaniia malykh predpriiatii, *Voprosy statistiki*, No. 2, 2001.

Osnovnye itogi sploshnogo iedinovremennogo obsledovaniia malykh predpriiatii po rezul'tatam raboty za 2000 god (predvaritel'nye dannye), typescript.

Parshev, A P, 2000, *Pochemu Rossiia ne Amerika*, Moscow, Forum.

Pipes, R, 1974, *Russia Under the Old Regime*, New York, Charles Scribner's Sons.

Redding, S and Venables, A, 2002, The economics of isolation and distance, *Nordic Journal of Political Economy* (Conference Volume), 28:2, pp. 93–108.

Rosen, K T and Resnick, M, 1980, The size distribution of cities: an examination of the Pareto law and primacy, *Journal of Urban Economics*, Vol. 8.

Rosenthal, S S and Strange, W C, 2004, Evidence on the nature and sources of agglomeration economies, In: Henderson, J V and Thisse, J-F, eds, *Handbook of Regional and Urban Economics. Volume 4. Cities and Geography*, Amsterdam, North-Holland.

Rosstat, 2005, *Rossiia v tsifrakh 2005*, Moscow.

SBA1, US Small Business Administration, Office of Advocacy, Employer Firms, Establishments, Employment, and Annual Payroll by Firm Size, and State, 2002 http://www.sba.gov/advo/stats/st.pdf

SBA2, US Small Business Administration, Office of Advocacy, Nonemployer Firms and receipts by state http://www.sba.gov/advo/stats/ne_st.pdf

Transparency International—Russia, Regional'nye indeksy korruptsii 9 October 2002. http://www.transparency.org.ru/proj_index.asp

US Census Bureau, *Statistical Abstract of the United States*, 2003.

Wheeler, C H, 2004, Wage inequality and urban density, *Journal of Economic Geography* Vol. 4.

D. POLITICAL ISSUES

9

A FROZEN VENEZUELA? THE RESOURCE CURSE AND RUSSIAN POLITICS

William Tompson[1]

Introduction

A growing body of empirical research suggests that countries endowed with great natural resource wealth tend to lag behind comparable countries in terms of long-run real GDP growth, a finding that has given rise to widespread debate about a so-called 'resource curse' or a 'paradox of plenty'.[2] Explanations of the resource curse focus on a wide range of economic and political factors. The most prominent lines of argument emphasize the impact of resource wealth on the competitiveness of other tradables ('Dutch disease'); the impact of commodity-price volatility, particularly on fiscal revenues; the interaction of commodity-price volatility with financial market imperfections, which can lead to inefficient specialization; and the impact of resource wealth on the quality of institutions, political processes and governance.[3] Significantly, the major *economic* explanations of resource-exporters' poor growth performance are all, at least in principle, treatable: governments have at their disposal policy tools to mitigate, if not eliminate, such economic hardships as 'Dutch disease'. The fact that they so often fail to do so suggests that consistent policy failure lies at the root of the problem.[4]

---

[1] The opinions expressed in this paper are those of the author and do not necessarily reflect the views of the OECD or its member states.

[2] See the classic statement of the resource curse hypothesis by Sachs and Warner (2001); on the 'paradox of plenty', see Karl (1999).

[3] For an overview of these explanations, with particular emphasis on the issue of weak financial markets, see Hausman and Rigobon (2003).

[4] See, for example, Lal and Myint (1996), who see policy failure as the prime cause of underperformance of natural resource-based economies. See also the overview of this literature in Ross (1999). Of course, part of the reason for this may be that less diversified economies have less margin for economic policy error: in other words, a highly resource-dependent economy arguably needs even *better* policy than a more diversified one (see Ahrend 2006).

If this is indeed the case, then the most promising approaches to the resource curse are likely to be those relying on political economy explanations, for the key must lie in understanding *why* resource-based economies are more likely than others to suffer from bad policies. The answer must be that resource wealth somehow distorts their politics in such a way as to produce institutional and policy failures. A number of possible explanations for such a link have been proposed, but because the literature has focused on political and governance issues as *intervening* variables, there is often a tendency to infer causation from association rather than to explore the causal links between economic structure and either the nature of the political system or the quality of governance. This tendency is particularly pronounced in large-scale cross-national studies, which are by their very nature ill-equipped to examine actual political processes closely in order to assess the extent to which they conform to the hypotheses advanced on the basis of quantitative analyses of data.

This chapter seeks to examine closely the links between resource wealth and politics in the context of contemporary Russia. It addresses two relatively simple questions. First, do we have compelling reason to believe that Russia's political life would have been substantially healthier—that politics would have been more democratic or governance less corrupt and more effective—if Russia had begun its market transformation without such large minerals sectors? Second, what can we say about the impact of Russia's natural resource endowments on its political development?

Russia's Resource Riches: A Political Curse?

At first glance, the answer to the first of the two questions posed above would seem to be a resounding 'yes'. Russia undoubtedly suffers from many of the governance problems identified in the political economy literature as typical of resource-rich states. To some, indeed, it seems to present a perfect illustration of the political economy of the resource curse at work.[1] When he was still presidential economic advisor, Andrei Illarionov spoke about Russia's 'petro-politics' and about the 'Venezuelanization' of Russia.[2] For Illarionov, 'Venezuelanization' suggested a combination of stalled reform, populist spending and growing nationalization of energy-sector assets. Nevertheless, a close examination of the Russian case suggests that it is difficult to attribute too much significance to Russia's resource-dependent economic structure

---

[1] See, for example, the views expressed by various analysts cited in Bush (2005). See also the discussion in Erochkine (2005).

[2] Illarionov presented his 'Venezuelanization' thesis to the *Euromoney*-sponsored 'Russia & The CIS Investment Forum 2005: Moving Towards A Balanced Economy', at the Radisson Slavyanskaya Hotel, Moscow, 13 September 2005.

when explaining the ills that afflict its body politic. Indeed, there is little reason to believe that the Russian polity would be substantially healthier had the country begun its market transition with less resource wealth.

The discussion that follows considers Russia in relation to a number of specific hypotheses advanced in the political economy literature on the resource curse. It finds that Russia does *not* conform to the expectations generated by several important strands of the literature. In a number of other cases, Russia does indeed appear to confirm the theory, in that it suffers from the kind of political pathologies associated with resource-based economies, such as pervasive rent-seeking and corruption. However, some of these problems would appear to be over-determined in the Russian case—we would expect to find them even in a resource-poor Russia.

Russia as a Resource Economy

On the measures conventionally employed in the resource curse literature, Russia undoubtedly qualifies as a heavily resource-based economy. Fuel and metals together accounted for an estimated 65 per cent of value added in industry in 2000. In 2003, hydrocarbons, metals and other raw materials accounted for 76 per cent of total exports, equivalent to 31.5 per cent of GDP.[1] This undoubtedly qualifies Russia as a resource-based economy on the criteria used by such authors as Sachs and Warner (2001), Auty (2004) and Narain *et al.* (2003). However, Russia is not a 'typical' resource-based economy. Much of the literature assumes, implicitly or explicitly, that the typical resource-dependent economy is a developing economy, with a large agrarian sector, low levels of urbanization and low overall levels of education. Russia's situation is more analogous to that facing highly industrialized economies following the discovery of major new resource wealth, such as The Netherlands or the United Kingdom in the 1970s and 1980s. The 'resource shock' in Russia resulted not from the discovery of new resources but from the adjustment of relative prices at the start of the post-Soviet transition. The relative prices of raw materials, having been held at artificially low levels under central planning, soared after prices were freed and foreign trade was liberalized. This triggered a radical reallocation of the resource rents derived from Russia's primary sector, a reallocation that is still being contested.

Clearly, a country's *ex ante* institutions will have a powerful impact both on how new-found resource wealth is used and on how it affects politics. It is therefore worth identifying a few of the peculiar features of Russia's institutional environment that might be relevant. First, as an economy in

---

[1] Oil and gas alone constitute over half the country's export bill.

transition, Russia is—quite apart from its resource endowments—an extremely 'rent-rich' environment. Property rights are still relatively weak and fluid, and the economic distortions inherited from the Soviet system—or created by incomplete reforms—have generated substantial 'transition rents'. Second, Russia started the post-Soviet period with a large state bureaucracy but, paradoxically, a weak state.[1] Finally, political accountability, social capital and the rule of law—the three main sanctions against antisocial governance—are all in short supply.

The foregoing suggests that many of the political pathologies that are identified in the resource curse literature and that are found in contemporary Russia are probably over-determined. There is no doubt, for example, that struggles over control of Russia's resource wealth have generated large-scale corruption. However, it seems overwhelmingly likely that Russia would have had very high levels of corruption in recent years anyway—as even a cursory look at some of its resource-poor neighbours would seem to confirm. Similarly, state weakness tends to increase agents' incentives to engage in rent-seeking rather than production, whatever the sphere of activity (Chakraborty and Dabla-Norris 2005).

Rent-seeking

The simplest line of argument linking natural resource dependence to poor governance is that which argues that resource wealth tends to create incentives for rent-seeking. Both state and private actors in resource-rich economies may focus on capturing the resource rents rather than on wealth creation and may favour the development of institutions geared to rent-seeking rather than entrepreneurship.[2] Control contests over resource rents may well constitute the central axis of political conflict. Economic performance is likely to suffer, since such contests are unproductive.

The nature of the resources in question matters. Case studies suggest that an abundance of point resources, such as mineral deposits, is more likely to lead to weak political systems and consequent economic disadvantage than are diffuse resources, like fisheries or forests (Deacon and Mueller 2004, p. 26). Point resources are potentially easier to monopolize,[3] so contests to control

[1] McFaul (1997) identifies three criteria of state strength: internal ideological and institutional cohesiveness; relative autonomy from society (i.e., the degree to which state structures are or are not captive to particular interests); and the ability of the state to implement policy effectively. On all three counts, the post-Soviet Russian state was exceptionally weak.

[2] See, e.g., Auty (2004), Robinson et al. (2002), and the overview of the 'rentier state' literature in Ross (1999, pp. 312–13).

[3] Diffuse resources, of course, may pose a different problem: if they are open access resources, then failure to establish an effective property rights regime may lead to overexploitation and a 'tragedy of the commons'.

them are more likely to be zero-sum and more likely to be won by whoever is in control of the state. Larger, more concentrated rents are thus likely to give rise to greater polarization and fiercer, more protracted control contests than smaller, more diffuse ones (Auty 2004).

A related, but nevertheless distinct, issue concerns the capital-intensive nature of resource extraction in many sectors, which is likely to mean that resource industries will tend to be dominated by fewer, larger firms.[1] This, in turn, increases the incentives for state elites to nationalize those industries, especially where they loom very large in the national economy. Otherwise, political leaders may fear that such powerful private companies could prove 'unmanageable'. It is perhaps not surprising, then, that so much of the resource curse literature focuses on minerals: they are point resources, with highly capital intensive production and, in many cases, substantial scale economies. Such sectors are likely to be characterized by higher levels of (state or private) ownership concentration than most others. Given Russia's enormous mineral wealth (chiefly hydrocarbons, metals and precious stones), the literature would lead us to expect fierce contests over rents.

Of course, the implications of such conflicts for politics and governance depend on the pre-existing institutional environment (Deacon and Mueller 2004). Rent-seeking is likely to be especially attractive in any environment in which property rights are weak and institutions are unstable. In such an environment, agents will have good reason to discount the future heavily. This shortening of time horizons will tend to make rent-seeking more attractive than production, since the immediate pay-offs will be greater.[2] In such a situation, a weak legal order will probably be unable to contain control contests, which will then be settled by extra-legal means. Those in power are likely to focus on capturing resource rents and using them in order to shore up their own positions.

This is precisely what we find in Russia. Conflict over resource rents has been one of the central facts of Russian political life over the last decade and more. Such conflicts must, however, be seen in the context of Russia's transition, which has provided opportunities for rent-seeking in virtually every sector and which has witnessed contests over the property rights to every imaginable sort of enterprise, large or small. In such an environment, contests for control over oil or aluminium deposits are likely to be longer and perhaps bloodier than those waged over local shops, but the roots of the problem lie in the general weakness of property rights rather than the nature of the assets. This becomes

---

[1] Capital intensity is partly a function of the nature of the resource, but it is also a function of technological change (fishing, for example, has become much more capital intensive in recent decades), and should therefore be seen as a distinct variable.

[2] In any case, productive activities, if successful, will tend to attract predators (Chakraborty and Dabla-Norris 2005).

clearer when we contrast Russia with Norway, a country characterized by democratic governance and the rule of law prior to the discovery of its North Sea oil. Norway has been able to manage its resources and to resolve conflicts over resource rents within a stable democratic framework.

No Representation without Taxation?

A second hypothesis holds that resource-rich states tend to suffer from under-developed extractive institutions.[1] The state's ability to derive substantial revenues from the primary sector reduces its incentive to develop any more elaborate fiscal institutions. This ensures that the state remains over-reliant on primary commodities for its revenue base—and may therefore be subject to sharp pro-cyclical swings in fiscal policy. Politically, the state's ability to run on resource rents may also serve to make it less accountable than it would other-wise be to those it governs.[2] While this freedom from constraint may suit rulers in the short run, the long-term cost can be considerable. North and Thomas (1973) argue that the flow of silver and gold from the New World in the sixteenth century freed the Spanish crown from the constraints of the Cortes. British monarchs, by contrast, had to negotiate tax rises with parliament. This ultimately strengthened the British state, since it gave rise to institutions such as annual parliaments and later helped secure property rights. The Spanish monarchy's freedom from such constraints contributed to institutional stagnation and thus to political decline. More recent work on rentier states focuses on the twentieth-century petro-states of the Middle East and elsewhere, but reaches a similar conclusion: government is far less likely to be accountable to the governed when rulers can finance their activities—and even provide generous benefits to their subjects—without having to tax those whom they rule.[3]

Intriguing though they are, these arguments do not shed much light on post-Soviet Russia. Indeed, Russia's recent past has witnessed the opposite of what the literature suggests. Russia started the post-Soviet era with catas-trophically weak extractive institutions. Instead of merely appropriating the surpluses generated by state-owned firms, the post-Soviet Russian state had to learn to tax effectively. This has not been easy and the process still has some way to go, but there is no doubt that the Russian state's extractive capabilities

[1] See, e.g., Chaudhry (1989) and Karl (1997).
[2] See Ganev (2001, p. 14): 'Only when elites are forced to renegotiate the terms of extraction will the "organisational residue" engendered as a by-product of the dominant elite project be harnessed for the purposes of good governance.'
[3] See, e.g., Isham *et al.* (2003), Ross (2001), Entelis (1976), Vandewalle (1998) and Bazresch and Levy (1991).

have improved dramatically over the last decade, in terms not only of its ability to raise revenue but of its ability to do so without unnecessarily distorting markets or restricting economic activity.

Nor are Russian fiscal institutions too specialized on capturing resource rents. Indeed, Russia initially focused on introducing a wide range of general taxes and arguably paid too *little* attention to capturing resource rents. Vasil'eva and Gurvich (2005) find that the total effective tax burden on the fuel sector in 2000 amounted to just 31.8 per cent of the sector's value added. The corresponding figure for non-fuel industry was 43.7 per cent, while that for transport and communications was 40.8 per cent. Non-fuel resource sectors also enjoyed far lower effective tax burdens than did major manufacturing sectors.

Tax changes introduced during 2000–03 served to correct the situation somewhat, as the effective tax burden on the fuel sector rose by an estimated 7.7 per cent while the burden on non-fuel industry fell by 8.4 per cent of value added. Quite apart from formal changes in tax legislation, the Yukos affair brought about both a change in the informal rules governing oil companies' tax behaviour and an increase in the state's ability to appropriate oil rents directly as a result of its expropriation of Yukos assets. However, these changes have focused overwhelmingly on the fuel sector. No attempt has been made to capture a larger share of the rent in other natural resource sectors, which have enjoyed further tax reductions—the metallurgy and forestry, pulp and paper sectors now enjoy the lowest overall tax burdens of any major industrial sectors.

Finally, it would be hard to argue that Russia has become a rentier state, free of any need to negotiate the terms of extraction with society. While the state's income from resource extraction has grown markedly in recent years, in fiscal terms it is no petro-state. Export duties and resource taxes accounted for only about 20 per cent of revenues in 2003, far less than either social taxes (22.2 per cent) or taxes on consumption (29.5 per cent). Value-added tax remains by far Russia's most important single tax, accounting for 35.8 per cent of federal revenues in 2004. And while there has been a definite authoritarian drift under Vladimir Putin, it would be difficult to link this with any changes in the structure of taxation. Indeed, the post-crisis (i.e., post-1998) period has witnessed a major effort to improve tax discipline across the economy.

If resource rents do indeed contribute to the erosion of political accountability in Russia, this probably owes less to the nature of taxation than to state elites' ability to appropriate and allocate resource revenues by other means. On this view, the increase in direct state control over oil-sector assets, in particular, should cause some concern: whatever the defects of Russia's budgetary system, the overhaul of the tax system after 1999 and the establishment of a treasury system of budgetary execution do appear to have increased substantially the transparency and efficiency of fiscal processes. By contrast, the governance of state-owned companies remains opaque and there are doubts about to whom—and to what extent—insiders are really accountable. It is widely believed that such financial opacity enables Russia's rulers to use state-controlled companies to fund activities they prefer to keep off-budget. If resource riches are undermining political accountability, it is more likely to be via the growth of direct state control over resources than via the fiscal system.

Policy Complacence

A third line of argument concerning the impact of resource wealth on politics and policy touches on what Ross (1999, p. 309) calls 'myopic sloth'. In essence, the argument is that resource wealth gives rise to a certain complacence in policy-makers and/or private agents. Such complacence can lead to excessively lax policies and a neglect of structural and other measures needed to foster diversification. Excessive spending in the good times necessitates sharp retrenchment when commodity prices fall, thus aggravating the impact of shifts in the terms of trade. The evidence suggests that policy-makers in resource-rich countries appear to be well aware of the dangers of boom-and-bust cycles, but often find it difficult to resist pressures for fiscal relaxation.[1]

Here, Russia is no exception: the economic bloc of the cabinet is acutely aware of the need to maintain macroeconomic discipline across the commodity-price cycle, and during 1999–2004, Russia demonstrated exemplary fiscal discipline (Ahrend 2004). The government, acutely aware of the lessons of the 1998 financial collapse, also undertook an ambitious and wide-ranging programme of structural reforms during 2000–03. Far from seeing the recovery of oil and metals prices after 1998 as an excuse to postpone reforms, the authorities initially seemed to view the boost to Russia's terms of trade as a window of opportunity to pursue reforms that would have been more difficult in other circumstances.

Nevertheless, there has been growing political pressure to spend an ever larger share of oil windfalls, as prices have remained high and memories of 1998 have faded. The government's fiscal hawks have come under increasing pressure to spend (or cut taxes) from the cabinet's spending ministries, from special interests seeking federal support for their priorities and from a Kremlin determined to maintain the pressure on the government to double GDP quickly. The real difficulty is that no one yet knows what part of the recent rise in oil prices will be more or less permanent. If the long-run average price has risen, then it makes sense for Russia to spend more, but betting too heavily on a much higher long-run price risks creating serious problems when prices fall. Even as spending pressures have

---

[1] See Ross (1999, p. 309), especially the references in notes 40–2.

mounted, structural reform has stalled. It appears unlikely that further major reforms will be launched before the next electoral cycle.

Like rent-appropriation contests, policy indiscipline tends to be worse in a poor institutional environment. Time horizons are shorter in such circumstances, and the more heavily agents discount the future, the weaker are the incentives to remain prudent. Moreover, if rulers are uncertain of their own tenure, then they will have a greater incentive to appropriate and manipulate resource rents more aggressively in order to retain power. In Russia, it is not difficult to see such incentives at work in the growing tendency to use oil windfalls to shore up support for the regime via tax cuts and increases in budget-sector wages and pensions, as well as to appease social protest where it emerges. The reaction to the monetization protests of January 2005 and the subsequent freezing of virtually all potentially sensitive reforms would tend to suggest that the authorities are indeed becoming more risk-averse, as Karl (1997) suggests, and starting to use oil windfalls for current consumption rather than to underpin forward-looking reforms.

Bloated Bureaucracies and Rent-dependent Industries

The issue of what state leaders *do* with resource rents when they control them is the focus of a fourth set of arguments about the impact of resource wealth on governance. As noted above, rulers will rationally tend to use such rents to strengthen their hold on power. Robinson *et al.* (2002) emphasize the use of rents as a patronage resource, arguing that leaders' use of this resource tends to result in a politically motivated expansion of the state bureaucracy.[1] The rent-driven growth of the bureaucracy, however, is only part of the story. Auty (1994; 2004), Mahon (1992) and others emphasize the use of resource rents to sustain a growing subsidy- and/or protection-dependent secondary urban sector. The growth of a secondary sector that relies on protection and/or subsidies will affect politics, for it will give rise to a social constituency with a vested interest in the *status quo*. Thus, numerous studies of import-substitution industrialization in Latin America suggest that the beneficiaries of subsidies and protection were a major source of resistance to reform.[2]

At first glance, Russia seems to conform all too well to the model just outlined. The growth of the state bureaucracy since 1992 has occasioned much comment, and resource rents have indeed been used to prop up distressed non-resource sectors. On closer inspection, however, the picture in Russia looks rather more complex.

[1] This view is shared by Auty (2004), among others.
[2] See the overview of this literature in Ross (1999, pp. 310–11). See also Gelb *et al.* (1988) and Treisman (2002) on 'dependent urbanization'.

The size of the bureaucracy has indeed grown, but by no means as rapidly as many think. In fact, the number of officials employed in public administration grew by just about 13.6 per cent during 1994–2001, with sub-national administrations accounting for most of the increase. The number of federal employees posted in the regions grew slowly, while the central federal administrative apparatus actually shrank. In fact, the public administration overall employs an unusually small portion of the labour force when compared with most OECD and transition countries, which makes it difficult to argue that Russia conforms to the rent-bloated bureaucracy hypothesis.[1] A large part of the growth at regional level appears to have resulted from the desire of financially *weak* regional authorities to extract subsidies from the federal centre—which means that it is unlikely to be related to resource wealth.[2] Nevertheless, a look at regional-level data suggests that resource wealth may play a role in fuelling the growth of sub-national bureaucracies. Between 1995 and 2003, employment in regional and municipal administrations grew by 22.5 per cent across the federation. In the ten federal subjects with the highest ratio of minerals extraction to gross regional product (GRP), however, the corresponding figure was 51.6 per cent, reaching 68 per cent for the six federal subjects in which minerals extraction accounted for over 30 per cent of GRP.[3]

The issue of the protected secondary sector is particularly interesting in the Russian case. On the whole, Russia's secondary sector has enjoyed surprisingly little formal protection—trade policy since 1992 has generally been fairly liberal, although informal barriers have sometimes made the Russian market less open than it appeared to be on formal criteria. Nevertheless, a large part of Russian industry was kept afloat via subsidies throughout the first decade of transition. This reflected both the power of industrial managers as a lobby and fear of the social consequences of structural change. Direct subsidies from the budget and soft credits from the central bank had largely been eliminated by the mid-nineties, but they were increasingly replaced by implicit subsidies, the most important of which involved unpenalized arrears and non-monetary payments to the state-controlled gas and electricity monopolies.[4] After the crisis, cash payments rapidly became the norm again, but gas and electricity prices were frozen for several years and

---

[1] See Brym and Gimpel'son (2004, pp. 92–100) for details. It should be noted that comparisons across time and countries are complicated by problems of definition, including the creation of new types of officials and the reclassification of others in conjunction with the transition.

[2] See Gimpel'son and Treisman (2002).

[3] Significantly, what matters here seems to be not the absolute volume of a region's mineral (hydrocarbons and metals) production but the relative weight of that production in gross regional product. In other words, it is resource-*dependence* rather than resource wealth that counts.

[4] Enterprises also 'borrowed' increasingly from workers, the state and other suppliers, via wage, tax and payment arrears. For details, see Woodruff (1999) and Tompson (1999).

thus fell sharply in real terms, dropping well below cost-recovery levels.[1] By contrast, the oil industry's support for the secondary sector was minimal. Since the authorities were officially committed to curtailing explicit subsidies, all that could really be done was to use restrictions on exports to hold down the domestic prices of crude oil and petroleum products. Given that Russia consumes far less crude than it does gas, this constituted a less onerous burden on the industry. Other major resource sectors—notably timber and metals— appear to have done even better, as they shared in the subsidies provided to the secondary sector.[2]

Up to this point, Russia might appear to conform quite well to hypotheses about a dependent urban sector. However, since 2000, there has been a dramatic reduction in the implicit subsidies provided to Russian industries and households. As OECD (2004) shows, the gas and electricity subsidies have been diminishing rapidly in recent years, while Russian enterprises' payment discipline—with respect to the budget, employees and suppliers—has greatly improved. It remains to be seen if this progress will be sustained through the next downturn, but recent years have seen a marked shift away from the subsidy-dependent industrialization model.

Any discussion of Russian leaders' use of resource rents to secure political support would be incomplete without a discussion of privatization. At first glance, Boris Yeltsin's readiness to privatize Russia's oil and metals industries so quickly—and so cheaply—might look rather surprising, especially as his admin- istration was not even able to tax them effectively. In the case of Gazprom, Yeltsin simply allowed insiders to appropriate a large share of gas rents, even while the company remained in state ownership. The political leadership seemed to surrender these spectacular rents without a fight. One might, of course, simply put this down to the weakness of a regime that had in any case found it impossible to assert effective control over state enterprises or to resist pressure to alienate its most valuable assets. However, Yeltsin's behaviour may make sense if one assumes that his time horizons were relatively short. Whatever its economic merits, the rapid privatization of the state's most valuable companies offered two major political benefits to Yeltsin as he fought for his political life in the mid-1990s. First, it helped secure the support of the country's richest tycoons for his re-election. Second, it helped ensure that, even in the event of defeat, his opponents would face powerful opposition to any attempt to reverse course in economic policy.[3] Putin, by contrast, has

[1] For an estimate of the scale of this implicit subsidy in the early post-crisis period, see OECD (2002, pp. 121–32). For an estimate of the natural gas subsidy in 2004 see Chapter 3.
[2] Aluminium producers, in particular, benefited greatly from cheap electricity.
[3] When political leaders adopt policies that effectively curtail their own power, it is often because their tenure is uncertain and they hope to bind their successors.

hitherto faced no such immediate threat to his tenure, and he is thus more interested in securing control over a much larger share of Russia's resource rents on an on-going basis, whether by means of taxation or direct state control over assets.

Corruption

A number of authors argue for a link between resource wealth and official corruption, not least because of the temptation to manipulate state institutions to secure resource rents.[1] However, the link between resource wealth and corruption in the Russian case is anything but clear. There is compelling evidence to suggest that the problem of official corruption has grown markedly worse since 1991,[2] but it would be difficult to attribute this development to the resource curse, given the many other factors at work.

If there were a strong link between mineral resources and corruption, we might expect to find that corruption was worse in resource-rich regions than elsewhere. The *Regional Corruption Indices 2002* of Transparency International–Russia are the one relatively rigorous assessment of corruption at regional level based on comparable sociological data. Unfortunately, they are available for only 40 of Russia's 89 federal subjects, and many of the most resource-dependent regions are not covered (Transparency 2002). Nevertheless, they do not, at first glance, provide any support for the proposition that resource-rich regions are more corrupt than others. The most striking feature of TI-Russia's 'corruption map' is that corruption appears to be substantially worse in border regions than elsewhere—hardly a surprising result, given the scale of contraband trade in Russia and the fact that ports in most countries tend to have higher levels of crime and corruption than other cities. This is not to say that resource regions are *not* corrupt—one of the striking features of the indices is the limited degree of variation among federal subjects. On most indicators, corruption was found to be high across the board, and the best regions were not a great deal better than the worst.

The recent joint study by the polling institute VTsIOM and the small business lobby OPORA likewise fails to show much of a link (OPORA Rossii 2005). Their survey of small and medium entrepreneurs did not ask about

---

[1] See, e.g., Mauro (1995), da Cunha Leite and Weidmann (1999), Easterly (2001) and Ahrend (2004).
[2] Estimating corruption levels is, of course, a notoriously difficult business, and few of the indicators available allow for an assessment of trends across time. Transparency International's 'Corruption Perceptions Index', despite its limitations, does now at least offer almost a decade of coverage of Russia. It suggests some gradual improvement during 2000–04, but Russia's recent scores, in the 2.7–2.8 range on a ten-point scale, show that it continues to be regarded as a highly corrupt place.

corruption specifically but rather asked respondents about 'transaction costs' incurred when interacting with the bureaucracy. This rubric covered not only bribes and kickbacks, but also such issues as procedural violations during inspections and difficulties with registration. To the extent that it taps forms of official predation, however, the transaction costs indicator looks like a reasonable proxy for corruption. Ranked on this indicator, Russia's most resource-dependent regions range from 6th to 78th. There is no evident clustering of metals- or fuel-producing federal subjects in the distribution. The survey results do, however, show that the propensity of officials to take 'illegal payments' from businesspeople is far greater in the Southern Federal District (not a resource-rich region) than anywhere else in Russia.

The failure to establish any apparent link between resource wealth and corruption levels does not by any means imply that competition for resource rents has not fuelled corruption in Russia. It may be that the inclusion of more resource-dependent regions in the sample would have yielded a different result; the index does not cover many of the most resource-dependent economies in Russia. Moreover, contests over resource wealth may be concentrated at the federal level and thus have little impact on regional perceptions of corruption. However, it seems likely that corruption in Russia is simply over-determined. Had Russia embarked on its market transformation with no significant resource endowments, one would still expect to find high levels of corruption during the transition—and, indeed, Russia's resource-poor CIS neighbours do not appear obviously less corrupt than Russia.

The growth of official corruption since the late 1980s reflects a large number of factors, including the breakdown not only of the political and bureaucratic controls that existed in the Soviet system but also of the norms and beliefs that supported the old order.[1] Another critical factor is the very low pay received by officials, particularly as many low-paid functionaries find themselves disposing of very valuable state assets or managing substantial financial flows. Corruption is also facilitated by the traditional opacity of state bodies in Russia.[2] More generally, cross-country research shows that both the rule of law and the development of civil society (including a free press) are strongly and negatively correlated with the level of corruption.[3] Their weakness in post-Soviet Russia has probably facilitated the growth of corruption. In short, the larger institutional environment within which officials operate in Russia is relatively 'corruption-friendly'.

[1] See Huskey and Obolonsky (2003). This is a key point: the role of informal norms has been little studied, but it is difficult to believe that changes in norms and values do not form part of the explanation here.
[2] Ahrend (2002).
[3] Brunetti and Weder (2003).

Resource Wealth and Russian Politics: A 'Tillyan' View

Clearly, then, there are good reasons to be sceptical about some of the hypothesized links between Russia's resource wealth and its politics. Yet it would be a mistake to conclude that no significant links exist. If politics is, in the conventional definition, about 'who gets what, when, how', then it would be surprising to find that the economic structure of a polity did *not* have an impact on its political institutions and practices. The nature of the principal sources of national wealth in any society—not only one heavily dependent on resource extraction—is likely to affect the framework for political decision-making, including goal formation, the locus of authority and the types of institutions adopted or created (Karl 1997, p. 44–5). With respect to resource-based economies, in particular, one might expect their natural endowments to affect the dominant mode of resource extraction employed by rulers. The discussion that follows seeks to understand the relationship between resource extraction and governance in contemporary Russia, drawing in particular on the work of Charles Tilly (1992) on the emergence of state structures in Europe.

State-building and Modes of Appropriation

Tilly views the state as a mechanism for appropriating resources and directing them towards the ends determined by the elite—the 'dominant elite project'. Since Tilly's focus is on the rise of the early modern state, the dominant elite project is more or less given: it is war. Much of Tilly's work therefore addresses the other half of the equation—elite strategies for the appropriating the goods of others. One critical question must therefore be: where are the resources which dominant elites strive to appropriate 'located' (in socio-economic no less than spatial terms) and what does it take to 'extract' them? Tilly's argument is that elites need to enter into a variety of social relations to secure the resources they need and that these varying modes of engagement propel the rise of different types of structures that may be used as instruments of governance. For our purposes, it is not necessary to delve into the detail of Tilly's three-fold classification of extraction strategies in the early modern period. The critical point is to recognize that the nature of the resources to be appropriated can shape the extraction strategies that elites pursue. Thus, the possibility of extracting large resource rents at relatively low cost is likely to shape the kinds of institutions political elites create.

The characteristics of the resource sectors in question may also play a role here. Shafer (1994) argues that when a state's production and export profile is highly concentrated, the characteristics of its leading sector can significantly influence its political economy. Where the leading sector is dominated by a small number of players, with high barriers to entry and exit, and a high degree of asset specificity, Shafer argues, it is likely to be both politically powerful and rather inflexible. Powerful but inflexible sectors in turn are likely to place exceptionally strong demands on the state. The state is likely to suffer from an erosion of its own autonomy, and state capacities are likely to be distorted, as the state develops specialized institutions and practices to deal with the leading sector while failing to develop effective mechanisms for governing, or addressing the needs of, other sectors. Intuitively, one would expect this to be especially true of minerals sectors, such as oil, gas and metals—as noted above, they are point resources, with highly capital intensive production and, in many cases, substantial scale economies, making entry difficult and increasing the likelihood that they will be dominated by a few large players.

Jones Luong (2004), however, focuses not on the nature of the industry *per se* but on the question of ownership and control. She argues that the choice of governance structure is largely determined by domestic politics, rather than factors intrinsic to the nature of the sector, such as capital intensity or concentration. While her analysis of the domestic political determinants of such choices is illuminating, the predominance of state ownership in major minerals sectors over the last forty to fifty years—despite wide variation in the political circumstances of minerals-exporting states—suggests that the characteristics of minerals sectors are nevertheless important in structuring the choices politicians make in response to the kind of domestic political opportunities and constraints she describes.[1]

It may well be that the presence of large, concentrated sources of rent, such as are found in many minerals sectors, constitutes a political problem to which the easiest (if not the most economically efficient) solution for many states is nationalization. The capital intensive nature of most large-scale resource extraction is likely to mean that the sector will be dominated by a small number of very large players, whether private or public, domestic or foreign. If private ownership prevails, the danger for state elites is that the political system might not be robust enough to contain conflicts among such influential private agents or that the state might not have the capacities needed to regulate the behaviour of private resource companies and to capture resource rents effectively. Provided the state disposes of the necessary force, nationalization may simply be easier than trying to govern powerful private players. Moreover, greater direct control will undoubtedly make it easier for state elites to appropriate and allocate resource rents than such indirect means as taxation

---

[1] Economically, of course, many developing countries were advised that nationalization would help them gain independence from foreign multinationals and would better enable them to use resource rents for economic development. See, e.g., Cardoso and Faletto (1979), Hirschman (1958) and Baldwin (1966).

and regulation. The irony here is that while weak states may be more likely to opt for nationalization precisely because of their limited capacities, under-developed state capacities make it more likely that nationalized resource industries will be poorly managed.

The State-ownership Curse?

This point is extremely important in the larger resource curse debate, as Jones Luong (2004), Auty (2004), Ross (1999) and others suggest that state ownership rather than resource wealth *per se* lies at the root of resource exporters' appar-ently chronic under-performance. State ownership of resource industries may soften states' budget constraints and encourage fiscal indiscipline. In any case, there are grounds for thinking that state-owned minerals producers are likely to be less efficient and less transparent, and also to be subject to more political interference. The resource curse might well be a state ownership curse. This proposition has not undergone much empirical analysis, for the simple reason that most of the literature focuses on minerals sectors in the period from the 1960s through the 1990s—a time during which the vast majority of mineral-rich countries opted for state ownership and control of mineral reserves.

While one cannot generalize on the basis of a single case, Russia's experience would seem to be entirely consistent with this view. OECD (2004) contrasts the striking divergence in performance between Russia's oil and gas sectors. The oil sector was broken up and privatized, while the gas sector remained overwhelm-ingly a state-controlled vertically integrated monopoly. The obviously flawed nature of oil privatization notwithstanding, the result was a dynamic oil industry that emerged as the most important driver of Russia's strong post-crisis growth. The gas industry's overall contribution to growth (in value added) during 1999–2004 appears by contrast to have been slightly *negative* (Gurvich 2005).

Our concern, however, is with politics. If the presence of rich natural (and particularly mineral) endowments tends to create incentives for politicians to pursue state ownership, this will undoubtedly have consequences for politics. However, the nature of these consequences will depend on the existing political order and the quality of the institutional environment. A country such as Norway, where the democratic accountability of the rulers to the ruled is well established and the rule of law is relatively strong, has a far better chance of creating a reasonably well-governed country.[1] Where political accountability and the rule of law are weak, however, the creation of large state companies in the most lucrative sectors is much more likely to be associated with greater opacity, corruption and rent-seeking by insiders. Politically, the resources placed at the

---

[1] One should not, however, be naïve about the Norways of this world: decision-making in and around Norsk Hydro and Statoil can be as opaque as anything found in Russia.

THE RESOURCE CURSE AND RUSSIAN POLITICS

state elite's disposal in this manner may well make it easier for them to resist, or buy off, pressure for change. In short, one might hypothesize that direct control over large resource rents would enable the governing elite both to enrich itself and to entrench itself, especially if the mechanisms for monitoring the management of those rents are weak or non-existent. None of these conclusions are likely to sound in any way surprising or controversial to observers of Russia's gas monopoly or other large, state-owned oil and gas companies in the CIS.

However, the argument goes even further. Jones Luong (2004, p. 11) argues that each of her four forms of ownership and governance 'fosters a different set of incentives for institution-building by creating a different set of primary actors and form of business-state relations'. She continues:

> Three basic patterns emerge. First, where the main actors are state elites and bureaucrats, business-state relations are blurred and symmetrical, their incentives for building discretionary institutions are likely to converge, and thus, institutions are likely to be weak in terms of both their ability to constrain and predictability... Second, where the main actors are state elites and domestic owners, business-state relations are clear and symmetrical, and thus, their incentives for building institutions that act as formal guarantees are likely to converge such that strong (i.e., broadly effective and stable) institutions emerge. And third, where the main actors are state elites and foreign investors, business-state relations are clear and asymmetrical; their incentives for institution-building are thus likely to diverge, resulting in hybrid institutions—or institutions designed specifically for the mineral sector that are effective but not stable.

The foregoing would suggest that the institutional implications of growing state control over Russia's major resource sectors are disturbing indeed.

These claims take on added significance if we accept that the institutional requirements of the 'leading sector' are likely to shape the economic and, to some extent, the political institutions of the society as a whole. A development strategy based largely on state control over natural resource sectors (or, for that matter, over the other 'commanding heights' of the economy) is likely to be far less demanding in its institutional requirements than many other development paths (Ahrend and Tompson 2005a). The development of civil society, the quality of the contracting environment (and, hence, of the rule of law), the security of property rights and the development of human capital all matter less than they would in an economy seeking to develop on the basis of private enterprise. The relatively lax institutional requirements of this strategy may, indeed, make it more attractive to rulers in settings where institutions are *ex ante* weak. The problem is that, in addition to being a strategy which is less promising in economic terms than many others, it is one which tends to reduce the incentives for *improving* institutions. The coping strategy thus risks becoming an impediment to any real resolution of the problem of weak institutions.

Russia Reconsidered

The argument towards which the foregoing has been leading us thus runs something like the following. The rulers of a resource-rich state will understandably be concerned to capture a large share of the economic surplus generated by its resource sectors. While personal cupidity and corruption (of politicians or officials) may play a role, it need not: following Tilly's logic, the focus on the appropriation of resource rents is the obvious, rational strategy for state elites to pursue. However, the mechanisms of appropriation they employ will depend on the tools at their disposal: it is here that the nature and quality of institutions comes into play. States whose regulatory, administrative and other capacities are generally weak are more likely to succumb to the temptation to nationalize outright, or at any rate to rely on their coercive power to sustain a tight grip over the resource sector. Such a solution is likely to prove economically inefficient but it has undoubted political advantages for rulers.

How well does this line of argument fit contemporary Russia? Vladimir Putin's 'dominant project' comprises the reconstitution of state power in Russia and the restoration of Russia's international 'great power' status following the travails of the 1990s. Moreover, he has publicly expressed his view that Russia's hydrocarbon wealth, in particular, is critical to re-establishing its geopolitical position in the world. It is therefore hardly surprising that Putin has been concerned to tighten the state's grip on Russia's resource-exporting oil and gas sectors, which constitute the single biggest potential source of wealth to sustain both his state-building project at home and his drive to enhance Russian power and prestige abroad. Putin, after all, inherited a state that had only a short time earlier been effectively bankrupt and that was still in a precarious financial position. The question of resources was thus an urgent one. And there can have been little doubt about where to find the richest resources he might hope to tap—in Russia's export-oriented natural resource sectors and, above all, in its hydrocarbon sectors. He had already expressed quite clearly his own belief that the state should appropriate a larger share of the economic surplus generated by these sectors and that such a step was critical to Russia's long-term revival.[1] The question facing him, therefore, was how best to secure that surplus.

[1] This line of argument was advanced in the future president's candidate of sciences thesis on 'The Strategic Planning of the Reproduction of the Mineral Resource Base of a Region in Conditions of the Formation of Market Relations' at the State Mining Institute in the 1990s, and in an article based on the thesis that appeared in the institute's journal in 1999. See Putin (1999) and Olcott (2004).

Economically, the optimal solutions would probably have involved a market-oriented restructuring of the largely unreformed gas sector,[1] along with better regulation and taxation of the predominately private oil industry. Instead, Putin moved to tighten his grip on the vertically integrated state-controlled gas monopoly, OAO Gazprom, and to expand considerably the state's direct involvement in the management of the oil sector. In the case of Gazprom, which had become something of a state within the state during the 1990s, this proved difficult enough: the new management team installed by Putin in 2001 did not find it easy to secure real, effective control over the company, but gradually the old guard was displaced. As is well known, Putin initially did little to regain control over the oil sector, but from mid-2003, the state reasserted itself in somewhat ham-fisted fashion. By late 2005, around 15 per cent of oil production had shifted, or was in the process of shifting, from private to state hands, and there was every likelihood that, when the onslaught against Yukos was finally over, the state would have raised the share of oil production directly under its control from around 17 per cent in 2003 to perhaps 45 per cent.[2] At the same time, the formal tax burden on the oil sector had been raised substantially, while tax administration had grown tougher, thus ensuring that the state would capture a much larger share of oil windfalls than previously.

A great many things seem to have influenced Putin's approach to the energy sector, including conjunctural political factors and his own ideological predilections. There has been nothing inevitable about the state's expansion into the oil sector: political leadership and choice remain key variables. Nevertheless, it would be a mistake to overlook the importance of both the sectoral characteristics described above and the weaknesses of Russian state institutions. The Russian state's administrative and regulatory capacities were and are weak. Its extractive capacities—its ability to tax effectively—have improved dramatically in recent years but are still rather clumsy. Hence the reliance in many cases on forms of taxation that are acknowledged to be economically sub-optimal but that are easier to administer and collect.[3] However, whatever its other weaknesses, the Russian state's coercive capacities are considerable. They are, indeed, developed out of all proportion to any of its other capabilities. And if all the state is really good at is coercion, then one can expect the state to coerce. To be sure, forceful methods undoubtedly serve the interests of many who are close to Putin, but it is difficult to deny that

---

[1] On gas sector reform, see Ahrend and Tompson (2005b).

[2] This is not the place for a detailed analysis of the so-called 'Yukos affair'. I have examined the case and its implications at length in Tompson (2005).

[3] This is the main reason that oil-sector taxation, in particular, remains focused on turnover and physical volumes rather than profit.

there is a large element of truth in Kraus's (2004) assertion that, in taking forceful action against Khodorkovskii and Yukos, Putin was merely employing the only really effective tools at his disposal. A state characterized by weak regulatory and rule-enforcement capabilities but enjoying a hypertrophied capacity for the use of force can be expected to use force.

This suggests that the roots of the problem lie, in the final analysis, in Russia's institutional weaknesses. These weaknesses did not predetermine the course of action taken by the Kremlin towards the oil industry in 2003–05, but they certainly made it a relatively more attractive option—quite apart from the personal and factional interests involved. It is not hard to see the vicious circle that may now take shape. Weak institutions prompt rulers to opt for feasible, if sub-optimal, solutions—in this case, a reliance on direct control and coercion rather than contract, regulation and taxation. The solutions adopted, in turn, create obstacles to institutional improvements, as second-best solutions often help to entrench the very weaknesses that gave them birth. And those very same institutional weaknesses ensure that, from an economic point of view, those most likely to nationalize are those least equipped to manage nationalized industries well. For a time, before 2003, Russia appeared to be struggling to break this mould—to create institutions capable of regulating, and mediating conflict within, a powerful, dynamic and privately owned oil industry. The events of the Yeltsin era and the early years of Putin show that this was never an easy process—the oil barons would not be so easily 'tamed'. In the end, therefore, the authorities seem to have fallen back on time-honoured methods of coercion and direct control.

This does not by any means imply that economic reform in Russia is dead, or that Russia is racing headlong back into the Soviet past. The authorities' approach to other sectors remains much more liberal and market-friendly. In principle, it is possible that the state might try to create different institutions for, and to pursue different policies towards, non-resource sectors (see also Chapter 6). As Sutela (2005) observes, Russia cannot be another Kuwait; it is simply too big to prosper on the basis of natural resources alone. The country needs a successful secondary sector that can provide employment if the great mass of its population is to enjoy a decent standard of living. As noted above, one danger is that protection and subsidies will be used to foster the development of this 'B' sector, as Sutela calls it. Alternatively, the authorities could try to create conditions for the development of an open and competitive sector of small and medium-sized businesses. Given the dual structure of the economy, Sutela argues that there is not *necessarily* a contradiction between two lines of policy that have emerged in recent years—the tightening of the state's grip over the resource sector, on the one hand, and attempts to create a better environment for SMEs on the other.

There are, however, good reasons to doubt that such a 'neo-NEP' would work in practice. First, much of the non-resource sector will continue to push for protection and, given its socio-political importance and economic weakness, it may get it. Yet such protection is more likely to impede than to facilitate the development of new activities and products that might be more competitive. Second, as Sutela observes, the dividing line between the 'A' and 'B' sectors is fluid and actions taken with respect to the former could have unexpected knock-on effects for the latter. To take but one recent example, the central authorities' use of the tax service and the prosecutors against the country's largest private company does appear to have encouraged lower-level officials to step up the pressure on small and medium businesses. Finally, there is a very real danger arising from the fact that the notion of 'strategic' sectors is proving rather elastic and may come to be applied to an ever larger part of the economy—as already appears to be happening in fields like metallurgy, machine-building, aviation and even banking.

Conclusion

Claims that Russia is turning into a frozen Venezuela are greatly exaggerated. Viewed from a political perspective, what is striking about Russia is not how well it conforms to the stereotype of a resource-based political economy but how successfully it has so far resisted many of the institutional and political pathologies commonly associated with resource-based development. In many cases, moreover, there are good reasons to believe that a resource-poor Russia would suffer from many of the same problems. Nevertheless, it seems that Russia's resource wealth does pose dangers to its political development. The crucial issue is not the nature of the resources themselves but the location of those resources in an institutional environment that is ill-equipped to cope with the pressures and problems that such wealth can create.

Bibliography

Ahrend, R, 2002, Press freedom, human capital and corruption, *DELTA Working Paper 2002–11*, February.

Ahrend, R, 2004, Accounting for Russia's post-crisis growth, *OECD Economics Department Working Paper No. 404*, September.

Ahrend, R, 2006, How to sustain growth in a resource-based economy: the main concepts and their application to the Russian case, *OECD Economics Department Working Paper*.

Ahrend, R and Tompson, W, 2005a, Russian institutions and possible development paths, mimeo, June.

Ahrend, R and Tompson, W, 2005b, Unnatural monopoly: the endless wait for gas-sector reform in Russia, *Europe–Asia Studies*, 57:6, September.

Auty, R, 1994, Industrial policy reform in six large, newly industrializing countries: the resource curse thesis, *World Development*, 22:1, January.

Auty, R, 2004, Patterns of rent-extraction and deployment in developing countries: implications for governance, economic policy and performance, Paper Prepared for the Poverty Reduction and Economic Management Unit Seminar, World Bank, April.

Baldwin, R E, 1966, *Economic Development and Export Growth: A Study of Northern Rhodesia, 1920–1960*, Berkeley, University of California Press.

Bazresch, C and Levy, S, 1991, Populism and economic policy in Mexico, 1970–82, In: Rudiger, D and Sebastian, E, eds, *The Macroeconomics of Populism in Latin America*, Chicago.

Brunetti, A and Weder, B, 2003, A free press is bad news for corruption, *Journal of Public Economics*, 87, pp. 1801–24.

Brym, R and Gimpel'son, V, 2004, The size, composition and dynamics of the Russian state bureaucracy in the 1990s, *Slavic Review*, 631:1.

Bush, J, 2005, Russia: the curse of $50 a barrel, *Business Week*, 16 May.

Cardoso, F H and Faletto, E, 1979, *Dependency and Development in Latin America*, Berkeley, University of California Press.

Chakraborty, S and Dabla-Norris, E, 2005, Rent seeking, *IMF Working Paper WP/05/43*, March.

Chaudhry, K A, 1989, The price of wealth: business and state in labour remittance and oil economies, *International Organization*, 43:1, Winter.

da Cunha Leite, C A and Weidmann, J, 1999, Does mother nature corrupt? Natural resources, corruption, and economic growth, *IMF Working Paper No. 99/85*, June.

Deacon, R T and Mueller, B, 2004, Political economy and natural resource use, *Departmental Working Paper 01–04*, San Bernardino, Department of Economics, UCSB, January.

Easterly, W, 2001, *The Elusive Quest for Growth. Economists' Adventures and Misadventures in the Tropics*, Cambridge, MIT Press.

Entelis, J P, 1976, Oil and wealth and the prospects for democratization in the Arabian peninsula: the case of Saudi Arabia, In: Naiem, A S and Mark, A T, eds, *Arab Oil: Impact on the Arab Countries and Global Implications*, New York.

Erochkine, P, 2005, Russia and its oil: friends or foes?, In: Jennifer, M, ed., *Blueprint for Russia*, London, Foreign Policy Centre.

Ganev, V, 2001, Post-communism as a historical episode of state-building: a reversed Tillyan perspective, *University of Chicago Department of Political Science Working Paper No. 289*, November.

Gelb, A and associates, 1988, *Oil Windfalls: Blessing or Curse?*, New York, Oxford University Press for the World Bank.

Gimpel'son, V and Treisman, D, 2002, Fiscal games and public employment: a theory with evidence from Russia, *World Politics*, 54, pp. 145–83, January.

Gurvich, E, 2005, Ustal li 'lokomotiv' rossiiskoi ekonomiki?, *Neft' Rossii* 2, February.

Hausman, R and Rigobon, R, 2003, An alternative interpretation of the 'resource curse': theory and policy implications, *NBER Working Paper No. 9424*, January.

Hirschman, A O, 1958, *The Strategy of Economic Development*, New Haven, Yale University Press.

Huskey, E and Obolonsky, A, 2003, The struggle to reform Russia's bureaucracy, *Problems of Post-Communism*, 50:4, July–August.

Isham, J, Woolcock, M, Pritchett L and Busby, G, 2003, The varieties of resource experience: how natural resource export structures affect the political economy of economic growth, mimeo, Harvard University, Middlebury College, and World Bank.

Jones Luong, P, 2004, Rethinking the resource curse: ownership structure and institutional capacity, Paper prepared for the Conference on Globalization and Self-Determination, Yale University, May 14–15.

Karl, T-L, 1997, *The Paradox of Plenty: Oil Booms and Petro-States*, Berkeley, University of California Press.

Karl, T-L, 1999, The perils of the petro-state: reflections on the paradox of plenty, *Journal of International Affairs*, 53, pp. 31–48.

Kraus, E, 2004, There will be life after Yukos, *Moscow Times*, 1 September.

Lal, D and Myint, H, 1996, *The Political Economy of Poverty, Equity and Growth*, Oxford, Clarendon Press.

Mahon, Jr, J E, 1992, Was Latin America too rich to prosper?, *Journal of Development Studies*, 28 No. 1, January.

Mauro, P, 1995, Corruption and growth, *Quarterly Journal of Economics*, 90, pp. 681–712.

McFaul, M, 1997, When capitalism and democracy collide in transition: Russia's 'weak' state as an impediment to democratic consolidation, *Working Paper No. 1, Program in New Approaches to Russian Security*, Cambridge, MA, Harvard Russian Center.

Narain, A, Rabanal, P and Byskov, S, 2003, Prudential issues in less diversified economies, *IMF Working Paper* WP/03/198, October.

North, D C and Thomas, R P, 1973, *The Rise of the Western World: A New Economic History*, Cambridge, Cambridge University Press.

OECD, 2002, *OECD Economic Surveys: Russian Federation*, Paris, OECD.

OECD, 2004, *OECD Economic Surveys: Russian Federation*, Paris, OECD.

Olcott, M B, 2004, Vladimir Putin and the geopolitics of oil, Paper prepared for the James A. Baker III Institute for Public Policy, October.

OPORA Rossii, 2005, Conditions and factors affecting the development of small entrepreneurship in the regions of the Russian Federation, June (http://www.opora.ru/live/investigations.asp?id=34083).

Putin, V, 1999, Mineral'no-syr'evye resursy v strategii razvitiya rossiiskoi ekonomiki, *Zapiski Gornogo Instituta*, January.

Robinson, J A, Torvik, R and Verdier, T, 2002, Political foundations of the resource curse, *CEPR Discussion Paper No. 3422*, June.

Ross, M L, 1999, The political economy of the resource curse, *World Politics*, 51, pp. 297–322, January.

Ross, M L, 2001, Does oil hinder democracy?, *World Politics*, 53:3, pp. 325–361.

Sachs and Warner, 2001, The curse of natural resources, *European Economic Review*, 45.

Shafer, D M, 1994, *Winners and Losers: How Sectors Shape the Developmental Prospects of States*, Ithaca, Cornell University Press.

Sutela, P, 2005, The political economy of Putin's Russia, *BOFIT Russia Review* 3, March.

Tilly, C, 1992, *Coercion, Capital, and European States, AD 990–1992*, Oxford, Basil Blackwell.

Tompson, W, 1999, The price of everything and the value of nothing? Unravelling the workings of Russia's 'Virtual Economy', *Economy and Society*, 28:2, May.

Tompson, W, 2005, Putting Yukos in perspective, *Post-Soviet Affairs*, 21:2, April–June.

Transparency International—Russia, 2002, *Regional Corruption Indices 2002* (http://www.transparency.org.ru/proj_index.asp).

Treisman, D, 2002, Post-communist corruption, *Department of Political Science Working Paper*.

Vandewalle, D, 1998, *Libya since Independence: Oil and State-Building*, Ithaca, NY.

Vasil'eva, A A and Gurvich, E T, 2005, Reglament nalogooblozheniya neftegazovogo sektora, *Neft' Rossii* 3, March.

Woodruff, D, 1999, *Money Unmade: Barter and the Fate of Russian Capitalism*, Ithaca, Cornell University Press.

LIST OF CONTRIBUTORS

Rudiger Ahrend is an economist in the OECD Economics Department; email: rudiger.ahrend@oecd.org

Michael S. Bernstam is a research fellow at the Hoover Institution, Stanford University, USA; email: bernstam@hoover.stanford.edu

Michael Ellman is professor of economics at the Amsterdam School of Economics, Netherlands; email: m.j.ellman@uva.nl

Evgeny Gavrilenkov is senior economist and managing director of Troika Dialog brokerage, Moscow, Russia, & professor of macroeconomics at the State University—Higher School of Economics, Moscow; email: Evgeny_Gavrilenkov@troika.ru

Gregory Khanin is professor of economics in Novosibirsk, Russia; email: galinasu@rol.ru

Vladimir Kontorovich is professor of economics at Haverford College, USA; email: vkontoro@haverford.edu

Sergiy Maslichenko is president of UCELA (Ukrainian Centre for Economic and Legal Analysis, Kyiv, Ukraine); email: maslichenko@ucela.org.ua

Peter Oppenheimer is an economist and student (fellow) of Christ Church (college), Oxford University, UK; email: peter.oppenheimer@chch.ox.ac.uk

Alvin Rabushka is the David and Joan Traitel Senior Fellow at the Hoover Institution, Stanford University, USA; email: rabushka@hoover.stanford.edu

Shinichiro Tabata is professor of economics at the Slavic Research Center, Hokkaido University, Japan; email: shin@slav.hokudai.ac.jp

William Tompson is a senior economist for the NIS and South-east Europe, Economics Department, OECD; email: william.tompson@oecd.org

INDEX

Anthem Studies in Development and Globalization

Rangaswamy, Vedavalli *Energy for Development* (2006)
Buira, Ariel *Reforming the Governance of the IMF and the World Bank* (2005)
Ringmar, Erik *Surviving Capitalism* (2005)
Ritzen, Jo *A Chance for the World Bank* (2004)
Fullbrook, Edward (ed.) *A Guide to What's Wrong with Economics* (2004)
Chang, Ha-Joon *Kicking Away the Ladder* (2003)